Lexical Borrowing and its Impact on English

Hituzi Linguistics in English

No. 1   Lexical Borrowing and its Impact on English   Makimi Kimura-Kano
No. 2   From a Subordinate Clause to an Independent Clause
                                                            Yuko Higashiizumi
No. 3   ModalP and Subjunctive Present   Tadao Nomura

Hituzi Linguistics in English No. 1

Lexical Borrowing and its Impact on English

with Special Reference to Assimilation Process of Newer Loanwords from Japanese and German and Impact on the Existing Lexical System in English

Makimi Kimura-Kano

Hituzi Syobo Publishing

Copyright © Makimi Kimura-Kano 2006
First published 2006

Author: Makimi Kimura-Kano

All rights reserved. Except for the quotation of short passages for the purposes of criticism and review, no part of this publication may be reduced, stored in a retrieval system, or transmitted in any form or by any means, electronic, mechanical, photocopying, recording or otherwise, without the written prior permission of the publisher.
In case of photocopying and electronic copying and retrieval from network personally, permission will be given on receipts of payment and making inquiries. For details please contact us through e-mail. Our e-mail address is given below.

Book Design © Hirokazu Mukai (glyph)

Hituzi Syobo Publishing
5-21-5 Koishikawa Bunkyo-ku Tokyo, Japan 112-0002

phone +81-3-5684-6871   fax +81-3-5684-6872
e-mail: toiawase@hituzi.co.jp
http://www.hituzi.co.jp/
postal transfer 00120-8-142852

ISBN4-89476-268-4
Printed in Japan

Contents

Acknowledgments	ix
1 Introduction	1
1.1 General Outline: Loanwords in English	1
1.2 Purpose of This Study	3
1.2.1 Generalizing the Assimilation Process of Loanwords	3
1.2.2 The Impact of Loanwords on the Existing Lexical System	4
I Assimilation Process of Loanwords	7
2 Previous Studies and Associated Problems	9
2.1 Studies on Japanese Loanwords	9
2.1.1 Studies before 1980	9
2.1.2 Studies by Japanese Researchers	11
2.1.3 Studies by Cannon	14
2.1.4 Problems with Studies by Cannon	20
2.2 Studies on German Loanwords	20
2.2.1 Studies by Cannon	21
2.2.2 Stubbs (1998)	25
2.2.3 Problems with the Studies on German Loanwords	26
2.3 Other Studies Referring to the Assimilation Processes of Loanwords	27
2.3.1 Umegaki (1963)	27
2.3.2 Koura (1992)	27
2.3.3 Daulton (2002)	28
2.3.4 Problems on Studies on Assimilation Processes of Loanwords	29

3 Assimilation Process of Japanese Loanwords — 31

- 3.1 Introduction — 31
  - 3.1.1 Suggested Solutions to the Problems — 31
  - 3.1.2 Definition of Japanese Loanwords — 31
- 3.2 Dictionary-based Approach — 32
  - 3.2.1 Procedure — 32
  - 3.2.2 The Four Stages of the Assimilation Process — 38
  - 3.2.3 Stage 1: Adaptation of Pronunciation and Orthography — 40
  - 3.2.4 Stage 2: Restricted Attributive Use of Nouns — 42
  - 3.2.5 Stage 3: Acquisition of Productivity — 42
  - 3.2.6 Stage 4: Semantic Shift — 44
  - 3.2.7 Cyclic System — 46
  - 3.2.8 Summary — 46
- 3.3 Corpus-based Approach — 48
  - 3.3.1 Procedure — 48
  - 3.3.2 Unassimilated Loanwords — 50
  - 3.3.3 Morphological Observation — 51
  - 3.3.4 Semantic Observation — 55
  - 3.3.5 Verification Results — 61
  - 3.3.6 Comparison of Usage in the Two Corpora — 64
  - 3.3.7 Summary — 65
- 3.4 Characteristics of Secondary Loanwords — 66
  - 3.4.1 Loan Translation — 66
  - 3.4.2 Re-borrowing of Words of English Origin from Japanese — 69
  - 3.4.3 Summary — 70
- 3.5 Sense and Context of Japanese Loanwords in English — 71
  - 3.5.1 Materials and Methodology — 72
  - 3.5.2 Results — 73
  - 3.5.3 Discussion — 76
  - 3.5.4 Summary — 82

4 Assimilation Process of German Loanwords — 85

- 4.1 Introduction — 85
  - 4.1.1 Purpose of This Chapter — 85

		4.1.2	Definition of German Loanwords	85
	4.2	Dictionary-based Approach		86
		4.2.1	Comparison between Loanwords from Various Languages	86
		4.2.2	Procedure	90
		4.2.3	Pronunciation and Orthography	91
		4.2.4	Orthography	96
		4.2.5	Irregularity of Plural Forms of Nouns	97
		4.2.6	Attributive Use	98
		4.2.7	Acquisition of Productivity	99
		4.2.8	Semantic Shift	99
		4.2.9	Assimilated German Loanwords	102
		4.2.10	Other Characteristics	107
		4.2.11	Summary	107
	4.3	Corpus-based Approach		109
		4.3.1	Procedure	109
		4.3.2	Unassimilated Loanwords	111
		4.3.3	Assimilated Loanwords	116
		4.3.4	Summary	122

5 Comparison of Assimilation Processes of Japanese and German Loanwords   125

II Impact of Loanwords on the Existing Lexical System   129

6 Introduction and Previous Studies   131

	6.1	Introduction		131
	6.2	Studies on Vocabulary Expansion		131
		6.2.1	Studies by Finkenstaedt *et al.*	132
		6.2.2	Studies by Cannon	134
		6.2.3	Jucker (1994)	136
		6.2.4	From the Introduction Section of Recent Dictionaries	137
	6.3	Previous Studies on Synonyms and Collocations		139
		6.3.1	Konishi (1976)	139

		6.3.2	Firth (1951)	141
		6.3.3	Jucker (1994)	141
		6.3.4	Biber (1996)	142
		6.3.5	Inoue (2001)	142
		6.3.6	Stubbs (2001)	143
	6.4	Purpose of Part II of the Study		143

7 Coexistence of Old Vocabulary with Newer Loanwords — 145

	7.1	Introduction		145
	7.2	Definition and Purpose of This Chapter		145
	7.3	Materials and Methodology		147
	7.4	Results and Analyses		151
		7.4.1	Restricted Range of Use of Newer Loanwords	152
		7.4.2	Wider Range of Use of Newer Loanwords	157
		7.4.3	Overlapped Range of Use	159
		7.4.4	Exclusive Range of Use	160
	7.5	Summary		163

8 A Case Study of Synonym Pair: *Magnate* and *Tycoon* — 165

	8.1	Introduction		165
	8.2	Methodology		166
		8.2.1	Materials	166
		8.2.2	Procedure	166
	8.3	Usage of *Magnate* and *Tycoon* as Seen in the *OED2*		167
		8.3.1	*Tycoon* in the *OED2*	167
		8.3.2	*Magnate* in the *OED2*	171
		8.3.3	Differences between *Tycoon* and *Magnate* Derived from *OED2*	173
	8.4	Verification and Detailed Analyses Using the *BNC*		174
		8.4.1	*Magnate*: Diachronic Shift in Sense	176
		8.4.2	*Tycoon*: Similarities to the Modern Use of *Magnate*	179
		8.4.3	The Difference in Collocation	179
		8.4.4	The Difference in Connotation of *Tycoon*	181
		8.4.5	The Difference in Usage: Apposition Patterns *etc.*	183

		8.4.6	The Difference in Referents	184
		8.4.7	The Difference in Number: Singular or Plural	185
		8.4.8	The Different Distribution: Domains and Media	186
		8.4.9	Other Synonymous Words of *Tycoon* and *Magnate* . . .	188
	8.5	Summary		192

9 Concluding Remarks and Future Perspectives   195

Bibliography   199

Dictionaries and Corpora   208

Summary in Japanese   211

Appendices   227
A	Productive Forms of Japanese Loanwords in *TIME Almanac*	227
B	Productive Forms of Japanese Loanwords in *The Times*	229
C	Japanese Loanwords in English Dictionaries	232
D	Unchanged and Anglicized Phonemes of German Loanwords	249
E	Productive Forms of German Loanwords in English Dictionaries	252
F	Selected German Loanwords in English Dictionaries	255

List of Tables

2.1	The Distribution of Part of Speech	22
2.2	The Distribution of Degree of Assimilation	25
3.1	Japanese Loanwords Found in the *OED2*	37
3.2	Japanese Loanwords Found in Other Dictionaries	38
3.3	The Degree of Assimilation of Japanese Loanwords	39
3.4	Examples of Assimilation Process	40
3.5	Three Types of Semantic Shift	45
3.6	An Example of Cyclic System	46
3.7	Japanese Loanwords Found in Corpora	48
3.8	Occurrence of the Assimilated Loanwords	52
3.9	Verification of Productivity (Stage 3 Items)	62
3.10	Verification of Productivity (Stage 4 Items)	62
3.11	Verification of Semantic Shift	62
3.12	Three Types of Semantic Shift (Revised)	64
3.13	The Degree of Assimilation of Japanese Loanwords (Revised)	64
3.14	Occurrence of Loan Translation in *The TimesCD*	68
3.15	Occurrence of Re-borrowing in *The TimesCD*	70
3.16	Semantic Categorization of Japanese Loanwords	75
3.17	Context Categorization of Japanese Loanwords	75
4.1	The Transition in Number of Loanwords from Top 11 Languages	87
4.2	Japanese/German/Spanish Loanwords First Attested in the *OED2* Later than 1940	88
4.3	The Characteristics of German Loanwords	91
4.4	Examples of Unchanged and Anglicized Phonemes of German Loanwords	95
4.5	Frequency of Unassimilated German Loanwords in the *BNC*	112
4.6	Frequency of Assimilated German Loanwords in the *BNC*	116

List of Tables

6.1	Etymology of New Vocabulary (from Cannon 1987, abbreviated)	135
6.2	The Distribution of Etymological Sources (from Algeo 1991)	138
7.1	Distribution of *Tsunami* and *Tidal Wave* in Frequency per Million	153
7.2	Domains of *Angst* and *Anxiety*	161
7.3	Collocations of *Angst* and *Anxiety*	161
8.1	Example of KWIC-formatted Results	168
8.2	Characteristics of *Magnate* and *Tycoon* as Seen in the *OED2*	174
8.3	Frequencies of *Tycoon* and *Magnate* in Each Sense	175
8.4	Characteristics of *Tycoon* and *Magnate* as Seen in the *BNC*	175
8.5	Transition of the Sense of *Magnate*	176
8.6	Co-occurring Words of *Magnate* in the *BNC*	178
8.7	Co-occurring Words of *Tycoon* in the *BNC*	180
8.8	Three Types of Use of *Tycoon* and *Magnate*	184
8.9	*Tycoon* and *Magnate* Used in Different Domains	186
8.10	*Tycoon* and *Magnate* Used in Different Media	188

List of Figures

1.1	The Flow of Language Borrowing	1
3.1	Assimilation Process	47
3.2	Sense-Context Matrix (1): Compelete b-II	77
3.3	Sense-Context Matrix (2): Quasi b-II	78
3.4	Sense-Context Matrix (3): Column (a)	80
3.5	Stage 1 and Stage 2 Items: Extreme a-I	81
3.6	Stage 3 Items: a-I and a-II	82
3.7	Semantic and Contextual Transition of Japanese Loanwords	83
4.1	The Spectrum of Unchanged and Anglicized Phonemes	96
5.1	Japanese Assimilation Process	126
5.2	German Assimilation Process	126
6.1	Distribution of Total Number of Vocabulary (from Finkenstaedt *et al.* 1969)	132
6.2	Expansion of Vocabulary after Shakespeare (from Finkenstaedt *et al.* 1970)	133
7.1	Search Result in KWIC	148
7.2	Distribution Option	149
7.3	Collocation Option	150
7.4	Restricted Range	152
7.5	Wider Range	158
7.6	Overlapped Range	159
7.7	Overlap Patterns	160
7.8	Exclusive Range	161
8.1	Domain of *Tycoon* and its Synonyms	190
8.2	Collocation of *Tycoon* and its Synonyms	191

Acknowledgments

This book is a revised version of my Ph.D dissertation "Dynamics of Language Contact: Assimilation Process of New Loanwords and Impact on the Existing Lexical System with Special Reference to Japanese and German Loanwords in English," submitted to the Graduate School of Language and Culture of Osaka University (Kimura-Kano 2004).

Here, I would like to express my appreciation to everyone who made various kinds of contribution to this work. I am especially grateful to my advisers and the members of the dissertation committee, Hikaru Nakanishi, Hajime Narita, Nobuo Okada, and Emi Takita for their crucial comments in the course of developing and completing the dissertation. I am indebted to Hideki Watanabe and Takao Gunji for giving me plenty of invaluable suggestions. I would like to express my gratitude to Tomoji Tabata, who kindly let me access his corpus server and also assisted me with launching mine, Sebastian Hoffmann for his assistance on the installation of BNCweb, and Randi Reppen and Douglas Biber for providing me an opportunity to use ARCHER corpus. I thank all the members of *LCCC (Gengo Kogaku Kenkyu Kai)*, *OCLA (Denshika Shiryo Kenkyu Kai)*, and *Keiryo Gengogaku Kenkyu Kai*, whose helpful suggestions inside and outside of meetings have been my impetus to move forward with my research. I also thank *JAECS (Japan Association for English Corpus Studies)* and *Society for the Study of Language and Culture (Gengo Bunka Gakkai)* for giving me the opportunity to present my studies in the conferences and provided me with helpful suggestions.

I am also thankful to many people around me: Mitsumi Uchida, Yuka Mitoya, Jane Takizawa, and Akira Kitaura. They longed for the successful completion of my dissertation, encouraged me, and gave me many pieces of advice. Special thanks to all of my family members, friends, colleagues and students for encouraging me all this while. I gratefully acknowledge the support from JSPS and Hituzi Syobo Publishing for enabling my dissertation to be published.

Finally, I would like to thank my husband, Hiroshi Kano, who has been cooperative all this while. Without his support, I could never have completed this work.

All the remaining inadequacies in this book are mine.

The publication of this book was supported by JSPS Grant-in-Aid for Publication of Scientific Research Results (No. 175140).

Chapter 1 Introduction

1.1 General Outline: Loanwords in English

Every language has some contact with other languages. Whenever two languages meet, they influence each other in various ways. Borrowing is one example. English has been open to such foreign influence, and has borrowed many words from other languages, mainly from Latin and French. Borrowing has been one of the major sources of new vocabulary in the history of the English language. According to Finkenstaedt (1964), only 22 percent of the English vocabulary in the *Shorter Oxford English Dictionary* (1933) can be counted as native, while 30 percent comes from Romance languages and 28 percent from Latin. Once a lexical item is borrowed into English, it goes through various changes and gradually establishes an independent status of full membership in the English vocabulary as shown in Figure 1.1.

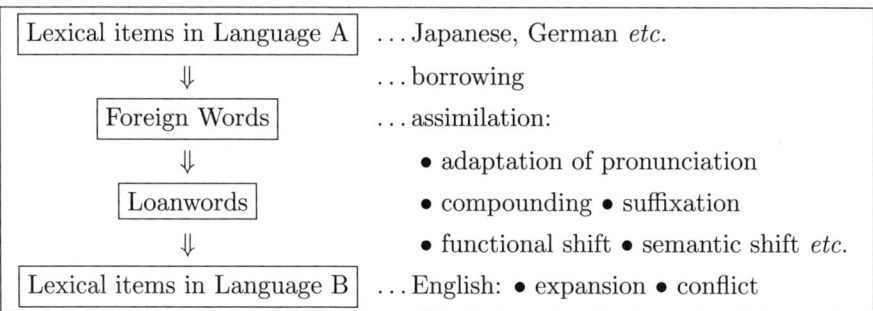

Figure 1.1: The Flow of Language Borrowing

In the Old English period, English borrowed several words, but the only major foreign influence on Old English vocabulary was Latin. In Middle English, the major loanwords were from European languages, such as Scandinavian, French, Latin, and Celtic, with a handful of loanwords coming into English from non-European languages, such as Arabic and Persian, for the first time. They were borrowed via European languages, coming into English indirectly through French or Medieval Latin. In Early Modern English, the number of loanwords from non-European languages increased greatly, due to the encounter with the New World. Native American languages, Asian languages, Middle Eastern languages, and African languages were major sources of such words.

It was during this time that Japanese loanwords first appeared in English. But Japan then politically closed its borders to foreign intrusion, so its influence on the English lexicon was relatively slight. Japanese provided a few terms like *Mikado* 'the title of the emperor of Japan,' *sake* 'a Japanese fermented liquor,' *shogun* 'Japanese commander-in-chief,' and *soy* 'a sauce prepared from soybeans.' The involvement of English-speaking peoples with the rest of the world has continued to the Present-day English period, and loanwords from exotic languages have continued to increase. After the reopening of Japan, the number of Japanese loanwords soared. Of the Asian languages, Japanese has become the largest contributor to the English vocabulary in Present-day English. What is more, according to Cannon (1994b), Japanese is said to be the second largest source of loanwords in the recent English vocabulary, though still far behind French.

In the meanwhile, German loanwords into English were never especially heavy before late Early Modern English partly because Germany was late in achieving political unification, hence in developing a standard language. It provided some terms in geology and mining, such as *cobalt*, *quartz*, and *zinc* in the 18th century. However, in Present-day English, German loanwords increased because of a number of factors: Germany's unification and emergence as a major international power, its early supremacy in graduate education, and the heavy German immigration into the United States during the 19th century. It provided many educational or intellectual loanwords, such as *seminar* 'a select group of advanced students associated for special study in universities,' *kindergarten* 'a school for the instruction of young children,' and *gestalt* 'an idea of object perception forms in the school of psychology.'

1.2 Purpose of This Study

In order to reveal the behavior of loanwords, this study deals with loanwords from two aspects; generalizing the assimilation process of loanwords (Part I) and identifying the impact of loanwords on the existing lexical system (Part II).

1.2.1 Generalizing the Assimilation Process of Loanwords

Bloomfield (1933) stated that there are mainly three forms of borrowing:

(1) a. cultural borrowing

  b. intimate borrowing

  c. dialect borrowing

Borrowing from Japanese is almost always 'cultural borrowing,' in which a foreign word is introduced to English when it encounters a new and unknown culture. Japanese words, once borrowed into English, go through several shifts and gradually gain an independent status as full members of the English vocabulary. Such changes include adaptation of pronunciation, suffixation, functional shift, and semantic shift. Although many loanwords remain unfamiliar to most English-speakers, some gain wide acceptance and frequent use among ordinary people.

Part I of this study aims to generalize the process through which loanwords become assimilated in the English vocabulary, and to examine the degree of assimilation. After reviewing the previous studies on the assimilation process of loanwords in Chapter 2, the four stages of assimilation process of Japanese loanwords are established in Chapter 3, as a result of investigating the English dictionaries, such as the *Oxford English Dictionary* 2nd ed., the *Shorter Oxford Dictionary* 5th ed., the *Oxford Dictionaries of Foreign Words and Phrases*, *Webster's Third*, and the *Random House* (Section 3.2),[1] and in Section 3.3, the results of dictionary research are verified using two corpora, *TIME Almanac* and *The Times and the Sunday Times* Internet Edition, and the description of

---

[1] Section 3.2 is based on (Kimura 2000), and the data were updated using the most recent edition of dictionaries.

the dictionaries are modified.[2] The characteristics of the secondary loanwords (*i.e.*, loan translation and re-borrowing) are also investigated (Section 3.4[3]). Section 3.5 deals with the context in which Japanese loanwords are used, and reveals the relationship between their sense and context, using a corpus called *Wordbanks* online.[4]

Furthermore, in Chapter 4, German loanwords are also analyzed as an example of loanwords from a language other than Japanese to see the differences between the assimilation process of German loanwords and that of Japanese loanwords. Section 4.2 is a dictionary-based research,[5] in which the same dictionaries are used as in Section 3.2, and Section 4.3 is a corpus-based research, in which the *British National Corpus* was utilized to verify and update the dictionary-based research.[6] Finally, Chapter 5 aims to identify which characteristics are unique to Japanese loanwords, and which are common among the loanwords in general.

1.2.2 The Impact of Loanwords on the Existing Lexical System

There are many possible effects of loanwords on the existing lexical system. They may affect the size of the English vocabulary or the regularity of English inflection. Further, though borrowing usually takes place when there is no equivalent vocabulary to express the new concept coming into English, it is sometimes the case that a word with a similar meaning already exists in English when a loanword is borrowed. Some loanwords come to have synonyms after they have gone through the stages of the assimilation process, and have come to possess a new sense as a result of a semantic shift. In these cases, loanwords rival with the existing vocabulary, and may affect the existing lexical system by replacing or coexisting with the existing vocabulary.

The purpose of Part II of this study is to clarify the distinctions between the

---

[2] Section 3.3 is based on (Kimura 1998), and further developed so that it reflects the recent data from the dictionaries.

[3] Issues of secondary loanwords were discussed in Kimura (1997a, 1997b and 1998). Those studies are the basis of Section 3.4.

[4] Kimura (2002) is the basis of Section 3.5.

[5] The basic idea of Section 4.2 is from Kimura-Kano 2003 , and it has been greatly modified and detailed.

[6] The study of Section 4.3 was supported by MEXT Grant-in-Aid for Young Scientists (B) (No. 15720117).

newer loanwords and the existing English vocabulary by comparing and analyzing them in the following aspects: sense, frequencies, domain and medium of texts in which they are used, co-occurring words in context, number (singular/plural), usage patterns, connotation, referents, and so on. This will reveal the usage patterns of synonymous loanwords and existing vocabulary, the nature of these words, and the similarities and differences between them, and show how the seemingly synonymous loanwords affect the existence of the equivalent older vocabulary and the English vocabulary system itself. The previous studies on vocabulary expansion, synonyms and collocation are reviewed in Chapter 6. In Chapter 7, an overview of the conflict patterns of synonymous pairs is introduced,[7] and a synonym pair, *tycoon* and *magnate* is investigated in detail as a case study in Chapter 8.[8]

By considering loanwords from both sides, as mentioned above, in regards to the changes of loanwords as they get assimilated and the changes in the English vocabulary system affected by the loanwords, this study will be able to capture the entire picture of loanwords.

---

[7] Chapter 7 is summarized in Kimura-Kano (2005a) .
[8] Chapter 8 is based on Kimura (2003) and further developed in Kimura (2004b). Section 8.4.9 has been newly added, which is included in Kimura-Kano (2005a).

Part I

Assimilation Process of Loanwords

Chapter 2 Previous Studies and Associated Problems

2.1 Studies on Japanese Loanwords

Several researchers have studied Japanese loanwords in English, but only a few have referred to their assimilation process. Among these, Garland Cannon, who has done a series of research on loanwords from Japanese and other languages, proposed a 'naturalization scale' to measure the assimilation degree of these words. His study, however, reveals some problems which require resolution. The following sections will review the previous studies on Japanese loanwords, look at Cannon's study in greater detail, and point out some associated problems.

2.1.1 Studies before 1980
2.1.1.1 A Study on *Webster's Third*
Knowlton (1970) studies words attributed to Chinese, Japanese, and Korean origin in *Webster's Third New International Dictionary of the English Language* (1961), and criticized them in regards to the following points:

(2) a. There were no outside consultants for etymologies from Japanese.

b. The morphological analysis of loanwords was inconsistent.

c. It does not indicate the distinctive pitch or vowel length of the Japanese etyma.

d. The guidelines for Japanese loanwords were unclear, only occasionally indicating whether a given term reflected a Sino-Japanese tradition or an indigenous one.

2.1.1.2 A Study on the *A Supplement to the OED*
Burchfield, the editor of the *A Supplement to the Oxford English Dictionary*, gives a list of Japanese loanwords which should have been included in the *OED*

but were too late for inclusion in Volume I (A-G) of the *A Supplement to the OED*. He considers the period of time in which Japanese words were borrowed in English, and states that in the second half of the 19th century, the most fertile period for Japanese loanwords, "just one half of all Japanese loanwords became lodged in the English language, representing every aspect of Japanese life" such as 'poetry,' 'drama,' 'art,' 'pottery,' 'clothing,' and other general words. However, in publishing the *OED2* in 1989, not all of these terms were included in the new edition. His choice of new entries includes the following terms:[1]

(3) *adzuki*∗ 'dark red edible beans'; *ama*∗ 'a Japanese woman diver'; *amado*∗ 'a set of shutters'; *andon* 'a Japanese type of lamp'; *Arita*∗ 'a variety of porcelain'; *betto* 'a groom or ostler'; *biwa* 'a four stringed Japanese musical instrument'; *Bizen* 'a hard unglazed pottery'; *bu* 'an old Japanese coin or unit of value'; *bugaku* 'a Japanese classical dance form'; *Buké* 'the military class or family in feudal Japan'; *buraku(min)* 'certain people politically treated as an inferior caste'; *chadai* 'a present of money to inn and restaurant'; *cha-no-yu* 'the Japanese tea ceremony'; *cho* 'a Japanese unit of length'; *chonin* 'a member of the merchant class in feudal Japan'; *chu* 'the duty of loyalty to a superior'; *daikon* 'the Japanese radish'; *dotaku*∗ 'a prehistoric bronze bell-shaped object'; *emakimono*∗ 'a Japanese scroll containing pictures'; *furoshiki* 'a square of fabric for wrapping'; *gaijin* 'a foreigner'; *giri* 'a system of obligation in Japan.'

2.1.1.3 Problems with Studies before 1980

These studies share certain problems:

(4) a. They are mostly out of date and do not reflect recent tendencies in loanwords from Japanese.

b. They are not systematic, merely listing Japanese loanwords registered or due to be registered in English dictionaries.

c. They focus on what kinds of words have been borrowed but fail to consider the linguistic shifts in loanwords after borrowing.

---

[1] Only the items with asterisks (∗) were registered in the *OED2*.

2.1.2 Studies by Japanese Researchers

In the 1990s, Japanese researchers have done some research on Japanese loanwords. They list Japanese loanwords, as did the studies before 1980, and some briefly mention the assimilation of Japanese loanwords. In this section, I will review various ways suggested to measure the degree of assimilation of Japanese loanwords.

2.1.2.1 A Study on *Newsweek* and *TIME*

Ishimaru (1990) deals with the Japanese loanwords which appeared in the two news magazines, *Newsweek*, and *TIME* from 1978 to 1985. He categorizes them into several semantic groups, observes the forms of adding gloss (transliteration preceding, translation preceding, and indirect explanation), and discusses the reasons for using Japanese loanwords in the articles (to explain Japanese indigenous events or objects, to be realistic, and to express 'local color').

He then establishes two standards of stability for Japanese loanwords in English:

(5) a. written in Roman style instead of italic.

b. not glossed before or after the word.

He gives a list of words which he considers to satisfy these standards as follows:

(6) *banzai* 'a shout to the emperor'; *bonze* 'the Buddhist clergy of Japan'; *geisha* 'a Japanese girl whose profession is to entertain men by dancing and singing'; *harakiri* 'suicide by disembowelment'; *judo* 'a refined form of ju-jitsu'; *kabuki* 'a traditional form of Japanese drama'; *kamikaze* 'The wind of the gods'; *karate* 'a Japanese system of unarmed combat'; *kimono* 'a long Japanese robe with sleeves'; *samurai* 'a class of military retainers in the feudal period'; *sayonara* 'good-bye'; *shogun(ate)*; *sushi* 'a small ball of cold rice with slice of fish'; *tycoon* 'the title of the shogun of Japan described to foreigners'; *yen* 'the monetary unit of Japan'; *zen* 'a school of Mahayana Buddhism.'

He also gives a list of words which he considers to be on the borderline between the stable and the unstable as follows:

(7) *bonsai* 'a Japanese potted plant or small tree'; *haiku* 'a form of Japanese verse'; *ikebana* 'the art of Japanese flower arrangement'; *No(h)* 'the traditional Japanese masked drama'; *sake*; *sashimi* 'a Japanese dish consisting of thin slices of raw fish'; *shinto* 'the native religious system of Japan'; *sumo* 'a form of Japanese wrestling'; *tatami* 'a rush-covered straw mat'; *tempura* 'a Japanese dish of deep-fried prawn and shrimp *etc.*'; *torii* 'a ceremonial gateway in front of a Japanese Shinto shrine.'

He observes that all the stable loanwords but *sayonara* are the words which signify Japanese indigenous events/objects. However, he fails to consider the morphological aspects of words (suffixation and functional shift *etc.*) as a standard for stability of Japanese loanwords.

2.1.2.2 A Study Focused on Historical Aspects

Matsuda (1991) divides Japanese loanwords into various semantic groups such as 'art,' 'food' and 'military affairs,' and analyzes them in detail. He especially focuses on the historical sequence of each item; when and by whom it was first used in English, and how it prevailed among the English-speakers. He mentions six points that can be considered as criteria of stability for Japanese loanwords as items in the English vocabulary:

(8) a. no need to be written in italic or with quotation marks.

b. inflecting regularly, taking *-s* for the plural form of a noun.

c. used metaphorically and attributively.

d. semantic shift after borrowing.

e. functional shift, for example, from noun to verb.

f. having one or more derivational form(s).

The remarkable point is that his criteria include not only the appearance in books but also morphological and semantic aspects. However, the order in which Japanese loanwords undergo these changes was not considered.

2.1.2.3 Studies on the *OED2*

Owada has continuously investigated and updated Japanese loanwords mainly in the *OED2*. Owada (1995 and 1998) researches the Japanese loanwords registered in the *OED2* and the three volumes of the *OED Additions Series*, respectively. He divides them into semantic categories and finds that 'food and drink,' 'art and craft,' and 'plant' are the three largest categories in the *OED2*, and 'sports' and 'economy' in the *OED Additions Series*. He also analyzes the date, authors and number of citations.

Owada (1996) deals with the orthographic and morphological aspects of Japanese loanwords, including spelling shifts and variations, and functional shifts and derivatives. For example, he points out the following characteristics as to the spelling shifts:

(9) a. alternation of consonants ($h \Leftrightarrow f$);

b. alternation between voicing and unvoicing ($s \Leftrightarrow z$, $d \Rightarrow t$, $k \Leftrightarrow g$);

c. repetition of consonants (-*kk*-, -*nn*-, -*tt*-);

d. alternation of a vowel ($e \Leftrightarrow i$) etc.

Owada (1997) deals with Japanese loanwords with special reference to Engelbert Kæmpfer, who contributed many Japanese words to the *OED*. He antedates several Japanese words and points out the transcription errors in the *OED2*.

He widens the range of the investigation to the recent Oxford Dictionaries, such as the *Oxford Dictionary of Foreign Words and Phrases*, and the *New Oxford Dictionary of English* in Owada (1999). He not only updates the list of Japanese loanwords, but also compares the description of the words in dictionaries and finds that some of the older loanwords are updated with derivatives and compounds in the newer dictionaries.

Though he observes some transitions of forms of Japanese loanwords to some extent, his observation is limited to those described in the definition section, and he does not consider other variations appearing in the citations. Moreover, he does not apply them to the general concept of the assimilation process.

Finally, the latest study on Japanese loanwords in the *OED2* is Hayakawa (2003), in which he antedates about 260 of the 550 Japanese loanwords in the *OED2*.

2.1.2.4 Summary of Studies by Japanese Researchers

Most of the studies done by Japanese researchers are relatively recent, and their observation of Japanese loanwords is detailed. Though some discuss the assimilation process or stability of Japanese loanwords in English, the generalized order of the process has not been fully investigated.

2.1.3 Studies by Cannon

Cannon has repeatedly studied the recent English vocabulary including loanwords. Among loanwords in general, he notes that Japanese loanwords are playing an important part in the new vocabulary of English. Cannon's study is the only one that suggests a phased and ordered assimilation process for loanwords. In this section, I will review Cannon's study on Japanese loanwords in detail, especially in the following seven aspects:

(10) a. Japanese loanwords among the new loanwords;

b. General characteristics of Japanese loanwords;

c. Orthographic system;

d. Semantic categories;

e. Pluralization;

f. Recent tendency;

g. The naturalization scale.

2.1.3.1 Japanese Loanwords among the New Loanwords

Cannon (1979) analyzes 473 loanwords in *Merriam-Webster's 6000 words* (1976) and *The Barnhart Dictionary of New English since 1963* (1973). He provides the following statistical facts and observations:

2 Previous Studies and Associated Problems   15

(11) a. Japanese has now become the third largest source of loanwords, furnishing seven percent of the total, following French (30%) and Latin (8%).

b. Of the first ten languages in the ordering, Japanese is the only non-Indo-European language.

c. Japan's economic and cultural ascendancy since World War II can explain the rapid growth in English loanwords.

d. Japanese is now clearly the largest non-Indo-European source of loanwords.

2.1.3.2 General Characteristics of Japanese Loanwords

According to Cannon (1981a), the English dictionaries he studies (the *OED*, the *OED Supplement*, *Merriam-Webster's 6000 words*, *The Barnhart Dictionary of New English since 1963*, *The Random House Dictionary of the English Language*, *Funk & Wagnalls Standard Dictionary of the English Language*) cite 462 nouns, 52 adjectives, and two interjections (*arigatou* 'thank you' and *banzai*) from Japanese. He also discovers "587 main entries of Japanese province and another 216 items derived from the old borrowing *Japan*" (Cannon 1981a). He points out the following characteristics of Japanese loanwords:

(12) a. Use of nouns as verbs (e.g., *karate, randori* 'a informal practice in Judo') or adjectives (e.g., *kamikaze, Shinto*).

b. Abridged forms (e.g., *Hirado* ← *Hirado ware* 'a rich elaborate white porcelain,' *kiku* ← *kikumon* 'the crest of the imperial family in Japan').

c. Compounds originally in Japanese (e.g., *akamushi* ← *aka* 'red' and *mushi* 'bug').

d. Formation of new compounds (e.g., *soy bean*).

e. Suffixation (e.g., *urushiol* 'An oily liquid of the Japanese lacquer tree').

f. Loan translation (e.g., *Linked verse* ← *renga* 'a form of Japanese verse contributed by different poets in turn').

g. Re-borrowings (e.g., *beddo* 'various beds designed in Japan' ← 'bed').

h. Slang in the American armed forces (e.g., *honcho* 'the leader of a small group or squad' (← *hancho*), *hootch* 'a shelter or dwelling' (← *uchi*), *moose* 'a young Japanese or Korean woman' (← *musume*)).

2.1.3.3 Orthographic System

The loanwords generally retain the orthographic system of the original language. Japanese loanwords are easy to spell faithfully since Japanese has fewer vowels and consonants than English. In some cases, however, the spellings have shifted. Cannon (1981a) reports several orthographic variants, for example, *daimyo* and *daimio* 'the title of the chief territorial nobles of Japan,' *jinricksha, jinrikisha,* and *jinriksha* 'a vehicle drawn by one or more men.' *Mus* is a slang term GIs used in Japan when the U.S. occupied Japan after World War II. The word means *musume*, 'a daughter' or 'a girl,' and Norman (1954) explains that GIs adopted *musume* to refer to a GI's wife or mistress. "To spell the word *mus* might be a good transcription from Japanese but would not sufficiently indicate the word's pronunciation" (Norman, 1954: 302). Later, *mus* was spelled as *moos* or *moose* by analogy with the animal.

2.1.3.4 Semantic Categories

Generally and not surprisingly, the majority of language borrowings are what Bloomfield (1933) calls culture loans: "what one nation taught another." Cannon (1981a) groups the Japanese loanwords into 16 semantic categories, and reports a somewhat different semantic distribution of loanwords from those considered in an earlier study (Cannon and Egle, 1979). 'Science' and 'art' are the two largest categories, followed by 'religion,' 'status,' 'food/drink,' and the 'martial arts.'

2.1.3.5 Pluralization

Cannon (1984) shows interesting research findings on the plural form of Japanese loanwords. Of 490 Japanese loanwords recorded in the standard English dictionaries, 311 are nouns, and 125 of these have not fitted comfortably into the regular pluralization system. This number drastically enlarges the total number of irregular plurals in English; 89 take zero plural suffixes, in which the plural form does not differ from the singular form such as *zori* 'thonged sandals' and *shakuhachi* 'bamboo flute,' 29 can take either zero or -*s*, and seven collective nouns occur only with zero plurals such as *burakumin*. Cannon (1984) considers the causes of such irregularity but comes to no firm conclusion. The causes he considers are:

(13) a. Length of time in the language
   Many items evidently took -*s* plural suffixes at the outset, including *sika*, 'deer,' which was recorded for the first time as *sikas* 'A small red deer native to Japan' in 1891, while many words of comparable age came in with zero plural and still retain it, such as *mochi* (1616) 'a cake made from rice' and *torii* (1727). Surprisingly, the first or at least quite early written occurrences of several items had the analogized -*s* before taking zero inflection. Words such as *hatamoto* and *katana* once had -s inflection but have reverted to the original Japanese phonemic form.

   b. Semantic characters
   The semantic distribution of zero forms differs from that of the total corpus. As mentioned above, 'science' and 'art' are the largest categories, followed by 'religion,' while 'status,' 'measurements,' 'ethnology,' 'occupation' and 'religion' are the major categories of zero plural nouns. 'Swords and sword-making' (all), 'status' (17 of 26), 'measurements' (all of ten), 'ethnology' (all of nine) are categories in which a large proportion are zero plural nouns. However, this can only account for 64 of the 125 zero forms.

   c. Phonological characteristics
   There is no phonological feature common to the 125 zero forms. Some words of unusual phonetic patterns take regular -*s* inflection, whereas many items quite close to English patterns take zero inflection.

   d. Morphological characteristics
   Usually zero plural nouns are monosyllabic or compounds, which are very common forms of Japanese loanwords. Among the zero forms, no items with English derivational suffixes or compounded with English nouns are observed.

e. Occurrence in everyday English

Among the 136 Japanese loanwords that are registered in the seven desk dictionaries and that are considered to be completely assimilated, 27 take zero inflection, occupying 21.8%.

As can be seen above, it seems that zero plural forms are no longer a minor exception. Independent of any linguistic features, some analogize and take the -*s* plural form and others retain the foreign grammatical quality. It is very interesting to consider the influence these words exert on the pluralization system of English.

2.1.3.6 On Recent Tendency

Cannon (1994b) updates the statistics of loanwords and shows new characteristics of Japanese loanwords in English. He finds that Japanese has become the second largest source of recent loanwords, supplying 275 recent (post 1949) items in standard and new-word dictionaries. He then compares loanwords from Spanish and those from Japanese, and finds that Spanish loanwords are quantitatively more productive today than are Japanese ones. This suggests that the speed of assimilation for Japanese loanwords is slower than that for Spanish. He also shows that Spanish loanwords are either regionally marked or socially labeled as slang/informal more often than Japanese loanwords. Other characteristics of recent Japanese loanwords he points out are:

(14) a. Most are monosemous.

b. Most are monosyllabic.

c. 40% of nouns take zero plural inflection.

d. There are four ways of borrowing:

1. phonetic transfer;

2. loan translation (total or partial translation, loose-translation);

3. re-borrowing;

4. combinations of the above.

Cannon (1995b) focuses on the special type of Japanese loanwords in English, and he calls them 'innovative Japanese borrowings.'[2] That is, English borrows vocabulary which Japanese coined using English lexical items such as *salaryman* and *Walkman*. He states that "in adopting these words, English has borrowed an English word to fill a semantic gap in existing English lexicon ..." He also refers to the assimilation process of those words as those which "have undergone no naturalization, are intuitively perceived as English neologisms, and thus were promptly accepted into English."

2.1.3.7 The Naturalization Scale

Cannon (1994b) applies the naturalization scale which is used to measure the degree of assimilation of loanwords from Malay. He divides post-1949 loanwords into four groups according to the four stages of the scale.

(15) 1. almost always glossed, italicized, or with quotation marks.

2. moving into the early stage of phonetic, grammatical, syntactic, and semantic adaptation.

3. recorded in all unabridged dictionaries, somewhat productive (affixation, compounding, shortening) but not fully absorbed into the general lexicon.

4. enjoying wide international usage, said to be a part of the general language, appearing in almost all the latest desk dictionaries, carrying various meanings including transferred, extended, or figurative senses.

He calls a word at the fourth stage "a true LOAN," and classifies the following twelve words into the fourth stage:

(16) *aikido* 'a Japanese art of self-defense'; *Atari*; *high profile* 'a conspicuous public image'; *karate*; *low profile* 'a low-keyed and unobtrusive policy'; *ninja* 'a Japanese warrior experted in ninjutsu'; *origami* 'the Japanese art of folding paper'; *Pac-Man* 'the name of a computer game'; *shiatsu* 'a kind of therapy with the thumbs and palms'; *teriyaki* 'a Japanese dish

---
[2] It is also called 're-borrowing' since English borrows back the vocabulary that has once been borrowed by Japanese from English.

of fish or meat marinated in soy sauce and broiled'; *Walkman* 'a small battery-operated cassette player'; *yakitori* 'a Japanese dish of grilled chicken.'

Cannon (1996) puts all his works on Japanese loanwords into the form of a historical dictionary with historical and linguistic analyses. Each entry of this dictionary is assigned a naturalization index with the modified criteria of a naturalization scale, which will be mentioned in Section 2.2.

2.1.4 Problems with Studies by Cannon

Though his series of studies on Japanese loanwords is the most detailed study and covers more aspects than any of the other studies reviewed above, certain problems remain.

(17) a. Lack of generalization from Japanese loanwords

His naturalization scale is designed to measure the degree of assimilation of Malay loanwords, not the process of assimilation generalized from the data of Japanese loanwords.

b. Missing detailed characterization of stages

His scale does not subdivide the process by which Japanese loanwords gain productivity. According to his scale, the words go through "an early stage of phonetic, grammatical, syntactic, and semantic adaptation" in Stage 2 and gain productivity in Stage 3, but he fails to specify what kind of change belongs to which stage.

c. Lack of data from the actual English texts

His corpus of Japanese loanwords consists only of items from English dictionaries; he does not investigate their actual usage in books.

2.2 Studies on German Loanwords

There are mainly two researchers who have studied German loanwords in English continuously; Garland Cannon and Michael Stubbs. In the following sections, studies of Cannon and Stubbs will be reviewed and problems with those studies will be pointed out.

2.2.1 Studies by Cannon
2.2.1.1 Cannon and Pfeffer (1994) and Before

Cannon and Pfeffer (1994) is a historical dictionary of German loanwords in English with some historical and linguistic overviews. The book is based on the Pfeffer (1987), which deals with the German loanwords on the English vocabulary. Before his book, the loanwords from German were said to be comparatively few, and the majority of these were characterized as technical items, especially in chemistry and mineralogy, which the ordinary speaker or reader of English would not encounter. However, Pfeffer (1987) collects over 3,000 German loanwords in American and British English, and changes this impression. Since it is written in German, there is only a limited access.

Pfeffer continued to collect German loanwords in English from various sources after his publication in 1987, and finally published the revised version written in English with more loanwords (5,380 items) and overview, coauthoring with Cannon (Cannon and Pfeffer 1994). There are two overviews in the book: historical overview by semantic field, and linguistic overview. In the historical overview, German loanwords are divided according to the sixty-nine semantic fields and ordered chronologically in each semantic field. It is revealed that three-tenths of the 5,380 loanwords are classified in mineralogy and chemistry, followed by biology, geology, and botany, which add up to another tenth.

In the linguistic overview, which is written by Cannon, German loanwords are analyzed in the following aspects: phonology and graphemics, grammar, word-formation processes, semantics, and degree of assimilation. His analyses on each of the aspects are summarized below.

Phonology and Graphemics

Since they do not include the pronunciation of entry in their dictionary, Cannon deals with phonology only to a limited extent. He states the general tendency of [x] replaced by [k] as in *Achtung* and [ts] replaced by [z] as in Tsarina (Czarina), and Americans' routine conversion of [r] from trilled and uvular German [R] to their flapped variety. He also mentions the replacement of voiced and unvoiced consonants such as the terminal -*s*, where it is pronounced as [s] in German and [z] in English. He concludes that "a language seldom borrows a new phoneme," and "[e]ven when the German sound is an existing variant of

22   I   Assimilation Process of Loanwords

an English sound, anglicization may occur," due to the analogy from English spelling-pronunciation rules.

As for graphemics, Cannon concludes that English has few problems transliterating German words except for a few punctuational differences: noun capitalization and umlauts. The capitals of nouns are mostly converted to lower case in English, and umlauts are occasionally retained as spelling variants, resulting in 305 main entries having two spellings.

Grammar

In the "Grammar" section, Cannon compares the distribution of the parts of speech of German loanwords and those from other languages (Table 2.1). Nouns are the great majority of all the parts of speech, followed by adjectives and then verbs, which is not very different from the loanwords from other languages.

Nouns are by far the largest group because of their least resistance and the greatest utility. Almost all of them take the English analogical plural *-(e)s*. 344 out of 503 adjectives contain a common English adjectival suffix (*-ic, -(i/y)al, -(i)ous, -oid* etc.). The distribution broadly exemplifies the pattern of Cannon's statistics of new items in English (1987), including loanwords but mainly non-loanwords. Only two German suffixes (*-lich* and *-isch*) are retained. As for verbs, there is a tendency for the German infinitive suffix *-en* to be dropped. Different from the statistics in Cannon (1987), there is a smaller proportion of words with *-ize*, while more items use *-ate* than are listed in the 1987 statistics. There are five affixes and 34 combining forms, which are quite productive in English (*amino-, -burger, morpho-, -ol* etc.).

Table 2.1: The Distribution of Part of Speech

	Noun (4)	Adj. (1)	Verb (2)	Adv.	others
German	88%	9.2%	1.1%	0.2%	1.5%
Chinese	83%	14.5%	1.9%	0.1%	0.5%
Japanese	89.5%	10.0%	—	—	0.5%
Malay	95.4%	4.4%	—	0.2%	—
American Norwegian	75.5%	3.4%	18.4%	n/a	n/a
Hindi and Urdu	89.0%	8.0%	1.2%	n/a	0.3%
Spanish	86.6%	12.7%	0.7%	—	—

Word-Formation Processes

Here, Cannon tries to answer the following questions: "In what proportions are the German forms adapted or translated?" and "What word-formation processes are involved?" The word formation process of nouns is straightforward. They lose the German case and gender designations when they are borrowed, and capitalization and umlauts gradually. Four common German noun patterns are usually eventually anglicized (*-ismus* → *-ism, -ie* → *-y* etc.). As for verbs, the process is less straightforward as it often utilizes considerable graphemic and phonemic changes. In addition to dropping the German *-(e)n* suffix, there are some forms automatically replaced by English forms (*-isieren* → *-ize*). Adjectives have considerable difficulty in being adapted to English, with all case and gender inflections immediately dropped. Suffixes are regularly replaced (*-isch* → *-ish* → *-ic*), proper adjectives are capitalized, and *-ous* or *-ic* is added to the items with no suffix. Overall, the anglicization or adaptation of any part of speech eventuates in an English spelling-pattern.

Cannon distinguishes three general alteration patterns of the German etyma:

(18) a. anglicization (slight change of the graphemic form).

b. adaptation (graphemic form not substantively altered).

c. translation (five types (15%): loanblend, full translation, express of semantic implication, translation to Latin/Greek technical items, loose translation).

However, he fails to discover a guiding principle as to which alteration happens to which items.

Semantics

In the "Semantic" section, Cannon discusses the semantics of names, trademarks and labels. As many as 473 items contain the names of real or imaginary beings, 337 of places, 19 more of peoples or ethnic groups, and 36 trademarks, occupying 15.5% of their corpus. Their originating names are usually transparent, and they are usually used as derivatives/compounds. Trademarks and proprietary names contribute to only a tiny percentage (0.7%). Cannon maintains that the frequent assignment of social, colloquial, or geographical labels indicates the limitation on the given items. On the contrary, he cites a loss of German context as a promise of gaining productivity, and this leads to the high achievement of assimilation.

Degree of Assimilation

Finally, Cannon deals with the degree of assimilation of German loanwords in English. He discovers that the general loss of native context promises a higher productivity in English, and no temporal, social, geographical restriction leads to the greater utility. He determines the degree of assimilation of each item in the dictionary in respect to whether they are registered in English dictionaries, and if so, in how many desk dictionaries, and whether they have productive forms such as derivatives and functional/semantic shift. Characteristics of the items at each stage are the following:

(19) **Stage 1:** an adapted item that is often newly adopted and almost always requires glossing and punctuation either in quotation marks or italics, noticeably foreign-looking, used by restricted groups of people. (Items in the Appendix in the dictionary are classified into this stage.)

Stage 2: partial adaptation of items enjoying a fairly wide range of usage, no glossing or special punctuation, yet have enjoyed little or no usage. Almost all the items are classified into this stage before they proceed to further stages.

Stage 3: generally finished adaptation, usually fits English morphological and phonological patterns, occurs without glossing or special punctuation, registered in enough desk dictionaries as to suggest that it is almost/partly a part of general English.

Stage 4: fully configured with English, registered in all the desk dictionaries, have productive forms, (semantic productivity), and high frequency, considered as a household word.

He also shows the distribution of the degree of assimilation according to the

Table 2.2: The Distribution of Degree of Assimilation

		Stage 2	Stage 3	Stage 4
4,795	nouns	4.0%	65.6%	*30.3%*
503	adjectives	3.0%	59.2%	*37.8%*
60	verbs	1.7%	53.3%	**45.0%**
21	interjections	23.8%	33.3%	**43.0%**
9	adverbs	33.3%	44.4%	22.2%
2	prepositions	50.0%	50.0%	—
1	conjunctions	—	100.0%	—
39	bound forms	—	62.0%	38.0%
20	unmarked	30.0%	60.0%	10.0%
	total	20.6%	55.7%	23.7%
	Malay	67.1%	23.4%	9.4%

parts of speech (Table 2.2). Verbs have the highest percentage of items in Stage 4, followed by interjections. Next come adjectives and nouns, which pose few surprises. One fourth of the items are general international English, which shows that German loanwords are more assimilated in English than Malay loanwords.

2.2.1.2 Cannon (1998b)

Cannon (1998b) updates the dictionary (Cannon and Pfeffer, 1994), adding 253 items dating from 1950 to 1993, and 326 post-1949 neologisms built from German loans. He not only enhances the data in the 1994 dictionary, but also points out the recent phenomenon of the roughly concurrent transfer of both a loanword and its loan translation into English, and the easy creation of neologisms from both pre-1950 and modern German loans.

2.2.2 Stubbs (1998)

Stubbs (1998) claims that there are many loanwords from German other than those which confirm national stereotypes, such as *Nazism* and *Gestapo*. He shows it by using the electric version of the *OED2* and corpora. Not only does he point out the pitfalls in collecting and interpreting the data from the *OED2*, but also he refers to *Cobuild English Dictionary* (1995) as a measure of which words are current in contemporary English. In the *OED2*, he finds 1,250 loanwords from German since 1900, and they can be classified as follows:

(20) a. historically motivated words;

b. names;

c. technical terms;

d. indirect words;

e. German words;

f. false hits.

Then, he searches for those words in a 2.7 million-word corpus and finds that only 15 of them occurred over ten times. Using a larger corpus, he shows the usage and connotation of *angst*. He concludes that although a word-form may not have been borrowed from German, many meanings have been greatly influenced by German-language philosophy, psychology and sociology.

2.2.3 Problems with the Studies on German Loanwords

As was pointed out in the section on Japanese loanwords, Cannon's naturalization scale has some problems.

(21) a. It is determined mainly by the number of dictionaries in which an item is registered and the number of the productive forms they have.

b. It lacks the subdivision of the process by which German loanwords gain productivity.

c. He fails to deal with the actual usage in English texts, judging the frequency of the items in English by the registration of major desk dictionaries.

Although Stubbs is aware of the distinction between loanwords and "words which just are German," he hardly comments on the assimilation of the German loanwords into English except his comment, "the vocabulary of a language is an open set, with words coming and going all the time."

2.3 Other Studies Referring to the Assimilation Processes of Loanwords

2.3.1 Umegaki (1963)

Umegaki (1963) proposes criteria of Japanization of loanwords as follows:

(22) a. whether there are changes in pronunciations, meanings, and usages.

b. whether they are borrowed in an old era or new.

c. whether their frequencies are high or not.

d. whether they are general words or technical.

e. whether they are accompanied by explanations and/or glosses or not.

f. whether they are written in 'hiragana' or 'katakana.'

g. whether they are written in Japanese characters or foreign.

h. whether they appear with 「 」 [quotation marks in Japanese] or not.

In dealing with loanwords in English, (22f) and (22g) are not valid criteria, but the others are applicable. However, he fails to mention which criteria are considered to show a greater degree of assimilation than others. That is, he does not distinguish the phenomena which tend to be observed at the early stages of assimilation, from those which occur at the later stages. As was the case of Cannon's naturalization scale, he does not subdivide the change by which Japanese loanwords gain productivity in (22a).

2.3.2 Koura (1992)

Koura (1992) proposes a point system to measure an assimilation degree of Japanese loanwords in Italian. He gives one point to a loanword if it satisfies one of the following six criteria, and attempts to show the assimilation degree by the sum of the points it earns:

(23) a. general Italian dictionaries register the item as a headword (one point per dictionary).

b. its foreign spelling is Italianized, and a foreign pronunciation which is hard for Italians to pronounce is replaced by an easier sound.

c. it has a derivative.

d. it has an Italian plural ending.

e. it is no longer italicized.

f. its stress is Italianized.

He investigates 36 Japanese loanwords in Italian using ten Italian dictionaries. As a result, *kimono* scores the highest (13 points) followed by *geisha* (12 points), *kaki* (11 points), and *harakiri* (10 points). The results may seem reasonable, but they will probably look differently if the way of giving points changes.

In his paper, all the criteria are dealt equally as one point, but it is unlikely for each of the criteria to show the same significance in measuring the degree of assimilation. Furthermore, in the criterion (23a), he gives one point to each appearance in Italian dictionaries, which can count up to ten points at maximum. Thus, the criterion (23a) seems to be weighted too much. Therefore, there needs to be more consideration and discussion as to how much weight each criterion should have to be able to measure the assimilation degree more accurately. To do so, further investigation of the changes of loanwords after borrowing will be necessary to determine which changes tend to occur more easily or less often than others in the assimilation process.

2.3.3 Daulton (2002)

Daulton (2002) discusses various aspects of the loanwords of English into Japanese, including the massive scale of borrowing, the transitions English words undergo to become *gairaigo* or loanwords, and their currency and usage among Japanese people. In dealing with the transformation of English words, he observes several phenomena in detail, such as "rephonalization," "shortening (truncation) and other morphological changes," "hybridization and coinage," "grammatical transformation," "phrase level transformation," and "semantic change." Although these are common changes when foreign words are assimilated into a language, he fails to mention which transformation is considered to occur at which stage of the assimilation process of English loanwords in Japanese.

2.3.4 Problems on Studies on Assimilation Processes of Loanwords

As we have reviewed in this chapter, there are many studies dealing with loanwords in general or in specific languages or from certain languages, with some mention of 'anglicized,' 'naturalized,' 'adapted,' or 'assimilated' items and the changes observed in those items, but the process in which loanwords get assimilated has not fully been investigated in a systematic way.

In Chapters 3 and 4, I will propose solutions to these problems and the definition of loanwords, and discuss the details of the assimilation processes of Japanese and German loanwords in English. Then in Chapter 5, the assimilation processes of the loanwords from these two languages will be compared, and the differences between them will be visualized.

Chapter 3 Assimilation Process of Japanese Loanwords

3.1 Introduction

3.1.1 Suggested Solutions to the Problems

To solve the problems mentioned above, this study will take the following approach to Japanese loanwords:

(24) a. Investigation of the definitions and citations in English dictionaries, mainly the *OED2*, to find out what changes each Japanese loanword has undergone, and generalize the process a Japanese loanword goes through as it becomes assimilated.

b. Establishment of the stages by which productivity is attained, focusing on phonological, morphological, and semantic aspects.

c. Verification of the generalized assimilation process using computerized texts: *TIME Almanac* (CD-ROM) and *The Times and the Sunday Times* (Internet Edition).

d. Search for other possible factors that can be regarded as criteria of assimilation or the factors that also change as the word proceeds in the assimilation process using a corpus called *Wordbanks* online that contains a wider range of English text than newspapers and news magazines.

3.1.2 Definition of Japanese Loanwords

Before going into specific discussion, I need to clarify the definition of 'Japanese loanword.' In this chapter, lexical items that fulfill the following conditions are assumed to be Japanese loanwords:

(25) a. Primary Loanwords

  Any English word or phrase whose etymology is Japanese including Sino-compounds, which are old Chinese loanwords but are considered to be fully assimilated in the Japanese language.

 b. Secondary Loanwords

  English words or phrases whose etymology is not Japanese but satisfy one of the following conditions:

  - Re-borrowing

    Words or phrases which are coined by the Japanese people using English vocabulary.

  - Literal loan translation

    Words or phrases which are totally or partially translated into English from Japanese words or phrases.

  - Loose loan translation

    Words, or usually phrases, which recently have come into use in English to denote Japanese expressions.

 c. Exceptions

  I do not consider the following items to be Japanese loanwords.

  - The word 'Japan' and its derivatives.

  - The technical term of a substance which was discovered or invented by a Japanese, but whose etymology is not Japanese, *e.g.*, Latin.

    However, I consider a term which contains a part-Japanese etymology a Japanese loanword, including the name of a discoverer or inventor.

3.2 Dictionary-based Approach

3.2.1 Procedure

The procedure I adopted in the dictionary-based part of this study is explained below.

3.2.1.1 Research with the *OED2* CD-ROM

Undoubtedly, the CD-ROM version of the *OED2* is very helpful in this kind of language study because it makes it easy to deal with such abundant data effectively and systematically. I used the *OED2* CD-ROM ver.3 for the search because it enables us to search not only the *OED2*, but also the three volumes of the *OED Additions Series*, which contain more recent loanwords. However, there are some problems with the searching method and etymology description. In this section, I would like to point out the problems I encountered during the research on Japanese loanwords, hoping that they will be improved in the next edition of the *OED*.

| Language Name Search |

On the *OED2* CD-ROM, the simplest way to search for loanwords is to use the **language names** option in the advanced search, which gives a list of loanwords from a target language simply by entering the name of the language (i.e., *japanese*) in the search window. Through this search, 420 possible Japanese loanwords were found. This number included items which did not fulfill the conditions for the definition of Japanese loanwords stated above in Section 3.1.2. 405 items were finally chosen as Japanese loanwords. The items which were excluded from the target were of the following types:

(26) a. The names of substances discovered in Japan which have etymologies of other languages, often Latin (e.g., *protoanemonin* 'a poisonous, vesicant, pale yellow oil').

b. The names of plants which inhabit Japan but have etymologies from other languages, often Latin (e.g., *metasequoia* 'a deciduous, coniferous tree of the genus').

c. The word 'Japan' and its derivatives (e.g., *Japanese, Japaneseness*).

d. The items borrowed from other languages but containing a reference to Japan in the etymology section (e.g., *Goanese* 'a native of Goa,' *Huk* 'a guerrilla movement in the Philippines').

These unwanted items resulted from a defect in the search software, which picks up every item containing the word 'Japanese' or 'Jap.' in the etymology section even if it does not indicate the Japanese origin.

Etymology Search

However, the search above did not pick up the items containing the word 'Japan' in the etymology section. Therefore, the **etymologies** option needed to be used to pick up such items. By entering 'jap∗' in the search window with the **etymologies** option, all the items that contain the word beginning with 'jap' in the etymology section can be searched. As a result, 460 items were extracted, and most of them were overlapped items from the search above, but 14 items were newly identified as Japanese loanwords. Characteristics of such newly found items are:

(27) a. local names which have come to indicate products for which they are well-known (e.g., *Akita* 'a medium-sized dog of Japanese breed,' *Satsuma* 'a kind of Japanese pottery, *Tosa* 'a type of fighting dog in Japan').

b. names of minerals composed of geographical names with suffixes *-ite/lite* (e.g., *ikunolite* 'a bismuth sulphide,' *todorokite* 'a hydrated oxide,' *Tokyoite* 'a native or inhabitant of Tokyo'[1]).

In this search, the software also produced more unwanted items which contained words starting with 'jap,' such as *Ashkenazim* (there is mention of a name 'Japeth' in the etymology section) and *jape* 'a trick, a device to deceive or cheat.'

Definition Search

The search with the **definitions** option picks up every item that contains a target word in the definition section including the etymology section. By entering 'jap∗,' all the items that contain the word beginning with 'jap' in the definition section can be searched for. As a result, it was established that words beginning with 'jap' occurred in the definition section of 512 headwords.

---

[1] *Tokyoite* is not the name of a mineral but the same suffix as minerals is added.

Omitting the items which had already been picked up and excluding unwanted items, it was revealed that 33 items were newly-chosen Japanese loanwords. The search with the **etymologies** option could not pick up these items because they did not have any indication of etymology in the etymology section. The excluded items were of the following types:

(28) a. names of plants/animals which inhabit Japan but have etymologies from other languages, such as Latin (e.g., *cryptomeria* 'An evergreen coniferous tree allied to the cypresses').

b. derivatives of the word 'Japan' (e.g., *Jap* (n.) 'Colloquial abbreviation of *Japanese*').

c. items unrelated to Japan which begin with 'jap' (e.g., *sard* (v.) = *jape* (v.)).

Characteristics of newly found items are:

(29) a. names of places or persons which have come to indicate products for which they are well-known (e.g., *Arita, Hirado* 'a kind of Japanese porcelain,' *Kōrin* 'a school of Japanese painting').
Of these, only *senryu* 'a type of Japanese verse,' *yuzen* 'a technique of dyeing silk fabric,' and *shimada* 'a young unmarried ladies' formal hairstyle' begin with a lower case letter.

b. technical terms for a discovery/invention named after the discoverer/inventor (e.g., *Hashimoto* 'a disease of autoimmune origin,' *Okazaki* 'fragments formed during the replication of chromosomal DNA,' *Shiga* 'the Gram-negative bacterium').

c. loan translation items (e.g., *bullet train* 'Japanese Shinkansen,' *nightingale floor* 'a floor that emits a high-pitched sound in Japan,' *martial art*).

d. others (e.g., *momme* 'a Japanese measure of weight,' *Nipponian* 'Japanese').

Among the items picked up by the search with the **definitions** option, *momme* is a unit of weight that does not derive from a proper noun. The etymology was indicated for other unit names, such as *to* 'a Japanese unit of capacity,' *ken* 'a Japanese unit of length,' and *sun* 'a Japanese unit of length,' and the search with the **etymologies** option could pick them up. Therefore, it may be concluded that the description of etymology is not totally consistent.

Full-Text Search

To make the list of Japanese loanwords more complete, a further search was attempted using the **full text** option. With this option, the software searches through the entire text of the *OED2*, including citations. By entering 'jap*' in the search window, all the entries that contain a word beginning with 'jap' under headwords are picked up. As a result, 'jap' occurred under 2085 headwords. From these, seven new Japanese loanwords were chosen. These newly found items have the following characteristics:

(30) a. spelling variations and derivatives of Japanese loanwords (e.g., *shoya* ← soy, *soyabean* ← soybean, *rick* ← jinrikisha).

b. secondary loanwords (e.g., loan translations: *black belt, tea ceremony*, and a proprietary name (re-borrowing): *Walkman*).

Manual Search

None of the searches mentioned above could pick up certain items; I needed to find them manually by looking at the entries before or after the Japanese loanwords. 11 items were newly verified through the manual search. These words were often loan translations (e.g., *acupressure* '= shiatsu,' *low profile, happy dispatch* '=hara-kiri'), or derivatives (e.g., *bonzess* ← bonze, *kojic* ← koji 'an enzyme preparation'), or spelling variations (e.g., *rickshaw* ← jinrikisha) of Japanese words. No search method could pick up these items because there was no associated etymology section or mention of Japan. The total number of Japanese loanwords found in the *OED2* is 465, and their distribution is shown in Table 3.1.

It is clear from Table 3.1 that there is no single search option which can create a complete list of loanwords from the *OED2* since each search option both produced many unwanted items and excluded many necessary ones. It is

Table 3.1: Japanese Loanwords Found in the *OED2*

Search Options	Items Found[a]	
Language Names	405	(420)
Etymologies	14	(460)
Definitions	34	(516)
Full Text	7	(2085)
Manual	11	—
Total[b]	465	—

a. The figures in parentheses are the number of the results given by each search method.
b. The total figure does not coincide with the sum of the results of the search options above since some items, such as spelling variations and derivatives are not counted separately but included in the main entry.

hoped that the next edition of the *OED* CD-ROM will have a more consistent description in the etymology section and to include software with more flexible search methods.

3.2.1.2 Research with Other Dictionaries

To expand the data, the following dictionaries were investigated:

(31) a. *The Random House Dictionary of the English Language* (1999);

b. *Webster's Third New International Dictionary of the English Language* (2000);

c. *The Oxford Dictionary of Foreign Words and Phrases* (1997);

d. *The Shorter OED 5th ed.* (2002).

The *Oxford English Dictionary* 2nd edition is obviously the largest historical English dictionary in the world with the dates of first appearance and chronological citations. Unlike the *OED2*, the *Random House* and *Webster's Third* are published in the United States, where Japanese loanwords are supposed to be in more frequent use than in the United Kingdom. These two dictionaries were investigated in the hope that they would reveal the American usage of Japanese loanwords omitted from the *OED2*. As a result, about 280 items were added to the data. Since the *Oxford Dictionary of Foreign Words and Phrases* and the *Shorter OED* are historical dictionaries and have been published quite recently, they helped to provide new loanwords, along with the

38   I   Assimilation Process of Loanwords

date of borrowing and chronological citations. They added 24 recent items to the data. The total number of the Japanese loanwords in English dictionaries finally counted up to 768. The number of Japanese loanwords registered in these dictionaries is shown in Table 3.2. Refer to Appendix C for the complete list of Japanese loanwords with the indication of dictionary registrations. Since the dictionaries have different treatments for spelling variations, derivatives, and compounds (some are headwords in one dictionary and sub-headwords in another), I counted all the spelling variations and word-formations as one item to avoid inconsistency. The figure in the right column of Table 3.2 is the figure after subtracting the overlapped items.

Table 3.2: Japanese Loanwords Found in Other Dictionaries

Dictionary	Search Result	Newly Identified
OED2	465	465
Random House	376	183
Webster	392	96
ODFWP	194	6
SOED5	447	18
Total	1874	768

I attempted to generalize the assimilation process for Japanese loanwords from the descriptions and citations in these English dictionaries. As will be mentioned in Section 3.2.2, I divided Japanese loanwords into four groups according to the degree of assimilation. The distribution of Japanese loanwords at each stage is shown in Table 3.3. The results will be discussed in detail in the following sections.

3.2.2   The Four Stages of the Assimilation Process

By tracing the citations for each Japanese loanword and by observing the forms, usages, senses, *etc.*, in these dictionaries, the phenomena occurring repeatedly with Japanese loanwords were extracted and listed in chronological order. As a result, I can now generalize that Japanese loanwords mostly go through the following four stages of the assimilation process:[2]

---

[2] The idea of dividing the assimilation process into stages is originated in Cannon (1994b), and developed further here to solve the problems pointed out in (17) (*i.e.*, lack of generalization from Japanese loanwords, missing detailed characterization of stages, and lack of data from the actual English text).

3 Assimilation Process of Japanese Loanwords 39

(32) a. Stage 1: Adaptation of pronunciation and orthography
(stressification, lengthening, diphthongizing, spelling adaptation).

b. Stage 2: Restricted attributive use of nouns
(noun compound = loanword + explanatory word).

c. Stage 3: Acquisition of productivity
(compounding, suffixation, functional shift from noun).

d. Stage 4: Semantic shift
(transfer of meaning, extension of meaning, metaphoric use).

The distribution of degrees of assimilation of Japanese loanwords is shown in Table 3.3. In the table, 'Others' include four items which do not satisfy the standard of Stage 1, and 26 items of secondary loanwords, which will be discussed in Section 3.4.

Table 3.3: The Degree of Assimilation of Japanese Loanwords

Degree	Observed Changes	Number
Stage 1	Pronunciation, Orthography	575 (74.9%)
Stage 2	Attributive Use of Nouns	99 (12.9%)
Stage 3	Productivity Acquisition	47 (6.1%)
Stage 4	Semantic Shift	17 (2.2%)
Others		30 (3.9%)
	Total	768 (100%)

Here, let us see the general assimilation process by using *kimono* and *soy* as examples. The word *kimono* first appeared in English in 1886, designating 'a long Japanese robe with sleeves' (Stage 1), and its derivative (*kimonoed*) was observed in 1894 (Stage 3), then the semantic shift occurred in 1902 (Stage 4), 'applied to a similar loose, wide-sleeved garment, worn as a dressing gown, coat, *etc.*, in Western countries.' *Soy* appeared in English in 1679 for the first time, meaning 'a sauce prepared from soybean' (Stage 1). In 1795, *soy sauce* was observed as a restrictive use (Stage 2). Then by 1815, more compounds were recorded, such as *soy bottle* and *soy frame* (Stage 3). In 1880, the word *soy* obtained a new sense as "the bean of Glycine max., grown for food" which is so-called 'soybean' (Stage 4).

It is not necessarily the case that every Japanese loanword goes through every stage of this process, but changes are most likely to occur in this order. More examples are shown in Table 3.4.

Table 3.4: Examples of Assimilation Process

	kimono	soy	rickshaw	kamikaze	tsunami
Stage 1	1886	1679	1874	1896	1897
	⇓	⇓	⇓	⇓	⇓
Stage 2	—	1795	1886	1946	1967
	⇓	⇓	⇓	⇓	⇓
Stage 3	1894	1815	1890	1960	—
	⇓	⇓	⇓	⇓	⇓
Stage 4	1902	1880	—	1963	1972

In the following sections, I will discuss each of the four stages of the assimilation process for Japanese loanwords in detail.

3.2.3 Stage 1: Adaptation of Pronunciation and Orthography
3.2.3.1 Pronunciation

Soon after a word is borrowed into English from Japanese, a stress is assigned to it. This is to be expected because polysyllabic words automatically acquire stress in English. Stress is indicated with almost all the Japanese loanwords registered in English dictionaries, though there are some exceptions. The words which do not have a stress indication are:

(33) *hatamoto* 'a vassal or member of the household troops of a Shogun'; *hanami* 'picnic to famous places to view certain flowers'; *hanashika* 'a professional story-teller'; *seoi nage* 'a kind of throw in judo.'

Stressed vowels are usually lengthened or diphthongized, while unstressed vowels are often weakened.[3]

(34) *seppuku* [sɛpúːkuː] (= hara-kiri); *sashimi* [sǽʃɪmɪ]; *zaibatsu* [zaɪbǽtsuː] 'a large capitalist organization in Japan'; *sasanqua* [səsǽnkwə] 'an evergreen shrub.'

---

[3] In this paper, the phonetic alphabets (IPA) are placed in [ ].

When there is sequence of vowels, [j] is often inserted.

(35) *bai-u* [báɪjuː] 'a seasonal rainfall in Japan'; *ukiyo-e* [ukɪjojéː] 'a Japanese wood-block prints.'

3.2.3.2 Orthography

Spellings usually change to make the pronunciation more predictable to the English-speaker as follows:

(36) a. abbreviation (e.g., *jinrikisha* → *rickshaw*);

  b. *ai, i* → *y* (e.g., *tycoon, hoochy*);

  c. final *e* → *i* (e.g., *saki, habutai* 'a fine soft Japanese silk');

  d. long vowel → *oo, ee, h* (e.g., *tycoon, mousmee, Noh*);

  e. *ch* → *tch* (e.g., *hootchie*);

  f. *kus* → *x* (e.g., *moxa* 'the dried leaves for burning on the skin').

Older loanwords tend to have several variations in spelling. For example,

(37) a. *samisen: shamishin, samisi, samishen, samisien, shamisen* 'a Japanese guitar of three strings';

  b. *soy: shoyu, shoya, soya.*

Other characteristics are:

(38) a. use of diacritics, such as *é* and *ō* to indicate the pronunciation (e.g., *Rōjū* 'the senior councillors in Tokugawa government,' *kakké* 'the Japanese name for beriberi').

  b. frequent use of hyphenation (e.g., *O-sotogari, hara-kiri*).

  c. non-capitalized proper nouns (e.g., *shimada, shimose* 'a form of lyddite made in Japan').

  d. capitalized common nouns (e.g., *Nanga* 'an intellectual style of Japanese painting,' *Go*).

e. repetition of consonants (e.g., *kattakanna* 'one of the two Japanese syllabic writing,' *norrimon* 'a kind of litter or palanquin used in Japan,' *yukatta* 'a light cotton kimono').

These adaptations of pronunciation and spelling are observed at a relatively early stage after borrowing. When a Japanese word is borrowed into English, several spelling variations are often observed. Once it has stayed in the English language for a long period of time, one particular variation becomes dominant, and gradually it gains acceptance as the standard spelling. Almost 75% of Japanese loanwords in the English dictionaries are considered to be at this stage.

3.2.4 Stage 2: Restricted Attributive Use of Nouns

At Stage 2, the nouns gain attributive use. Since most of the loanwords from Japanese are nouns, I consider this stage a first step to the stage of "Acquisition of productivity." Loanwords at this stage form compounds, almost always preceding a word which suggests its meaning, as is shown in (39):

(39) | noun compound of restricted attributive use
= *loanword* + **explanatory words**

I do not consider this attributive use fully productive because its use is very restricted, always appearing with the same one or two word(s). Many Japanese loanwords (*i.e.*, 12.9%) stop the assimilation process at this stage without going further. Here are some examples:

(40) *bonsai tree*; *adzuki bean*; *nunchaku sticks* 'a kind of a defensive weapon'; *kana characters* 'Japanese syllabic writing'; *kami religion* (= *Shinto*); *shoyu sauce*; *Sendai virus* 'a paramyxovirus identified in Sendai'; *Yagi aerial* 'a highly directional aerial.'

3.2.5 Stage 3: Acquisition of Productivity

As the assimilation process proceeds, a word obtains power to produce new forms in several ways: compounding, suffixation, and functional shift. A word at this stage can produce new words quite freely, and is not restricted to limited usages as in Stage 2. However, the number of words at this stage is very small, which makes up only 6.1% of the total data, implying that not very many Japanese loanwords are assimilated to this degree. The following is the list of the items which I classify as this stage:

(41) *Arita*; *hiragana* 'the cursive form of the Japanese syllabary'; *ricksha(w)*; *Jomon* 'a kind of very early hand-made Japanese pottery'; *judo*; *Kabuki*; *karaoke* 'a form of entertainment of singing against prerecorded backing'; *karate*; *Meiji* 'the name of the period (1868–1912) in Japan'; *Nippon* 'the Japanese name for Japan'; *Noh*; *Okinawan* 'A native of the Okinawa Islands'; *origami* 'Japanese art of folding paper'; *Ryukyu(an)* 'a native of the Ryukyu Islands'; *saké*; *sayonara*; *shiatsu*; *Shinto*; *shogun*; *Suzuki* 'a method of teaching violin'; *tatami*; *Tokugawa* 'the Japanese ruling dynasty (1603–1867)'; *ukiyo-e*; *Zen*; *Yayoi* ' a type of early Japanese pottery'; *Yukawa* 'the name of Japanese physicist.'

Here are examples of productive usage of these words:

(42) a. compounding

judo society/jacket/club/pyjamas;

kimono blouse/coat/gown/shirt/sleeve;

samurai code/ethic/order/spirit/sword/warrior;

soy biscuit/bottle/flour/jam/oil/protein.

b. suffixing

daimio: daimiate, daimioate, daimiote;

Shinto: Shintoistic, Shintoism, Shintoist, Shintonize;

shogun: shogunal, shogunate, shogunite, shogunship;

tycoon: tycoonate, tycooness, tycoonish, tycoonship.

c. functional shift

(adj.) Shinto; banzai; kamikaze.

(v.) honcho; jinrikisha; ju-jutsu; sayonara; karate.

Here, a functional shift to a noun is not included in the shifts at this stage because it always occurs at the very beginning of borrowing. Four items have

44   I   Assimilation Process of Loanwords

shifted to nouns from other parts of speech: two Japanese interjections (*sayonara*, *banzai*), a Japanese adjective (*shibui* 'appreciation of elegant simplicity'), and a Japanese verb (*tsutsumu* 'the Japanese art of wrapping') are used as nouns in English.

Though one might claim the regularity of inflection as one scale for assimilation as in Matsuda (1992), this is not always the case. As Cannon (1984) stated, Japanese loanwords are likely to retain the irregular inflection regardless of the length of time in English or the degree of assimilation. In the *OED2*, eight are collective nouns[4] (e.g., *amado*, *sumi-e* 'Japanese ink painting,' *yakuza* 'a Japanese gangster'), and 17 nouns have unchanged plural forms (e.g., *geisha*, *nisei* 'an American born of Japanese parents,' *samurai*). The words which have been borrowed for a long period of time and are considered to be quite assimilated in English such as *geisha* and *samurai* still retain this irregularity. This indicates that regularity of inflection cannot be considered as a stage of assimilation.

3.2.6   Stage 4: Semantic Shift

Up to Stage 3, loanwords are usually monosemous, carrying a narrower sense than the original in Japanese. However, at the final stage, a word goes through a semantic shift and becomes polysemic. Words at this stage are supposed to be widely known to and frequently used by English-speakers. I have identified 17 Japanese loanwords as being at this stage, and divided them into three groups in regard to their type of shift: extension of meaning, transfer of meaning, and metaphoric use. The type of shift of each word is shown in Table 3.5.

Here are the definitions from the *OED2* for the words at this stage:

(43)   a.   *banzai*: Applied to a reckless attack by Japanese servicemen.

   b.   *dojo*: In full *dojo mat*. A padded mat on which judo is practised.

   c.   *honcho*: ...hence, anyone in charge in any situation; the boss.

   d.   *geisha*: ...loosely, a Japanese prostitute.

   e.   *kamikaze*: *transf.* and *fig.* Reckless, dangerous, or potentially self-destructive (*lit.* and *fig.*).

---

[4] These are the nouns which the *OED2* labels as '*collect.*' or which have a mention of collective use in the definition section.

Table 3.5: Three Types of Semantic Shift

Extension	Transfer	Metaphoric
futon	*banzai*	*hara-kiri*
geisha	*dojo*	*ju(-)jitsu*
honcho	*hibachi*	*tsunami*
kimono	*kamikaze*	
moxa	*soy*	
samurai	*soya*	
shinkansen	*tycoon*	

f. *kimono*: Now freq. applied to a similar loose, wide-sleeved garment, fastened with a sash, and worn as a dressing gown, coat, *etc.*, in Western countries.

g. *moxa*: Any substance used like moxa for burning on the skin.

h. *samurai*: Also applied to any Japanese army officer.

i. *soy*: Bot.=soybean.

j. *tycoon*: An important or dominant person, esp. in business or politics; a magnate. Also attrib. orig. U.S. (as a nickname of Abraham Lincoln).

Three items contain no indication of an additional sense in definition but are used in shifted senses in the citation. (Underlines supplied in the examples hereafter.)

(44) a. *harakiri*: 1888 *Scott. Leader* 17 Mar. 4 The Liberal Unionist party... will hesitate long before committing hari-kari in that fashion.

b. *hibachi*: 1965 *Austral. Women's Weekly* 20 Jan. 27/1 The other indispensable came from a prolonged stay in Yokohama, a small serviceable iron hibachi, the original of the Western barbecue grill, but portable.

c. *ju-jitsu*: 1965 K. Briggs in Battiscombe & Laski *Chapelet for C. Yonge* 25 Practising a kind of spiritual ju-jitsu, in which by falling with the misfortune you overcome it.

d. *tsunami*: 1972 Science 11 Aug. 502/1 The Food and Drug Administration... is currently swimming through a tsunami of comments generated by its announced intention to alter the regulations concerning the dispensation of methadone.

Three items are from the definition of the *OED Additions Series*:

(45) a. *futon*: ... Hence, any thin mattress or low-lying bed deriving from or resembling the Japanese original.

b. *Shinkansen*: Also *transf.* (usually with lower-case initial) a similar train or system elsewhere.

3.2.7 Cyclic System

Among the loanwords at stage 4, some go back to the earlier stages with their new senses and produce a new series of additional word-formations. I call this phenomenon "a cyclic system of assimilation." The earlier example, *soy* can clearly show how the cyclic system works (Table 3.6). After going all the way through stages 1 to 4 and obtaining a new sense as 'soybean,' many word-formations occur with the new sense.

Table 3.6: An Example of Cyclic System

1679	*soy* (referring to a sauce)	←	Stage 1
	⇓		
1795	*soy sauce*	←	Stage 2
	⇓		
1815	*soy bottle, soy frame*	←	Stage 3
	⇓		
1880	*soy* (referring to beans)	←	Stage 4
	⇓		
1897	*soy flour, soy biscuits, ...*	←	Stage 3
			with the new sense

3.2.8 Summary

In this part of the study, I have presented the four stages of the assimilation process of Japanese loanwords as seen in English dictionaries. Five dictionaries were used to investigate Japanese loanwords: the *OED2v3* (2001), *Random*

House (1999), *Webster's Third* (2000), the *Oxford Dictionary of Foreign Words and Phrases* (1997), and the *Shorter OED 5th ed.* (2002). As the result of the research on these English dictionaries, I have extracted a generalized tendency as to how Japanese loanwords mostly go through the four stages of the assimilation process shown in Figure 3.1.

```
Stage 1    Pronunciation
           Orthography
              ⇓
Stage 2    Attributive Use  ←┐
              ⇓              │
           Productivity      │
           (Compounding)     │
Stage 3    (Derivatives)    ←┤
           (Functional Shifts)│
              ⇓              │
           Semantic Shift    │
           (Transferred)     │
Stage 4    (Extended)       ─┘
           (Metaphoric)
```

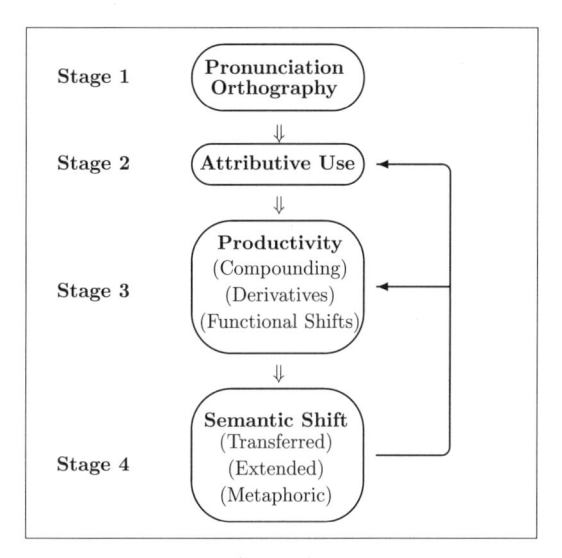

Figure 3.1: Assimilation Process

Soon after a word is borrowed into English from Japanese, a stress is assigned to it. Stressed vowels are usually lengthened or diphthongized, while unstressed vowels are often weakened. Spellings usually change to make the pronunciation more predictable to the English-speakers. At Stage 2, the nouns gain attributive use. Loanwords at this stage form compounds, almost always followed by a word which explains its meaning. As the assimilation process proceeds, a word obtains power to produce new forms in several ways: compounding, suffixation, and functional shift (Stage 3). At Stage 4, a word goes through a semantic shift and acquires a transferred or extended sense. Words at this stage are supposed to be widely known to and frequently used by English-speakers. As the arrow in the figure suggests, some go back to an earlier stage with their new sense and produce more word-formations.

I have also presented the problems I encountered while carrying out this research especially on the *OED2* on CD-ROM. I have pointed out the inconsistency of the descriptions in the etymology section and the inflexibility of the search method.

In Section 3.3, I will verify the assimilation process derived from English dictionaries using corpora.

3.3 Corpus-based Approach

3.3.1 Procedure

Here, I explain the procedure adopted in the corpus-based part of this study.

To verify the assimilation process generalized by the English dictionary-based research, two corpora were used, *TIME Almanac* on CD-ROM (henceforth *TIME*) and *The Times and the Sunday Times* Internet Edition (henceforth *The Times*). *TIME* is available on CD-ROM and contains all the articles published in *TIME Magazine* from 1989 to 1994, along with a supplement. *The Times* can search through the articles of 1996 and is updated everyday. The entire database of *TIME* and all the articles of *The Times* from January 1 to August 31, 1996 were used for this verification. Those Japanese loanwords which were determined to be relatively assimilated in Section 3.2, along with some unassimilated ones, were searched for in these corpora and their degrees of assimilation were examined. Respective distributions for the stages mentioned above are shown in Table 3.7.

In searching these corpora for Japanese loanwords, the following points were focused on:

(46) a. How (forms, gloss *etc.*) unassimilated words appear in corpora.

b. What kinds of word-formation are observed for assimilated words.

Table 3.7: Japanese Loanwords Found in Corpora

Stage	*TIME*	*The Times*
Stage 3	27 out of 47 items	24 out of 47 items
Stage 4	12 out of 17 items	13 out of 17 items
Total	39 out of 64 items	37 out of 64 items

c. In what sense they are used.

d. Whether these observed word-formations and semantic shifts reflect the results of the dictionary-based research.

e. Whether there are any new usages that could not be found in the dictionaries.

In the process, the following problems arose:

(47) a. Because the text of *TIME* is plain, with no indication of Italic or bold typefaces, such information could not be used as an indication of assimilation as suggested by Ishimaru (1990).

b. There is a considerable variation in the spelling of Japanese loanwords, which makes the word searches difficult and inaccurate.

c. In mechanical search, there is no way of distinguishing a Japanese loanword from an English native word if the spelling coincides with that of a frequently occurring English word (e.g., *do* 'the art,' *Go* 'a Japanese board game,' *No*, *sake*, *sen* 'a Japanese copper or bronze coin,' *to*).

d. It is difficult to find a new word or a new spelling variation in the corpora which has not been registered in dictionaries unless the researcher guesses in advance which words are likely to occur in English texts.

In regards to *sake*, among the 236 instances, I excluded such phrases as *for the sake of ...* and *for ...'s sake* and obtained twelve results which refer to the Japanese loanword, *sake*. Though other problems have remained unsolved, failure to find such items will not be expected to have much influence on the overall picture with Japanese loanwords. Hence, the number of instances collected from the corpora was considered to be sufficient for the subsequent verification process.

3.3.2 Unassimilated Loanwords

In the articles of news magazines or newspapers, Japanese loanwords which are not considered to be commonly-known usually appears with a gloss. Such words appear in these articles in the following ways:

(48) a. A sentence which explains the loanword is embedded in the article.
- *Minamata takes its name from a Japanese fishing village that was afflicted with industrially caused mercury poisoning, ...*
- *The yakuza is Japan's version of the Mafia, a shadowy mob brotherhood that often operates behind a shield of what appears to be legitimate business fronts.*

b. The word is used attributively, followed by an expression which explains the word.
- *... little has been done to help the estimated 70,000 Thai "hostesses" ... usually controlled by yakuza gangsters.*
- *Japanese-born painter Masami Teraoka combines elements of European art and Japanese ukiyo-e wood-block imagery.*
- *Unlike Japan's notorious juku cram schools, which concentrate on passing exams, ...*

c. The word is followed by an apposition of gloss.
- *It turned out to be run by the yakuza, Japan's organized-crime syndicate.*
- *The Japanese word ukiyo — "the floating world "— suggests the narrow bridges of Hiroshige or the frozen waves of Hokusai.*
- *Kumon Mathamatex, a math-teaching method developed by educator Toru Kumon to improve his own child's performance.*

d. The word is followed by a gloss in parentheses.
- *... "when parties take up really fundamental issues like karoshi (death from overwork) and unpaid overtime."*
- *Akebono, 25, the hefty U.S.-born sumo yokozuna (grand champion); ...*
- *If the Cali cartel makes an alliance with the yakuza (Japan's organized-crime network), ...*

e. The word is paraphrased followed by *or*.

- But the prevalence of the <u>nisei</u> giin, or second-generation politicians, has raised fears that Japanese politics is increasingly being restricted to an elite kinship.

As mentioned in Section 3.3.1, it was impossible to use an Italic typeface as an indication of non-assimilation because the text was plain. These unassimilated loanwords appear in the articles only a few times, and in every case, a gloss is attached in one of the ways listed above, implying that they are not sufficiently well-known to be used without a gloss. The usages of gloss observed here are difficult to detect in the dictionary because it is required to go beyond the lexical-level to sentence- or even passage-level observation to study gloss.

3.3.3 Morphological Observation

I searched for 64 items (47 Stage 3 items and 17 Stage 4 items) to investigate the productivity of these words in *TIME* and *The Times*. The frequencies are summarized in Table 3.8. The following three ways of producing new words are observed:

(49) a. Compounding;

b. Suffixation;

c. Functional Shift.

3.3.3.1 Occurrence in *TIME*

Compounding is the most frequently observed followed by suffixation. I found that *Zen* and *soy* produce the largest number of compounds followed by *kamikaze* and *samurai*. Here are examples:[5]

(50) **Zen:** *Zen Buddhist, Zen meditation, Zen garden, Zen teacher, Zen characters, Zen machismo, Zen archery, pseudo-Zen profundities, Zen state of suspended agitation, Zen instructor, Zen retreat,* etc.;

---

[5] The complete list of observed productive forms in *TIME* appears in Appendix A.

Table 3.8: Occurrence of the Assimilated Loanwords (*TI*: *TIME*, *Ts*: *Times*)

Item	TI	Ts	Item	TI	Ts	Item	TI	Ts
Arita	0	0	*karaoke*	8	98	*Shinto*	12	14
banzai	6	0	*karate*	27	123	*shogun*	15	16
dimio	0	0	*kimono*	8	11	*shoji*	0	0
dojo	0	1	*Meiji*	11	7	*soy*	101	84
futon	0	1	*moxa*	0	0	*soya*	0	29
geisha	8	16	*Nara*	0	0	*sushi*	22	31
hara-kiri	3	3	*Nippon*	27	67	*sukiyaki*	0	0
Hashimoto	0	0	*Nisei*	6	0	*Suzuki*	21	99
Heian	0	0	*Noh*	1	17	*tatami*	1	2
hibachi	0	0	*Okinawan*	23	0	*tempura*	1	12
hiragana	1	0	*origami*	1	8	*teriyaki*	4	2
honcho	20	5	*Ryukyu*	5	2	*Tokugawa*	1	0
Imari	0	0	*sake*	15	1	*tsunami*	25	1
inkyo	0	0	*samurai*	27	14	*tycoon*	139	284
Ishihara	0	1	*satori*	0	0	*Ukiyo-e*	3	6
jinrikisha	3	28	*sayonara*	4	34	*urushi*	0	0
Jomon	0	0	*shiatsu*	6	7	*yamato-e*	0	0
judo	10	201	*shiitake*	3	4	*Yayoi*	0	1
jujitsu	4	0	*Shin*	0	0	*Yeddo*	0	0
Kabuki	11	11	*Shingon*	0	0	*Yukawa*	2	0
Kamakura	0	0	*Shinkansen*	0	1	*Zen*	67	23
kamikaze	24	27						

soy: *soy sauce, soy bean, soy ink, soy milk, soy diesel fuel, soybean crop, soybean broker, soybean bran, soybean formula, soybean future price, soybean farmer*, etc.;

kamikaze: *kamikaze mission, kamikaze reputation, kamikaze competition, kamikaze attack, kamikaze airmen, kamikaze team*, etc.;

Nisei: *Nisei outcasts, Nisei students, nisei son*;

samurai: *samurai sword, samurai class, samurai warrior, samurai work ethic, pseudo-samurai businessman*, etc.;

sushi: *sushi bar, sushi chefs, sushi lovers, sushi eater, sushi deliveries, sushi waitress*.

There are also hyphenated compounds, none of which are registered in the dictionaries:

(51) *samurai-like; tsunami-sized; kamikaze-styled; karate-skilled; soy-based; Meiji-era; Zen-like, Zen-heavy, Zen-minded, Zenned-out.*

I found the following items with suffixation:

(52) *kimonoed; shogunate; shogunism; shogunist; tycoonery; karatecize; Okinawan; Nipponese; zenlike, Zenned.*

Functional shift is observed only with the following three items:[6]

(53) **kamikaze** (*adj.*): *"He's such a puppy dog off the ice, but give him a pair of skates and he turns kamikaze."*

karate-kick (*v.*): *As a blood-soaked Denny called for help, he was hit with beer bottles and karate-kicked in the head.*
Tom Laughlin ... and now the jowly actor wants to karate-kick his way into the White House on a platform of nuclear disarmament and middle-class tax cuts.

karate-chop (*v.*): *He looked rested, smiled frequently, radiated energy, frequently karate-chopped the air or formed a fist to make a point, ...*

Among the functional shifts above, only *karate-chop* as a verb is a new usage which could not be found in the dictionaries.
Among the 64 searched items, the following 25 do not occur at all:

(54) *Arita; daimio; dojo; futon; Hashimoto; Heian; hibachi; Imari; inkyo; Ishihara; Jomon; Kamakura; moxa; Nara; satori; Shin; Shingon; Shinkansen; shoji; soya; sukiyaki; urushi; yamato-e; Yayoi; Yeddo.*

---

[6] Since an attributive use of a noun and an adjective have the identical form, I only dealt with the predicative adjective.

54   I   Assimilation Process of Loanwords

Yukawa and *Suzuki* appear in *TIME* but only as proper nouns which show no productive forms. *Sayonara* does not provide any productive forms, either.

Moxa seems to have enjoyed its prevalence in English but is no longer used commonly, as can be seen from the fact that the latest citation for *moxa* in the *OED2* is 1877. *Shinkansen* does not occur because its loan translation, *bullet train* is already widely known and preferred in *TIME*. Since *futon* and *hibachi* are terms related to daily-life, rather than being newsworthy, they do not appear in such news magazines like *TIME*. Since most of the others are proper nouns and technical terms in certain fields, they are not likely to appear in a general news magazine. Thus, different kinds of books need to be examined to investigate the usage of these items.

3.3.3.2   Occurrence in *The Times*

Compounding is the most frequently observed and the other two ways of word formation are rarely observed. I found that *karaoke* and *karate* have the largest number of productive form of compounds, followed by *kamikaze* and *judo*. Here are examples:[7]

(55)   **karaoke:** *karaoke bar, karaoke channel, karaoke night, karaoke outing, karaoke song, karaoke party, karaoke session, karaoke restaurant,* etc.;

karate: *karate attack, karate champion, karate kick, karate pyjamas, karate techniques, karate expert,* etc.;

kamikaze: *kamikaze challenge, kamikaze mission, kamikaze attacker, kamikaze mood, kamikaze terrorism, kamikaze man,* etc.;

judo: *judo club, judo players, judo title, judo mat, judo nations, judo talent, judo champion,* etc.;

sushi: *Sushi restaurant, sushi knives, sushi box, Sushi chic, sushi bars, sushi chef, sushi rolls.*

There are also hyphenated compounds, none of which are registered in the dictionaries:

---

[7] The complete list of productive forms in *The Times* appears in the Appendix B.

(56) *soya-based; karaoke-fashion, karaoke-style, karaoke-entertainment; karate-kick, karate-like, karate-style, karate-type; noh-theatre; shiatsu-practicing; sushi-making.*

Shintoism, Nipponese and *origamist* were the only suffixed ones. Functional shift is observed with the following three items:[8]

(57) **kamikaze (*adj.*):** *It's where I'll probably be criticised if I lose it, People will say I went kamikaze all over the place.*

karate kick (*v.*): *... 1960s feminism who karate-kicked their way to equality; ... Honor Blackman karate-kicked her way across television screen in The Avengers.*

Zen (*adj.*): *Still, Gabrielle's being quite Zen about it all. She, like an stout British citizen, is blaming it on the weather.*

Among the 64 searched items, the following 27 do not occur at all:

(58) *Arita; banzai; daimio; Hashimoto; Heian; hibachi; hiragana; Imari; inkyo; Jomon; Jujitsu; Kamakura; moxa; Nara; Nisei; Okinawan; satori; Shin; Shingon; Shoji; sukiyaki; Tokugawa; urushi; yamato-e; Yayoi; Yeddo; Yukawa.*

Sayonara and *shogun* appear in *The Times* but showed no productive forms. The occurrence of each item in Stage 3 and 4 is summarized in Table 3.8.

3.3.4 Semantic Observation

In search of the 17 items which I classified as the loanwords in Stage 4, most of the items occur repeatedly in both its original and shifted sense. Here are some examples of these items with the number of occurrences and the different senses that appear in *TIME*:

(59) Occurrences in *TIME*[9]

---
[8] Again, since an attributive use of a noun and an adjective have the identical form, I only dealt with the predicative adjective.
[9] The numbers in parentheses indicate the occurrence times. ○: the original sense, ●: a shifted sense mentioned in the dictionaries, ×: a shifted sense the dictionaries mentioned but was not observed in the corpus, ★: a newly found sense in the corpus.

banzai: (6)

  ○ a shout to the emperor (2).
  ⋆ the title of a movie (2) *The Adventure of Backaloo Banzai.*
  ⋆ a cartoon character (1) *giddy Banzai.*
  ⋆ the name of the Japan vs. the U.S. baseball game (1) *Banzai Ball.*
  × a reckless attack.

harakiri: (3)

  ○ disembowelment (2).
  • suicidal (1) *harakiri tactic of Kamikaze.*

honcho: (20)

  • the president of a company, executives (in *pl.*), a head of an organization, a powerful person in economy (17) *show-biz honchos, real estate honchos, CAA honcho, S&L honcho.*
  • a political leader (3) *Democratic honchos.*
  × the leader of a small group.

jujitsu: (4)

  ⋆ a technique, strategy (3) *political jujitsu, social jujitsu.*
  ○ a kind of Japanese martial art (1).

kamikaze: (24)

  • reckless, suicidal, certain to fail; a small group attacking the big (20) *kamikaze band of less profitable owners to block an agreement.*
  ○ the suicidal attack by Japanese airmen during the war (2).
  ⋆ the name of a cocktail (1).
  ○ a divine wind (1).
  × a surfing term.

kimono: (8)

  ○ a Japanese traditional costume, wearing kimono (6).
  • kimono-like robe (1) *with black flowing bottoms and a leopard-spotted kimono.*

⋆ a barrier covering Japan (metaphorical) (1) *a Teflon kimono.*

samurai: (27)

- ○ a Japanese military caste in the feudal system (17) (often described as a loyal or noble or sadistic warrior).
- ⋆ an aggressive Japanese business man (4) ... *transform himself into a pseudo-samurai businessman.*
- ⋆ the name of a car (1) *Suzuki Samurai.*
- ⋆ a TV comic character (3) *samurai comic.*
- ⋆ a strong male image (2) *samurai biker.*
- × a Japanese army officer.

soy: (101) (88 of them occured as *soybean*)

- • a bean of *Glycine max.* (101) as grain, oil, commodities, merchandise in future market, a target for investment.
- ○ soy sauce.

There are several instances of 'Soya,' but all of them signify the strait of Soya in Japan.

tsunami: (25)

- ○ a tidal wave (16).
- • a large amount, a big movement. (metaphorical) (9) *A tsunami-sized wave of nausea rolled through him*; *a tsunami of Mickey Mouse trinkets, teriyaki burgers* ...

tycoon: (139)

- • a millionaire, a successful businessman (138) *office boy turned tycoon, whose $2 billion family fortune is one of the largest in the U.S.*; *oil tycoon*; *media tycoon*; *publishing tycoon.*
- ⋆ the name of a novel (1) *The Last Tycoon.*
- ○ × a virtual ruler in the feudal period.
- × an important person in politics.

Some items such as *futon, hibachi, moxa,* and *shinkansen* do not appear at all in *TIME*. The reason for this non-occurrence is already mentioned above. Some senses that dictionaries refer to do not appear in *TIME*. This suggests that certain senses obtain dominant uses as the assimilation process proceeds, while others go out of use. *Honcho, tycoon* and *soy* are used only in transferred or extended senses and *kamikaze* is used in a transferred sense except for two instances. It shows that these words have completely stabilized in English in these senses rather than in the original ones.

Besides these items, I found three items which are considered to have gone through a semantic shift: *shogun, judo,* and *Zen. Shogun* shows an extended sense of a ruler of any kind and a transferred sense of a powerful person in politics. *Judo* and *Zen* are used metaphorically. The details are shown below:

(60) **shogun:** (15)
- ○ a virtual ruler in the feudal period (5).
- ★ the title of a musical (5).
- ★ a ruler, a powerful person (3) ... *dominated by male shogunists*; *the shogun of the ruling Liberal Democratic Party.*
- ★ the title of a novel (1).
- ★ the title of a TV program (1).

judo: (10)
- ○ a kind of Japanese martial arts (5).
- ★ a fight (metaphorical) (4) *verbal judo, presidential judo battles.*
- ★ the name of a bull (1).

Zen: (67)
- ○ a sect of Japanese Buddhism (31).
- ★ philosophical, mysterious, paradoxical (metaphorical) (29) *Zen politics, Zen approach, Zen of golf.*
- ★ the name of a book (6) *Zen in America, Zen and the art of Motorcycle Maintenance.*
- ★ a literal expression (1).

The 17 items of Stage 4 from the English dictionaries and the three newly found Stage 4 items in *TIME* are examined in the same way, using *The Times*. Here are some examples of these items with the number of instances and the senses that appear in the articles of *The Times*.

(61) Occurrences in *The Times*[10]

futon: (1)

- a mattress (metaphorical) (1). *a futon of spinach with pine nut cushions*

One instace is observed for *futon*, while none is found in *TIME*.

harakiri: (3)

∘ disembowelment (1).

- suicide (metaphorical) (2) ... *commit hara-kiri by falling on their quill pens and voting themselves out of the limelight.*

honcho: (5)

- the president of a company, executives (in *pl.*), a head of an organization, a powerful person in economy (4) *head honchos at Post Office; advertising honcho.*
- a political leader (1) *he flew to Australia to tell arch-Thatcherite Rupert Murdoch and his head honchos that he and new Labour were the true heirs to the Thatcher revolution.*

× the leader of a small group.

Honcho is not as common an item in *The Times* as in *TIME*. This can be observed from the fact that it almost always occurs in the article accompanied by 'head' to specify its sense.

kamikaze: (27)

- reckless, suicidal, certain to fail; a small group attacking the big (19) ... *to conceive such a kamikaze campaign credible; they may send a kamikaze attacker to throw himself in front of Schumacher's car ...*

∘ the suicidal attack by Japanese airmen during the war (4).

⋆ the name of a race horse (4).

× the name of a cocktail.

× a surfing term.

∘ × a divine wind.

---

[10] The numbers in parentheses and symbols denote the same as above.

kimono: (11)

- ○ a Japanese traditional costume, wearing kimono (11).
- × loose, wide-sleeved garment.

Unlike *TIME*, no extended sense was observed.

samurai: (14)

- ○ a Japanese military caste in the feudal system (7) (often described as a loyal or noble or sadistic warrior).
- ★ a warrior (metaphoric) (2) *he is the stern Samurai of the baseball field.*
- ★ the name of a car (2) *Devon-based Samurai Motor Components.*
- ★ the title of a movie (3) *Samurai Cowboy.*
- × a Japanese army officer.

shinkansen: (1)

- ○ Japanese high-speed train (1).

There were 4 instances of a loan translation of *shinkansen, bullet train*, which will be discussed in the next section.

soy: (84) (62 of them occur as *soya*)

- • a bean of *Glycine max.* (84).
- ○ × soy sauce.

Soy is almost always used in the form of 'soy sauce,' though *soya* is the dominant use in other instances in *The Times*.

tsunami: (1)

- ○ a tidal wave (1).
- × a big movement.

tycoon: (284)

- • a successful businessman, millionaire (278) *media tycoon*; *publishing tycoon.*
- ★ the name of a race horse (5) *Gnome's tycoon.*
- ★ the name of a novel (1) *The Last Tycoon.*
- ○ × a virtual ruler in the feudal period.
- × an important person in politics.

As is so in *TIME*, *hibachi* and *moxa* do not occur in *The Times*. Unlike *TIME*, *futon* appears and *banzai* and *jujitsu* do not. *Honcho* occurs in both corpora, but much less frequently in *The Times*. There is also a difference in its usage as will be mentioned later. I also searched for *shogun*, *judo*, and *Zen* whose transferred senses are observed in *TIME*. Though I obtained 16 instances for *Shogun* and 201 instances for *judo* in *The Times*, no metaphorical use is observed. Most instances of *Shogun* indicate the name of Mitsubishi's car,[11] while two are used in the original sense. All the instances for *judo* indicate a Japanese martial art, which is the original sense. *Jujitsu* does not occur at all. Metaphorical use for *Zen* is observed as follows:

(62) **Zen:** (23)

- ○ a sect of Japanese Buddhism (15).
- ⋆ the name of a book (3) *Zen and the Art of Motorcycle Maintenance*.
- ⋆ intuitive, mysterious, paradoxical (metaphorical) (2) ... *being quite Zen about it;* ... *swam into his Zen*.
- ⋆ a proper noun (3) *Zen Video Theater, M Zen*.

3.3.5 Verification Results

As a result of the investigation of the two corpora, the assimilation process of Japanese loanwords derived from English dictionaries can be verified to a certain degree. More than half of the items which are considered to be assimilated also show frequent occurrence in corpora with a variety of word formations. The verification results of productivity is summarized in Tables 3.9 and 3.10, where items of Stage 4 are also examined to see if they satisfy the standard of Stage 3. In Table 3.11, the verification results of semantic shift are summarized. ○ denotes that the degree of assimilation for the item in question matches that indicated in the English dictionaries. △ denotes that the item in question appears in the corpora, but does not show the same degree of assimilation indicated in the English dictionaries. × denotes that the item never appears in the corpora. Failure to find some items in the corpora seems to

---

[11] It is sold as "Pajero" in Japan.

Table 3.9: Verification of Productivity (Stage 3 Items)

Items	TIME	The Times
Arita	×	×
daimio	×	×
Hashimoto	×	×
Heian	×	×
hiragana	△	×
Imari	×	×
Inkyo	×	×
Ishihara	×	△
(jin)ricksha(w)	○	○
Jomon	×	×
judo	○	○
Kabuki	○	○
Kamakura	×	×
karaoke	○	○
karate	○	○
Meiji	○	×
Nara	×	×
Nippon	○	○
Nisei	○	×
Noh	△	○
Okinawan	○	△
Origami	△	○
Ryukyu	△	○
sake	△	△
Satori	×	×
sayonara	△	△
shiatsu	○	○
shiitake	△	△
Shin	×	×
Shingon	×	×
Shinto	○	○
shogun	○	△
shoji	×	×
sushi	○	○
sukiyaki	×	×
Suzuki	×	△
tatami	○	○
tempura	△	△
teriyaki	△	△
Tokugawa	△	○
Ukiyo-e	△	△
urushi	×	×
yamato-e	×	×
Yayoi	×	×
Yeddo	×	×
Yukawa	△	×
Zen	○	○

Table 3.10: Verification of Productivity (Stage 4 Items)

Items	TIME	The Times
banzai	△	×
dojo	×	△
futon	×	△
geisha	○	○
harakiri	○	△
hibachi	×	×
honcho	△	△
jujitsu	○	×
kamikaze	○	○
kimono	○	○
moxa	×	×
samurai	○	○
shinkansen	×	△
soy	○	○
soya	×	○
tsunami	○	△
tycoon	○	△
Total	○ 24	○ 21
(Stage 3 and	△ 14	△ 17
4 Items)	× 26	× 26

Table 3.11: Verification of Semantic Shift

Stage 4 Items	TIME	The Times
banzai	△	×
dojo	×	×
futon	×	○
geisha	○	△
harakiri	○	○
hibachi	×	×
honcho	○	○
jujitsu	○	×
kamikaze	○	○
kimono	○	△
moxa	×	×
samurai	○	○
soy	○	○
soya	×	○
tsunami	○	△
tycoon	○	○
shinkansen	×	△

New Items	TIME	The Times
judo	○	△
shogun	○	△
Zen	○	○

Total	○ 13	○ 9
	△ 1	△ 6
	× 6	× 5

result from one of the following reasons:

(63) a. The dictionaries do not reflect the recent tendencies.
  b. The description of the dictionaries are slanted.
  c. The corpora are not representative enough.

There are some items which are not concluded to be assimilated in the English dictionaries, but appear in the corpora frequently and productively. These items should be added to the Stage 3 items. Here are some examples:

(64) **bonsai:** *bonsai plant; bonsai-club members; bonsai growers; bonsai trees.*
  kendo: *kendo master; kendo academy.*
  kudzu: *kudzu vine; kudzu starch.*
  sumo: *sumo wrestling; sumo wrestler; sumo stable master; sumo contenders; Sumo indigenous communities; sumo superstar; sumo fans; sumo tournament.*
  tofu: *tofued (v.)*
  yen: *yen falters; yen pit; yen traders.*

These items failed to be included as Stage 3 items because their usage is too recent for the dictionaries to pick up. Now, there needs to be some revision to the classification of Japanese loanwords to reflect the results of the research using corpora. (65) shows the revised list of the Stage 3 items, and Table 3.12, the revised version of the types of semantic shift. Table 3.13 is the revised version of the degree of assimilation of Japanese loanwords. The revised items are indicated in the Appendix C.

(65) The revised list of Stage 3 items: *bonsai, ricksha(w), Kabuki, karaoke, karate, kendo, kudzu, Meiji, Nippon, Noh, Okinawan, origami, Ryukyu(an), saké, shiatsu, Shinto, sumo, sushi, Suzuki, tofu, tatami, teriyaki, Tokugawa, yen.*

Table 3.12: Three Types of Semantic Shift (Revised)

Extension	Transfer	Metaphoric
futon	*kamikaze*	*hara-kiri*
geisha	*soy*	*jujitsu*
honcho	*soya*	*tsunami*
kimono	*tycoon*	*judo*
samurai	~~*banzai*~~	*Zen*
shogun	~~*dojo*~~	
~~*moxa*~~	~~*hibachi*~~	
~~*shinkansen*~~		

Table 3.13: The Degree of Assimilation of Japanese Loanwords (Revised)

Degree	Observed Changes	Number	−, +
Stage 1	Pronunciation, Orthography	596 (77.6%)	−3, +24
Stage 2	Attributive Use of Nouns	103 (13.4%)	−3, +7
Stage 3	Productivity Acquisition	24 (3.1%)	−29, +6
Stage 4	Semantic Shift	15 (2.0%)	−5, +3
Others		30 (3.9%)	
	Total	768 (100%)	

3.3.6 Comparison of Usage in the Two Corpora

There are several interesting differences in the usage of Japanese loanwords between the two corpora. Generally speaking, *TIME* supplies more items than *The Times*. However, the frequency of each item in the two corpora cannot be compared because they are different in size. Though instances for *judo* in *The Times* outnumbers those in *TIME*, this is probably because the Olympic Games were held in 1996 and corpus of *The Times* covers articles of the year. Going into more detail, the following differences are observed:

(66) a. Suffixation is observed more frequently in *TIME* than in *The Times*.

b. The items which form a large number of compounds are different; *Zen* and *soy* produce the largest in *TIME*, *karaoke* and *karate*, in *The Times*.

c. In *The Times*, *honcho* is mostly used as 'head honcho,' while in *TIME*, this collocation does not appear at all.

d. As for *soy*, *soy* is the only spelling in *TIME*, while *soya* is dominantly used in *The Times*, though both spellings are used.

e. In *TIME*, both *jujitsu* and *judo* are used, while *jujitsu* is not used at all in *The Times*.

f. Semantic shifts for *kimono, tsunami, shogun,* and *judo* are observed only in *TIME*.

g. *Futon, satsuma,* and *shinkansen* appear only in *The Times*, while in general, *TIME* supplies more items.

h. *Suzuki* occurs in both corpora, but the sense the dictionary (i.e., the *OED Additions Series*) cites ('a teaching method of instrument') only appears in *The Times*.

Though *TIME* is published in the United States and *The Times* in Britain, the differences between the two corpora do not directly indicate the differences between the English dialects of these two countries. That is because (1) these corpora cover articles of different years, and (2) one is a newspaper and the other is a news magazine, which may cover different kinds of topics and have different usages of words. However, the differences I stated here may suggest different usages of Japanese loanwords between American and British English.

3.3.7 Summary

To verify the assimilation process derived from the dictionary-based study, I used two corpora: *TIME* and *The Times*. In the articles of these corpora, a Japanese loanword which is not considered to be commonly-known usually appears with a gloss. Word formations such as compounding and suffixation are observed for the words at Stages 3 and 4 except some proper nouns and technical terms. The words at Stage 4 show transferred/extended senses and metaphorical uses. Some new usages and meanings are also observed. The comparison of the two corpora suggests a likely different usage of Japanese loanwords between American and British English.

There still remain problems to solve in the future. Because of the nature of the corpora used in this study, some items could not be found at all, or a sufficient number of instances could not be collected for some items. The use of a more representative corpus will be needed to obtain more accuracy. At the same time, this may help to distinguish the difference in usage between American and British English. Another problem is the lack of the degree of prevalence of Japanese loanwords. Since the corpus study does not provide information on the actual use by English-speakers, survey and interviews with English-speakers will be a necessary study to establish the total image of Japanese loanwords. It will also help to find those items which are commonly known but cannot be classified as being assimilated in this study.

3.4 Characteristics of Secondary Loanwords

The assimilation process of primary loanwords from Japanese has been observed in Section 3.2 and 3.3. In this section, I will present a result of investigation of the secondary loanwords from Japanese and determine if they follow the same process of assimilation as primary loanwords. As was defined in Section 3.1.2, secondary loanwords are the English words or phrases whose etymology is not Japanese, but are coined by Japanese using English vocabulary (re-borrowing), or are translated from Japanese words or phrases literally or loosely (loan translation). The same dictionaries as in Section 3.2 were used for the investigation. As for corpus, I used *The Times and the Sunday Times* CD-ROM Edition (1995, henceforth *The TimesCD*) since the two corpora used in Section 3.3 (i.e., *TIME* and *The Times*) did not supply enough variety of secondary loanwords.

3.4.1 Loan Translation

There are two kinds of loan translation: literal translation and loose translation. In the English dictionaries I studied, the following items are registered:[12]

(67) **Literal Translation:** *black belt** (← kuro-obi); *brown belt** (← cha-obi) 'the belt which shows a certain degree of proficiency next to black belt in judo'; *god-shelf* (← kami-dana) 'a shelf-like shrine of white wood in Japanese house'; *karate-chop** (← karate-shuto); *nightingale floor* (← uguisu-bari) 'a floor that emits a high-pitched

---

[12] Those which are asterisked appear in *The TimesCD*.

sound when it is trodden on'; *plum rain* (← bai-u); *stone* (← goishi) 'a round piece used in game of go'; *tea ceremony** (← chagi) 'the ritual preparation and consumption of green tea'; *yellow belt* (← ki-obi) 'the belt which shows a certain degree of proficiency in judo'; *white belt** (← shiro-obi) 'a belt making the rank of beginner in judo.'

Loose Translation: *acupressure** (← shiatsu); *bullet train** (← Shinkansen); *graphic novel** (← manga) 'a full-length of story of a comic strip'; *happy-dispatch* (← hara-kiri); *high profile** (← koushi-sei); *low profile** (← teishisei).

None of these but *plum rain* and *stone* have the etymology of the Japanese origin in the English dictionaries. There are more examples of loan translation in the literature[13] as follows:

(68) **Literal Translation** *Black Current* (← kuroshiwo); *black mist* (← kuroi kiri); *low posture, low silhouette* (← teishisei); *linked verse* (← renga); *hell camp* (← jigoku no kunren); *human-wave tactics* (← jinkai senjitu); *black curtain* (← kuromaku); *water trade* (← mizu shobai); *shadow shogun* (← kage no shogun); *flowery exit* (← hanamichi); *the flower-and willow world* (← karyukai); *strainer laws* (← zaru-ho); *forward-looking posture* (← maemuki no shisei); *certain victory hachimaki* (← hissho hachimaki); *sympathy vote* (← dojohyo); *bodily injury leading to death* (← shogai chishi); *the so-called 'sunset' industries* (← iwayuru shayou sangyou); *bone-picker charters* (← ikotsu shushu chataki); *barbarian-subduing generalissimo* (← seiitaishougun); *Old Man Thunder* (← kaminari oyaji).

Loose Translation *just-in-time** (← kanban); *the sound of one-hand-clapping** (← sekishu no koe); *stable** (← heya); *three wise monkeys* (← san-en).

Though many items are listed, few are actually used in the common vocabulary. Since an item of loan translation is composed of English vocabulary, it is often

[13] Cannon (1994b), Matsuda (1991), and Ishimaru (1990).

Table 3.14: Occurrence of Loan Translation in *The TimesCD*

Loan translation	Occurrence	Original Context	
black belt	17	marital arts	(16)
brown belt	2	marital arts	(2)
white belt	3	marital arts	(2)
acupressure	3	Japanese therapy	(3)
bullet train	4	Japanese transportation	(4)
comfort woman	16	Japanese war	(16)
graphic novel	2	Japanese comic	(0)
just-in-time	13	Japanese manufacturing	(5)
the sound of one hand clapping	3	Zen	(3)
tea ceremony	2	Japanese tradition	(1)
low profile	80	Japanese politics	(0)
high profile	141	Japanese politics	(0)
stable	1	sumo	(1)

hard to determine if it is actually borrowed from Japanese unless it appears in Japanese context. Table 3.14 shows the occurrence of loan translation in *The TimesCD*.

Most of the loan translations occur in the original context, such as martial arts and Japanese transportation, but *graphic novel*, *low profile*, and *high profile* never occur in the Japanese context. *Just-in-time* appears in many compound forms:

(69) *just-in-time deliveries; just-in-time techniques; just-in-time production schedules; just-in-time systems; just-in-time manufacturing; just-in-time production control; just-in-time manufacturing schedules.*

The usage of *low profile* and *high profile* are almost identical except that *low profile* has an additional use that refers to a kind of tire. They usually appear as 'keep/maintain/have a *high/low profile*.' Adjectival use of *low profile* is observed twice in the form, 'stay *low profile*.' A metaphorical use is observed in *black belt* as in *an administrative Black Belt*. No suffixation or irregular inflection is found.

3.4.2 Re-borrowing of Words of English Origin from Japanese

Re-borrowing is one form of loanword of English origin used in Japanese and later incorporated into English again. The following items can be found in English dictionaries:

(70) *shokku* (← shock) 'a shock or surprise in political or economic affairs concerning Japan'; *Beta(max)** (← beta 'all over' + maximum) 'a video-cassette format'; *karaoke** (← kara 'empty' + orchestra); *mama-san* (← Mom+san); *martial art** (← martial + art) 'fighting sports or skills mainly of Japanese origin'; *mechatronics* (← mechanic+electronics) 'a branch of technology which combines mechanical engineering with electronics'; *romaji* (← Roman+ji 'character') 'a system of Romanized spelling for the Japanese language'; *salaryman** (← salary+man) 'a white collar worker in Japan.'

The researchers[14] have found more examples which have not registered in English dictionaries as follows:

(71) *nighter** (← night+er); *co-prosperity* (← co+prosperity); *glocal, glocalize, glocalization* (← global+local); *beddo* (← bed); *eroduction* (← erotic+production); *Euroyen** (← European+yen); *yen bond* (← yen + bond); *zaitech* (← zaisan 'property' + technique); *sarakin* (← salary+kin 'money'); *demo** (← demonstration); *bebi hotel* (← baby + hotel); *feminisuto* (← feminist); *godoru girls* (← go 'five' dollar girls); *haro* (← hello); *heddo-hantaa* (← head + hunter); *janpingubodo* (← jumping+board); *kohi-shoppu* (← coffee + shop); *rajio* (← radio); *roman poruno* (← Roman + pornography); *saido bijinesu* (← side + business); *sarariman* (← salary + man); *sree* (← three); *takushi* (← taxi); *wandafuru* (← wonderful); *wapuro* (← word+processor); *biiru* (← beer); *kirishitan* (← Christian); *besuboru* (← baseball).

Similarly to the case of loan translation, many items were listed by the researchers, but very few are commonly used. The items that appear in *The*

---
[14] Cannon (1994b), Matsuda (1991), and Ishimaru (1990).

70   I   Assimilation Process of Loanwords

Table 3.15: Occurrence of Re-borrowing in *The TimesCD*

Re-borrowing	Occurrence	Original Context	
Beta(max)	65	Japanese technology	(7)
demo	39	political protest	(6)
Euroyen	5	Japanese Economy	(5)
martial arts	100	Japanese sports	(100)
mechatronics	1	Japanese technology	(0)
nighter	1	Japanese baseball	(0)
salaryman	12	Japanese business	(10)

TimesCD are asterisked. Table 3.15 shows the occurrence of re-borrowings in *The TimesCD*.

Beta and *demo* occur frequently because they have different senses that are not related to Japan (e.g., *beta version, beta carotene, demo tape, demo version*). I found that *Beta(max)* is often used to refer to an out-of-date, non-standardized system of any kind. For example,

(72) ... *the legal publishing equivalent of the Betamax video recorder;*
... *as trendy as owning a Betamax video;*
... *made Betamax obsolete;*
... *the computer equivalent of buying a Betamax video recorder instead of an industry standard VHS.*

Martial art was called 'martial sport' or 'martial exercise' before Japan National Railways first used the phrase 'martial art' in *Official Guide to Japan*; now this phrase has gained the dominant use and 'martial sport' and 'martial exercise' are no longer used. No suffixation or irregular inflection is observed.

3.4.3   Summary

In Section 3.4, I have demonstrated that the secondary loanwords do not follow the same process of assimilation as the primary loanwords. The secondary loanwords have the following characteristics:

(73) a. Dictionaries often fail to indicate the Japanese etymology.
   b. Most of them are phrases and not words.

c. Most of them are relatively recent lexical items.

d. Since they are composed of English-originated words, it is not necessary to adopt spelling or pronunciation.

e. They rarely produce new lexical items by compounding and suffixation partly because they are already phrases in most cases.

f. Irregular inflection is not observed since they have English word forms.

3.5 Sense and Context of Japanese Loanwords in English

In the previous sections, we have seen the changes in pronunciation, forms, parts of speech, productivity, and senses of Japanese loanwords in the process of assimilation. However, there may be other changes or phenomena that occur in the course of assimilation. The context in which the loanwords are used is an example. When a new word is borrowed from a foreign language into English, it is used in its original sense or a part of the original, in the text that explains the object or concept it designates. If it is borrowed from Japanese, it is used in the text bound tight to Japan, such as Japanese culture, customs, and food. Then, as the word gradually prevails in English, it begins to expand its use semantically and contextually. That is, the word is used in a newly developed sense in a text unrelated to Japan. In an extreme case, English speakers use the word without knowing its original sense or even the fact that it has originally been borrowed from Japanese.

In this part of the study, I take up the Japanese loanwords that appear in an English corpus frequently and investigate their senses and the contexts. Combining the results of the investigation from the two aspects, I will reveal how the Japanese loanwords expand the range of sense and context. In Section 3.5.1, the target words and the corpus employed here are introduced, and the procedure is explained briefly. Then, in Section 3.5.2, the search results will be presented along with the categorization of the results from the semantic and contextual aspects. Further, in Section 3.5.3, the discussion follows, dividing Japanese loanwords into three types, and finally in Section 3.5.4, a summary will be stated.

3.5.1 Materials and Methodology

3.5.1.1 The Target Words

The target words in this part of the study are the 14 words that have been classified as Stage 4 items as shown in (74). All the items in Stage 4 have gone through a semantic shift and gained one or more new senses.

(74) *futon; geisha; hara-kiri; honcho; judo; jujitsu; kamikaze; kimono; samurai; shogun; soy(a); tsunami; tycoon; Zen.*

3.5.1.2 The Corpus

The corpus employed in this part of the study is *Wordbanks* online. This corpus contains 56 million words of actual English from British, American, and Australian books, magazines, newspapers, radio broadcasts, and informal speech, divided into nine subcorpora. One can access it by telneting to the Collins server. It can provide the search result in KWIC (Key Word In Context) format and browse the context at a maximum of 512 letters around the target word. The results can be saved on the server and downloaded by FTP to one's computer. All of the nine subcorpora are used in this search.

3.5.1.3 The Procedure

The target words in (74) are searched for in *Wordbanks* online, and the retrieved instances are grouped according to their senses and contexts. From the semantic aspect, the instances are divided into three groups as in (75):

(75) a. The items used in the same sense as the original.

b. The items used in the shifted sense by extension or transfer.

c. Others, such as the items used as proper nouns.

For example, if there is an instance in which *kamikaze* is used in the original sense of 'one of the Japanese airmen who made suicidal attack in the war,' the instance is qualified as (a). If it is used in the shifted sense as 'reckless,' then it goes into the group (b). If it is a proper noun, such as the name of a racing horse, it is grouped as (c).

From the contextual aspect, the instances are divided into two groups as in (76), judging from the words before and after it.

(76) I: The items used in the context related to Japan.
II: The items used in the context unrelated to Japan.

If the retrieved instance contains any of the words, such as 'Japan,' 'Japanese,' a place name in Japan, or the name of a Japanese, or if the sentence obviously refers to Japan in some other ways, I categorize it as (I), and otherwise (II). For example, if *futon* is used to explain what Japanese *futon* is like or to describe a Japanese traditional inn, the instance is grouped into (I). If *futon* appears in the advertisement of a futon shop in Britain, showing the price or how to take care of it, or in the conversation of Americans describing their guest rooms, I consider that the context is ripped away from Japan, then I group it into (II). Another example is that if *kimono* is used in the sentence about a geisha wearing a *kimono*, the instance goes to the group (I), and if the word appears in a novel in which an American woman comes out of a shower room in a *kimono*, the instance is categorized as (II): the context unrelated to Japan. In this way, each instance is categorized from the two aspects. In Section 3.5.2, these two kinds of categorization will be combined to determine the dominant use of the Japanese loanwords.

3.5.2 Results

As a result of the search, I obtained the instances of each of the target words with the frequencies as shown in (77). It is divided into two groups according to the frequency.

(77) A: High frequency words: *futon* (49); *honcho* (17); *judo* (79); *kamikaze* (58); *kimono* (29); *samurai* (73); *soy(a)* (258); *tycoon* (469); *Zen* (125).

B: Low frequency words: *geisha* (27); *harakiri* (6); *jujitsu* (7); *shogun* (47); *tsunami* (23).

Geisha is categorized in (B) since 27 items out of 38 instances are derived from one source, failing to provide enough variety of instances for analyses. The word *shogun* is also grouped in the low frequency words in spite of its relative high frequency since it cannot be considered to have a wide usage in English. It is used as a proper noun in more than half of the instances, designating the name of a car or the title of a book, and the majority of the remaining are from one source, a book on Buddhism history in Japan. Similarly, *tsunami* is categorized in (B) as a proper noun and one source provided up to 18 instances out of 23.

In this study, only the high frequency words (*i.e.*, the group (A)) are used for analyses. The characteristics of each of the two categorizations will be stated in Sections 3.5.2.1 and 3.5.2.2.

3.5.2.1 Semantic Categorization

As a result of the search and the semantic categorization, the tendency of each word regarding in which sense it is mainly used is revealed. Some words, such as *judo*, *samurai*, and *Zen*, are mainly used in the original sense, while the dominant use of others, such as *futon*, *honcho*, *kamikaze*, and *tycoon* is in the shifted sense(s). The items used in both (a) and (b) are *kimono* and *soy*. The frequency in each category and the senses used in (b) and (c) for each word are shown in Table 3.16.

3.5.2.2 Contextual Categorization

The result of the contextual categorization is summarized in Table 3.17. The frequency of each group, together with some examples of contexts, are given in the table. From this table, one can learn the tendency of each word regarding in which context it appears the most often. The contexts of *honcho*, *judo*, *kamikaze*, *soy*, and *tycoon* are almost always grouped as (II): unrelated to Japan, and *futon* and *kimono* are also used often in context (II), though there are some instances that were used in (I): Japanese related context.

On the contrary, *samurai* and *Zen* were found to be used more often in context (I) than in (II). However, this cannot lead us to the conclusion that these two words are used mainly in (I), since many instances are retrieved from

Table 3.16: Semantic Categorization of Japanese Loanwords

Items	a. Orig.		b. Shifted		c. Others
judo	78	0	—	1	Nickname for J. Chirac
samurai	51	11	a weapon a man with sword	11	a TV program the name of a car or a horse
Zen	102	6	abstract philosophical	17	a song title the name of a restaurant
futon	4	45	a sofa bed sleep	0	—
honcho	0	17	a business leader	0	—
kamikaze	8	31	reckless suicidal	11	the name of a cocktail, a buster or a horse
tycoon	0	459	a magnate a millionaire	10	a book title the name of a horse
kimono	16	13	a robe, a gown	0	—
soy	97	160	soybean	1	the title of a picture

Table 3.17: Context Categorization of Japanese Loanwords

Items	I: Japan	II: Other	Examples
honcho	0	17	Business, Politics
judo	7	72	Sports, Crime, Theater
kamikaze	7	51	Sports, Horse racing, Politics
tycoon	2	467	Business, Politics
soy	13	245	Health, Cooking, Agriculture, Environment
futon	11	38	Advertisements, Guest rooms
kimono	10	19	Suspense novels, Theater
samurai	47	26	TV programs, Horse racing, Cars
Zen	84	43	Restaurants, Music

one source (28 instances out of 47 for *samurai*, 71 instances out of 84 for *Zen*), a book on the history of religions in Japan, and therefore the result may be skewed. Here, it is safe to say that *samurai* and *Zen* are used in both kinds of context.

3.5.2.3 Sense-Context Matrix

So far, we have seen the characteristics of loanwords from each aspect of sense and context. Now, we combine the two to find out which sense is used in which context. Each instance is labeled with the combination, such as a-I, and b-II, and placed in a matrix so that one can capture the features visually. A horizontal axis of a matrix represents the sense, and the vertical axis represents the context. A matrix is constructed for each word. As a result, it is revealed that the matrices can further be grouped into three types in respect to the distribution of instances: (1) all the instances gather in the b-II box (Complete b-II type), (2) most of the instances gather in the b-II box with some dispersion (Quasi b-II type), and (3) almost all the instances scatter in the column of (a) (Column (a) type). The items fall under the types as in (78):

(78) **Complete b-II:** *honcho, tycoon.*
    Quasi b-II: *futon, kamikaze, kimono, soy.*
    Column (a): *judo, samurai, zen.*

The matrices are shown in Figures 3.2, 3.3, and 3.4.[15]

3.5.3 Discussion
3.5.3.1 Complete b-II Type

As shown in Figure 3.2, complete b-II type matrices have almost all the instances in the box of b-II. The loanwords categorized in this type are never used in their original senses, but are always used in the context unrelated to Japan. The items *honcho* and *tycoon* are always used in the business context designating millionaires or business executives, in such phrases as *head honcho* and *media tycoon*. This type of loanwords has completely been cut off from the concept of 'Japan,' and accepted by English speakers in the shifted senses. Therefore, they can be considered as the most developed type of loanword. Some examples are given in (79).

(79) **honcho b-II:** *THE PUNTER'S favourite, Kelvin MacKenzie, former Editor of The Sun and now* head honcho *at Live TV, treats his*

---
[15] The alphabets in the boxes signify the genre of the text:
B: American or British books
E: Ephemera such as flyers and posters in the U.S. or in U.K.
N: Newspapers and magazines in U.K. or in Australia
S: Spoken (formal: TV/radio news, informal: telephone conversation *etc.*)
Each letter represents one occurrence. As for *tycoon*, N has been curtailed to ..... because of the overflowing number of instances. Each letter in the matrix for *soy* represents two occurrences.

honcho (17) *tycoon* (469)

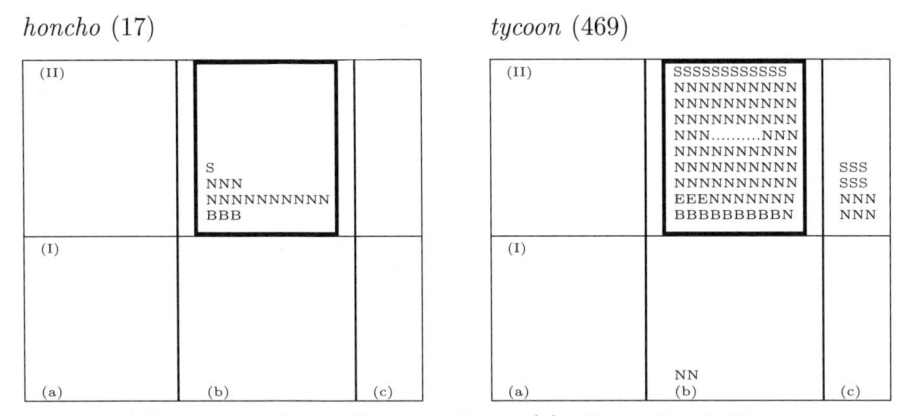

Figure 3.2: Sense-Context Matrix (1): Compelete b-II

employees as he does his own family. (N2000960130)

tycoon b-II: *Channel Nine, owned by media tycoon Kerry Packer, was forced to take action when rival Channel Seven chipped away at its audience figures with a bingo game offering £92,000 of prizes.* (N6000920826)

3.5.3.2 Quasi b-II Type

The second type has a similar tendency to the first one, but is not quite fully developed enough to be called a b-II type. Though there are some instances placed in other boxes as well, more instances fall into the box of b-II than in any other box (Figure 3.3). Therefore, it can be described that the dominant use of the items in this group is b-II: shifted sense and context unrelated to Japan. For example, *kimono* appears more often in the sense of 'long loose clothing like a robe or a gown' than in the sense of 'Japanese traditional clothing,' and its context is often unrelated to Japan, such as a scene of a suspense novel or a news article reporting an incidence in Britain. Since the words of this type still retain their original sense and context, they cannot be considered as fully removed from the concept of 'Japan,' but the smaller number of instances related to the original sense and context shows that they are losing their Japaneseness and at the same time becoming accepted as general vocabulary of English. (80) shows some examples of this type.

78   I   Assimilation Process of Loanwords

futon (49)

	(II)		
	SSSSSSSSS NNNNNN EE EEEEEEEEEE EEEEEEEEEE B		
(I)			
EEE B (a)	NNNN EEE (b)		(c)

kamikaze (58)

	(II)		
NNNN	NNNNNNNN NNNNNNNNNN NNNNNNNNNN BBB	NNN NNN NNN NNN E EEE	
(I)			
	BBBB (a)	(b)	NNN (c)

kimono (29)

	(II)		
NN	NN BBBBB BBBBBBBBBB		
(I)			
NNNNNN BB (a)	B (b)		(c)

soy (258)

	(II)		
NNN NNNNNNNNNN NNNNNNNNNN NNNNNNNNNN EEEEEE BB	SSS SSSSSSSSSSS NNNNNNNNNN NNNNNNNNNN NNNNNNNNNN EEEEEEEEEE EEEEEEEEEE BBB BBBBBBBBB	N	
(I)			
NNNN EE (a)	N E (b)		(c)

Figure 3.3: Sense-Context Matrix (2): Quasi b-II

(80) **futon b-II:** *The <u>Futon</u> Sofa-Bed is far ahead of all other types of Sofa-Bed, especially the foam filled type, which are notoriously uncomfortable both as bed and sofa.* (E0000001852)

kamikaze b-II: *They turned <u>kamikaze</u> to stop us from going five points clear - credit to them because they got a result from taking that risk.* (N6000911230)

kimono b-II: *I imagined her on the terrace of her flat wrapped into that red <u>mini-kimono</u> she so liked to wear before going to bed.* (B9000001447)

soy b-II: *In fact, one of the best sources of protein is the <u>soya bean</u> which contains all the essential amino acids and <u>soya beans</u> are one* *of the staples of the vegetarian diet - we don't all exist on carrots and lettuce.* (N6000920519)

3.5.3.3 Column (a) Type

The third type includes the items whose shifted senses are never or rarely observed (Figure 3.4). The items *judo, samurai,* and *zen* fall under this group. The items of this type have most of their instances in the column (a); either in a-I or a-II. Among them, *judo* is a word known worldwide as a sport or a martial art and rarely used in the context related to Japan. Thus, it is more of the a-II type than the a-I. The word *judo* has prevailed in English in the original sense, frequently used in the context of sports, such as news articles reporting the results of a tournament or the incident where a famous judo master was involved. However, its use is limited as it is seldom used in other senses and contexts.

As for *samurai* and *Zen*, the large number of the instances are placed in a-I. However, as already mentioned in Section 3.5.2.2, since many instances are retrieved from one source, a book on the history of religions in Japan, and therefore the matrices are biased, it is impossible to determine the tendencies assertively. It can only be said that *samurai* and *Zen* are used in both kinds of context in their original senses. Some examples are shown in (81).

(81) **judo a-II** *The 34-year-old heavyweight from Wolverhampton, seeking to become the first Briton to win a <u>judo</u> gold medal, was beaten in just 68 seconds of his first fight against Frenchman David Douillet.* (N6000920728)

samurai a-I: *A surgeon with the American forces in Japan during the 1950s, Rosin became obsessed with the <u>Samurai tradition</u> and its weaponry.* (N0000000487)

Zen a-II: *He says Lyle's approach to life was like a <u>Zen philosopher's</u>. His sensitivity to the natural world was easy to miss, Galvin says, because like most of his neighbors, Lyle wasn't a verbal person.* (S2000920803)

80   I   Assimilation Process of Loanwords

judo (79)

(II) SSSSS SSSSSSSSSSSS NNNNN NNNNNNNNN NNNNNNNNN NNNNNNNNN NNNNNNNNN EEEE BBBBBB			N
(I) NNNNN BB (a)	(b)	(c)	

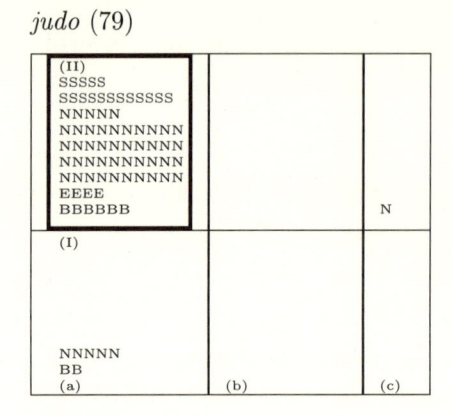

samurai (73)

(II) NN NNNNNNNNN BB		N B	N NNN NNN NNN
(I) NNNNNNNN BBBBBBB BBBBBBBBB BBBBBBBBB BBBBBBBBB (a)	N (b)	(c)	

zen (125)

(II) S NNNNNNNN EEEEEE BBBBBBB	NNNN E B	NS NNN NNN NNN NNN EE
(I) B BBBBBBBBB BBBBBBBBB BBBBBBBBB BBBBBBBBB BBBBBBBBB BBBBBBBBB BBBBBBBBB BBBBBBBBB (a)	(b)	(c)

Figure 3.4: Sense-Context Matrix (3): Column (a)

3.5.3.4   Comparison with Stage 1-3 Items

So far, we have seen the Stage 4 items in matrices. Here, let us turn to the unassimilated items (items in Stage 1 and 2) and compare the positions of instances in the matrices with those of Stage 4 items. By searching *Wordbanks* online for the items and placing the result in the matrices, the distinctive characteristics appear. That is, all the instances of the items in Stage 1 and 2 gather in a-I (Figure 3.5). This extreme a-I type could not be observed with the Stage 4 items. For example, *karoshi*, *tatami*, and *yukata*, the Japanese loanwords that are considered to be uncommon to English speakers occur in the corpus as few as four to eleven times, and all the instances (except two of *yukata*) are used in the context bound to Japan. This shows that the low

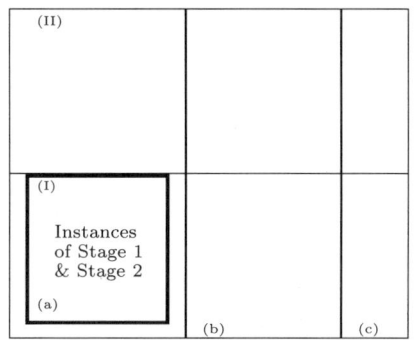

Figure 3.5: Stage 1 and Stage 2 Items: Extreme a-I

assimilation degrees are associated with the low frequency and the limited range in context. Some examples of unassimilated items are shown in (82).

(82) **karoshi a-I:** *CLINICS are being set up in Japan to prevent deaths from overwork. At least 1,000 people have died from the condition known as <u>karoshi</u>.* (N6000920826)

tatami a-I: *KYOTO, THE FORMER Japanese capital city, is a maze of traditional inns with <u>tatami mat</u> floors, ancient temples, castles and gardens.* (N0000000788)

yukata a-I: <u>*Yukatas*</u> *have been worn by Japanese men and women for centuries, but only recently have westerners discovered their lightweight comfort and elegant look for informal wear and as a dressing gown.* (E0000001613)

Another comparison was carried out using Stage 3 items. They are considered to be relatively assimilated into English but have no semantic variety. Among the Stage 3 items, some which have relatively high frequencies and wide prevalence, were picked up as targets for comparison: *bonsai* (43 instances), *shiatsu* (47 instances), *shinto* (38 instances) and so on. Two types: a-I and a-II emerged from the constructed matrices (Figure 3.6). Some items, such as *bonsai* and *shiatsu*, are almost always used in the context unrelated to Japan (*i.e.*, a-II type), while others, such as *shinto*, are mainly used in the context bound to Japan (*i.e.*, a-I type), for example, in an article on the issue of the Japanese Prime Minister's visit to Yasukuni shrine. Judging from the fact that some

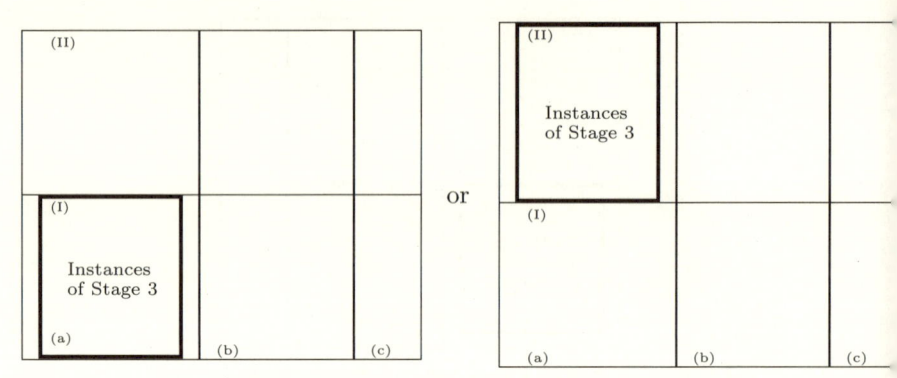

Figure 3.6: Stage 3 Items: a-I and a-II

Stage 3 items have a limited context as the items in Stage 1 and 2 do, and others have widened their range of use as Stage 4 items, it can be asserted that the expansion of context starts at around this stage. Some examples are shown in (83).

(83) **shinto a-I:** *But others say it works contrary to the spirit of the constitution by equating the state with the Shinto religion.* (S1000901027)

bonsai a-II: *Initially, this consists of regular watering and applying a bonsai fertilizer during the growing season.* (N9119980426)

shiatsu a-II: *At 3 00 pm you have a 60-minute Swedish massage by either a male or a female massage therapist adept also in shiatsu, acupressure, and reflexology.* (B9000000453)

3.5.4 Summary

As we have seen in this section, Japanese loanwords, after being introduced into English, gradually expand their range of use semantically and contextually, as they go through various changes in the assimilation process. Using sense-context matrices, the process of expanding context and sense from a-I to b-II was captured and visualized. As a result, the relationship between the assimilation process and the context expansion was revealed as follows. First, the items in Stage 1 and 2 have only restricted contexts, almost always used in the context related to Japan, and then the loanwords begin to be used in the context unrelated to Japan at Stage 3, though some of the Stage 3 items

(II)
 	
    Stage 4 ⇒
    Stage 3
       ⇑
	⇒ Stage 4	

(I)   ⇑
    Stage 3
    Stage 1, 2		

(a)	(b)	(c)

Figure 3.7: Semantic and Contextual Transition of Japanese Loanwords

remain restricted in context, and finally at Stage 4 as they gain the semantic varieties, the shift from the original sense to the shifted sense begins to take place. At the final point, they are totally cut off from both the original sense and context and accepted as general vocabulary of English, though the number of items which has achieved this status is very small. This transition can be illustrated as in Figure 3.7.

In this chapter, I have investigated the Japanese loanwords from various aspects on the basis of dictionaries and corpora, and established the assimilation process of Japanese loanwords. In the next chapter, the same kinds of investigations will be carried out on German loanwords to compare and contrast the assimilation process of Japanese and German loanwords.

Chapter 4   Assimilation Process of German Loanwords

4.1   Introduction

4.1.1   Purpose of This Chapter

In this chapter, the assimilation process of German loanwords will be investigated and compared with that of Japanese loanwords in English. I will determine whether the four-stage process of assimilation is unique to Japanese or also common to German loanwords. If there is a common part and a language-specific part, then I will examine what changes are shared among loanwords from various languages, and what changes are unique to Japanese or German. By comparing the assimilation process of loanwords from these two languages, one which is closely related to English, and the other which is totally distant from English, I aim to reveal a contrastive relation that could be a baseline for distinguishing the assimilation process of loanwords in general and language specific characteristics.

As was done in Chapter 3, the investigation will be carried out on the basis of both dictionaries and corpora.

4.1.2   Definition of German Loanwords

Before I go into detail about the research, I clarify the definition of a 'German loanword.' In this study, words that fulfill the following conditions are assumed to be German loanwords:

(84)   a. Primary Loanwords

Any English word or phrase whose etymology is German, including old loanwords from other languages which are considered fully established German lexical items.

b. Secondary Loanwords

English words or phrases whose etymology is not German but satisfy one of the following conditions:

- Re-borrowing
  Words or phrases which are coined by the German people using English vocabulary.
- Literal loan translation
  Words or phrases which are totally or partially translated into English from German words or phrases.
- Loose loan translation
  Words, or usually phrases, which come into use in English to denote German expressions.

c. Exceptions

I do not consider the following items to be German loanwords.

- The word 'German' and its derivatives.
- The technical term of a substance discovered or invented by a German but whose etymology is not German, *e.g.*, Latin.
  However, I consider a term which contains a part-German etymology a German loanword, including the name of the discoverer or inventor.

4.2 Dictionary-based Approach

4.2.1 Comparison between Loanwords from Various Languages

First, I introduce the transition of loanwords in English history to grasp an idea of the position of Japanese and German loanwords in English and to further compare them.

4.2.1.1 The Number of Loanwords in English

The time periods in which the loanwords were introduced into English are investigated using the *Oxford Dictionary of Foreign Words and Phrases* (1997). Table 4.1 shows the eleven largest suppliers of loanwords in English, and the number of the loanwords by time period. As can be seen in Table 4.1, the tendency of loanwords in the 20th century differs greatly from that of the preceding periods. Romance languages such as French, Latin, Italian, and Spanish increasingly supplied English with their vocabulary until the 19th century. Though the borrowing from such languages continues to occupy a higher position in the table, the number of words decreased in the 20th century. On the other hand, increases can be observed in German, Russian, Japanese, and Yiddish.

Table 4.1: The Transition in Number of Loanwords from Top 11 Languages

	Fr.	L.	It.	Sp.	G.	Gk.	Jp.	Ar.	Sk.	R.	Y.	Total
OE	1	9	0	0	0	0	0	0	0	0	0	10
ME	37	24	1	0	1	3	0	0	0	0	0	66
LME	97	136	0	0	0	9	0	0	0	0	0	242
15th	22	14	0	0	0	0	0	0	0	0	0	36
16th	123	289	54	39	1	19	0	11	1	5	0	542
17th	308	366	71	57	6	36	9	19	6	2	1	881
18th	485	175	183	40	13	23	17	20	32	6	0	994
19th	1041	284	229	215	192	63	67	56	46	27	30	2250
20th	615	118	136	126	<u>204</u>	49	<u>99</u>	18	18	<u>57</u>	<u>59</u>	1499
Total	2729	1415	674	477	417	202	192	124	103	97	90	6520

Fr.: French, L.: Latin, It.: Italian, Sp.: Spanish, G.: German, Gk.: Greek, Jp.: Japanese,
Ar.: Arab, Sk.: Sanskrit, R.: Russian, Y.: Yiddish

4.2.1.2 Recent Loanwords from Japanese, German, and Spanish

Here, the characteristics of loanwords from three languages are compared. The three languages are Japanese, German, and Spanish. I chose German and Spanish as targets of comparison: German because, like Japanese, there is an increase in the number of loanwords in the 20th century, and Spanish because it has the similar number of words borrowed into English as Japanese does. I deal only with recent loanwords that are currently going through the process of assimilation to find out what changes are observed in the earlier stages of assimilation.

The target words are those whose etymologies are "Japanese, German, or Spanish," and whose first attested dates are 1940 or later in the *OED2*.[1] The points in (85) are investigated, and the results are summarized in Table 4.2.

---

[1] The data from the *OEDAD* are not included.

88 I Assimilation Process of Loanwords

(85) a. labels of *slang* and *colloq.*

b. labels of technical terms, such as *Min.* (*i.e.*, Mineralogy) and *Path.* (*i.e.*, Pathology)

c. parts of speech

d. ‖ (*i.e.*, indication of 'not naturalized') before the headwords

e. changes of pronunciation and orthography

f. attributive uses

g. irregular inflections

h. productivity (compounding, suffixation, functional shifts)

i. semantic shifts

Table 4.2: Japanese/German/Spanish Loanwords First Attested in the *OED2* Later than 1940

	Japanese		German		Spanish	
Total[a]	68	(73−5)	122[b]	(215−93)	48	(54−6)
slang, colloq	4	(5.9%)	18	(14.8%)	5	(10.4%)
Technical Term	7	(10.3%)	33	(27.0%)	5	(10.4%)
Non-Noun	2	(2.9%)	19	(15.6%)	3	(6.3%)
Word with ‖	45	(66.2%)	52	(42.6%)	24	(50.0%)
Attributive Use	13	(19.1%)	8	(6.6%)	0	(0.0%)
Irregular Inflection[c]	2	(2.9%)	11	(9.0%)	3	(6.3%)
Foreign Pronunciation[d]	27	(39.7%)	32	(26.2%)	21	(43.8%)
Orthographic Change[e]	9	(13.2%)	18	(14.8%)	10	(20.8%)
Productivity (Compounding)	17	(25.0%)	18	(14.8%)	7	(14.6%)
Productivity (Suffixation)	4	(5.9%)	28	(23.0%)	1	(2.1%)
Productivity (Functional Shift)[f]	4	(5.9%)	11	(9.0%)	7	(14.6%)
Semantic Shift	3	(4.4%)	11	(9.0%)	1	(2.1%)

a. The numbers in parentheses are the results given by the *OED2* search and the excluded items.
b. The number includes 18 indirect German loanwords via Yiddish.
c. Irregular or ϕ plural forms of nouns indicated in the *OED2*.
d. Items with no stress or with foreign phonemes.
e. Only the changes that make the pronunciation imaginable or fit English rules.
f. The information is taken from the description in the *OED2*.

Table 4.2 describes well the characteristics of loanwords from the three languages. German is the largest source of the loanwords in English in recent decades among the three foreign languages. This is because German contributed heavily to modern science in such fields as mineralogy and chemistry, resulting in the borrowing of many technical terms (33 items), and because a large number of Jewish immigrants to the U.S. during the persecutions of Jews brought German-originated Yiddish words (18 items) to American English. German loanwords via Yiddish borrowed from Jewish immigrants can also explain the loanwords labeled as *slang* or *colloq.* (14 items out of 18) and non-noun loanwords (six items out of 19).

As shown in Table 4.2, Japanese loanwords have a higher percentage of ‖ (indication of 'not naturalized') and attributive use than the others, indicating that those Japanese loanwords are not yet assimilated in English. On the contrary, German has the highest percentage of irregular inflection, probably due to the fact that it has a different system of plural inflection from English, and therefore it may take longer to be assimilated than the ones from Japanese, which has no system of plural inflection. This will be discussed further in Section 4.2.5. Spanish loanwords have a low percentage of irregular plural inflection as Spanish has a similar system of pluralization to English, adding -*s* or -*es*, so it often coincides with the English plural form.

Loanwords from all three languages more or less retain foreign pronunciations. Here, I include only the words which have foreign phonemes such as [a], [o], [e:], [x], [ʏ], and [ø], or no stress indicated in the pronunciation section in the *OED2*, though there are other kinds of foreign features in the pronunciation, such as in the cases which violate the orthographical or stress assignment rules of English. This will be discussed in Section 4.2.3. Some loanwords from all three languages have gone through orthographical changes. Orthographical changes included here are the changes of spelling, so that the spelling represents the actual pronunciation in English more accurately, following the rules of spelling-pronunciation in English. This is more often observed in Spanish loanwords than others as they provide many cases of dropping of the final vowel. It is one of the easiest ways to anglicize Spanish words, since many of them look and sound more like English just by dropping the final vowel.

Compounding is the most widely observed way of producing new words for Japanese loanwords, while for German it is suffixation, due to the many technical terms consisting of the name of a scholar + a suffix (e.g., -*ite, -an*). As for semantic shift, not many cases were observed since I dealt here with only the new loanwords that were borrowed after 1940. However, eleven loanwords from German already show semantic shift, indicating that German loanwords have a different assimilation process, or a different speed of assimilation from Japanese loanwords.

In this section, I have demonstrated that loanwords from each of the three languages (*i.e.*, Japanese, German, and Spanish) have distinctive characteristics of changes after borrowing, implying that they have different assimilation processes. In the following sections, I will deal with German loanwords in English as a whole, not just limited to new vocabulary.

4.2.2 Procedure

From here on, I bring German loanwords into focus and discuss the assimilation process of them in detail. In this section, the way the target words are selected and the procedure of the research will be briefly mentioned. Then, in the following sections, I will describe the characteristics of the German loanwords, regarding the changes in the various aspects such as pronunciation, word-formation, semantic shift, and regularization of inflections, as a result of the dictionary-based research on them, as was done on Japanese loanwords.

Here, I deal with only the loanwords that are currently used and exclude the technical terms whose usages are limited to their fields. The source of the loanwords are as follows:

(86) a. *The Oxford Dictionary of Foreign Words and Phrases* (1997)

   b. *The OED Additions Series*, 3 vols. (1993 and 1997)

   c. *The OED* 2nd ed. (1993)

First, I extracted all the items from German in the *Oxford Dictionary of Foreign Words and Phrases*. Then, I referred to the *OED* 2nd ed. and the three volumes of the *OED Additions Series* to obtain more detailed information on the extracted words. I investigated the data obtained from these dictionaries and determined what characteristics German loanwords have, what changes they go through in pronunciation, part of speech, sense and other aspects, and how many of them have actually gone through the changes. Refer to Appendix F for the whole list of extracted items.

The results are summarized in Table 4.3. Each aspect of change after borrowing is described in detail in the following sections.

Table 4.3: The Characteristics of German Loanwords

Total	418	(100%)
Technical Terms	95	(22.7%)
Words with ‖	284	(67.9%)
Non-noun Loanwords	33	(7.9%)
New Concept/Object	213	(51.0%)
Loan Translation Counterpart	43	(10.3%)
Pronunciation Change[a]	186	(44.5%)
Irregular Inflection	106	(25.4%)
Attributive Use	21	(5.0%)
Productivity	121[b]	(28.9%)
— Compounding	100	(23.9%)
— Suffixation	38	(9.1%)
— Functional Shifts[c]	18	(4.3%)
Semantic shift	90	(21.5%)

a. Weakening or deletion of unstressed vowels and vowelized [r] are excluded, for it is often difficult to determine if it really occurred after borrowing or it was originally so in German.
b. This count is not equal to the sum of the following word-formations since some items can be formed in more than one way.
c. Functional shift of a noun to an adjective is not included unless it is used as a predicative adjective since a definitive adjective is indistinguishable from a compound-forming noun.

4.2.3 Pronunciation and Orthography

As for pronunciation, as one can easily predict, the German loanwords generally tend to change from the original to the one the English speakers imagine from the spelling, and this is caused by what is called 'analogy'; when one encounters a new word whose pronunciation is not known, he/she will pronounce it according to the rule of English orthography. Henceforth, this change will be referred to as "an analogy from the English spelling."

Though stress assignment was the obligatory change for Japanese loanwords, it is not often observed in German loanwords, for German words originally have a stress according to the stress assignment rule of the German language, and they tend to maintain their stress position even after borrowing (e.g., *Ursprache* ['uːrʃpraːxə], *Wehmacht* ['veːrmaxt]). Thus, the stress position changes are less likely to occur. Only 13 items, four of which have also gone through pronunciation changes, show this change (e.g., *frakt*u*r, l*ei*tmotiv, l*u*mpenproletariat, prägn*a*nz, sch*o*ttische, Schlamper*ei*).*[2]

Vowels are clearly distinguished, as German (and other foreign) vowels are [i], [e], [a], [o], [ɔ], [ø], [u], [ʏ] *etc.*, while English ones are [ɪ], [ɛ], [ɒ], [æ], [ʌ], [ə], [ʊ]. There are several patterns of change for each vowel, but, unlike Japanese loanwords, lengthening is not observed very often. These patterns can be largely divided into two groups: the ones in which the phonemes do not exist in English change, and those that change by analogy from the English spellings. The observed changes are summarized in (87).

(87) a. Non-existing phonemes in English:
  [e] → [ɛ] (e.g., *d*e*licatessen, Gedankenexp*e*riment*)
  [eː] → [eɪ] (e.g., *b*e*bung, heimw*eh*, jäger, leberwurst, l*e*derhosen*)
  [a] → [æ] ([ɒ], [ə]) (e.g., *A*bitur*, dr*a*ng, k*a*merad, kn*a*llglas*)
  [o] → [əʊ] (e.g., *aut*o*bahn, Bildungsr*o*man, d*o*cent*)
  [ɔ] → [ɒ] (e.g., *d*o*ppelgänger, dummk*o*pf, gl*o*ckenspiel*)
  [ø] → [əː], [eɪ], [əʊ] (e.g., *f*ö*hn, l*oe*ss, v*ö*lkerwanderung*)
  [yː] → [ʊː] (e.g., *einf*ü*hlung, flügelhorn, gl*ü*hweinm, m*ue*sli*)

 b. Analogy from the English spelling
  [au] → [ɔ] (e.g., *au*tobahn, *au*tomat, meersch*au*m)
  [ɛr] [ɪr] [ur] → [əː] (e.g., *d*i*rndl, *e*rsatz, t*u*rnverein, uri*r*nis, w*u*rst*)
  [uː] → [ʌ] (e.g., *bl*u*t, b*u*ckling, kr*u*mmholz, l*u*mpenproletariat, p*u*mpernickel*)
  [i] → [aɪ] (e.g., *g*i*ro*)

The German sound [r] is different from the one in English, the former being an uvular trill [ʀ] and the latter an alveolar approximant [ɹ], but the dictionaries do not distinguish them. The German [ʀ] is always automatically replaced

---

[2] The underlined vowels are German stress positions, and the vowels in bold face are anglicized ones.

by the English [ɹ] after borrowing (e.g., *rinderpest, graupel*) unless it is intentionally pronounced as German by someone who is familiar with the German pronunciation, and that is why the dictionaries do not mention this.

The consonants have a fewer number of change patterns than vowels, but they can also be divided into the same two groups as vowels: those that replace a non-existing phoneme in English, and those that change by analogy from the English spellings. The latter group of analogy is further divided into two subgroups: the analogy caused by the differences in English and German as to which alphabet stands for which phoneme, and the analogy caused by the different voicing rule of the spelling. In as many as 70 items, both the original pronunciations and their anglicized pronunciations are listed under the dictionary headwords. This indicates that the pronunciations of those items are in a transition period, and that pronunciation changes take time before completion. The other observed changes are summarized in (88).

(88) a. Non-existing phonemes in English:

[gn] → [n] (e.g., *gneiss*)

[pf] → [f] (e.g., *rauschpfeife, schreierpfeife*)

[ç] → [g], [k] (e.g., *Ewigkeit, Reich, spritzig*)

b. Analogy from the English spelling (designation of phonemes):

[f] → [v] (e.g., *turnverein*)

[j] → [ʤ] (e.g., *katzenjammer*)

[ʃp] → [sp] (e.g., *glockenspiel, kriegspiel, spritzer*)

[ʃt] → [st] (e.g., *alpenstock, Gestapo, Mittelstand, stoss, strudel*)

[t] → [θ] (e.g., *thalweg, thuringer*)

[ts] → [z] (e.g., *führerprinzip, panzer, zeitgeber, Zeitgeist, zugzwang*)

[v] → [w] (e.g., *wurst, nebelwerfer, schwa, wanderlust, wiener*)

c. Analogy from the English spelling (voicing rules):

[k] → [g] (e.g., *blitzkrieg, schlag, Sieg Heil, thalweg*)

[p] → [b] (e.g., *ablaut, abseil, erbswurst, liebchen*)

[s] → [z] (e.g., *bildungsroman, entscheidungsproblem, felsenmeer, lebensraum*)

[t] → [d] (e.g., *doctorand, goldwasser, kamerad, Karrenfeld, ländler,*

volkslied)

[z] → [s] (e.g., *Identitätsphilo<u>s</u>ophie, in<u>s</u>elberg, <u>s</u>auerkraut, <u>s</u>inter, <u>S</u>ängerfest*)

d. Others: [ks] → [xs] (e.g., *la<u>chs</u>schinken*)

If we shift the focus from the changed phonemes to the unchanged ones, it is noticeable that some words contain both German phonemes and anglicized phonemes in their pronunciations. When the pronunciations of these words are investigated, the tendency can be seen regarding which phonemes remain unchanged longer than the others, and which changes occur at an early stage of pronunciation assimilation. For example, *krummholz* is pronounced as [ˈkrumhɔlts] in German, but is described as [ˈkrʌmhɒlts] in the *OED2*. In this word, [ts] for 'z' letter remains unchanged, but the vowel changes ([u] → [ʌ], [ɔ] → [ɒ]) are observed.[3] This suggests that the non-existing vowels in English change first, and the consonant that can be changed by analogy from the spelling remains unchanged.

In this way, the anglicized and unchanged phonemes coexisting in a word are retrieved. The phonemes are grouped into three columns: unchanged, anglicized, and dual usage. I put the instances in the middle column 'dual usage' when they provide both the anglicized and the original version of pronunciation. Table 4.4 shows some examples. For a complete list of the unchanged and anglicized phonemes, refer to Appendix D.

From Table 4.4 and Appendix D, one can find that they are on a spectrum, at one end being phonemes the most likely to change (basic changes) and at the other end being phonemes the most unlikely to change (optional changes). An automatic replacement of [r] mentioned above can be considered to be on the very end of the basic changes on the spectrum. The other basic but less obligatory changes occur mostly with vowels (except [a]), especially with 'o' ([ɔ] → [ɒ]), and vocalized [r] after a vowel ('er' [ɛr] → [ɜː]), and these appear in the right column in Table 4.4. The number of the instances of consonant changes is not as great as those of vowels, so it is sometimes difficult to determine the tendency, but 'b' ([p] → [b]) and 'd' ([t] → [d]) seems to be included in the

---

[3] Henceforth, the orthographic transcription and its corresponding phonetic alphabet(s) are notated as 'orthographic transcription' [phonetic alphabet].

Table 4.4: Examples of Unchanged and Anglicized Phonemes of German Loanwords

Word	Unchanged	Dual Usage	Anglicized
ablaut	'a' [a]		'b' [p] → [b]
abseil		's' [z]/[s]	'b' [p] → [b]
		'ei' [aɪ]/[eɪ]	
glockenspiel		'sp' [ʃp]/[sp]	'o' [ɔ] → [ɒ]
goldwasser	'o' [ɔ]		'd' [t] → [d]
	'w' [v]		
Herrenvolk		'ol' [ɔl]/[əʊ]	
inselberg		's' [z]/[s]	'er' [ɛr] → [ɜː]
			'g' [k] → [g]
jäger	'j' [j]		'ä' [ɛː] → [eː][a]
leitmotiv	'v' [f]		'o' [o] → [əʊ]
streusel	's' [z]	'st' [ʃt]/[st]	
		'eu' [ɔʏ]/[ɔɪ][uː]	
thalweg	'w' [v]	'a' [aː]/[ɑː]	
	'th' [t]		
wanderlust		'w' [v]/[w]	
		'a' [a]/[ɑ]	
		'u' [ʊ]/[ʌ]	
zollverein	'z' [ts]		'o' [ɔ] → [ɒ]

a. This change may not be called an 'anglicization' but an modification, since [ɛː] is modified to [eː], but [eː] is not a English long vowel, either.

basic changes as well.

Toward the other end of the spectrum exist the consonant letters which indicate different sounds between German and English such as 'j', 'w', 'v', and 'z' German [j], [v], [f], and [ts], and English [ʤ], [w], [v], and [z], respectively. They tend to retain their original sounds after borrowing. The consonant 's' which changes their voicing status (*i.e.*, [z] or [s]) depending on their environment in German, also belong to this group. The vowel [a] appears often in the left column, indicating that the change occurs at the later stages of assimilation than other vowels.

In the middle column, some of the items are the same as the ones in the left column 'unchanged' (*i.e.*, 'a' [a], 's' [z], and 'w' [v]), indicating that they are pronounced with the original pronunciation in some cases and with anglicized phonemes (*i.e.*, [æ], [s], and [w], respectively) in other cases. These items

			'b' [b]	
'j' [j]	'a' [a]/[æ]	'sp' [ʃp]/[sp]	'd' [d]	
'v' [f]	's' [z]/[s]	'st' [ʃt]/[st]	'er' [ɜː]	
'z' [ts]	'w' [v]/[w]	'u' [ʊ]/[ʌ]	'o' [ɒ]	'r' [ɹ]

← unchanged   anglicized →

Figure 4.1: The Spectrum of Unchanged and Anglicized Phonemes

may have more resistance to change than the other non-overlapped items in the middle column (*i.e.*, 'st' [ʃt]/[st], 'sp' [ʃp]/[sp], and 'u' [ʊ]/[ʌ]), but not as much as the non-overlapped items in the left column (*i.e.*, 'j' [j], 'v'[f], 'z'[ts]). Those in the middle column are in a transitional period, so some of them will eventually be anglicized.

This spectrum can be visualized as in Figure 4.1.

4.2.4 Orthography

Next, let us go on to the orthographic changes of German loanwords. They tend to retain their original spellings in principle, though the same tendencies as pronunciation change can be observed; that is, the original spelling changes to the one by analogy by English speakers when the words have items which do not exist in English, such as the umlaut, or which do not follow the orthographic conventions of English, such as capitalization of the initial letters of common nouns and compounds spelled as one word. Examples are shown below:

(89) a. Nouns: coexisting capital and small initial letters (e.g., *Giro, giro* ← *Giro, Karst, karst* ← *Karst*)
adding a final -n^4 (e.g., *delicatessen* ← *Delikatesse, lederhosen* ← *Lederhose, palatschinken* ← *Palatschinke*)
dropping the final -*e* (e.g., *shaman* ← *Schamane*)

b. Compounds: inserting hyphens at the word boundary or dividing into two words (e.g., *natur-philosophie* ← *Naturphilosophie, Sacher Torte* ← *Sachertorte, Tafel Music* ← *Tafelmusik*)

---

[4] It might be the case that English borrowed the words in the plural form with the German plural ending -*n*.

c. Verbs: dropping the German verb ending -*en* (e.g., *abseil* ← *abseilen*)

d. Dropping umlauts (e.g., *b<u>u</u>ckling* ← *Bückling, doppelg<u>a</u>nger* ← *Doppelgänger, L<u>a</u>mmergeyer* ← *Lämmergeyer, vorl<u>a</u>ufer* ← *Vorläufer*)

e. Changing consonant letters: 'k' → 'c' (e.g., *delicatessen* ← *Delikatesse*), 'sch' → 'sh' (e.g., *shaman* ← *Schamane*), 'tsch' → 'tch' (e.g., *klatsch, klatch* ← *Klatsch*)

4.2.5 Irregularity of Plural Forms of Nouns

As for the irregularity of plural inflection, it is revealed that the German loanwords can be divided into the following three types:

(90) a. items retaining the original plural inflections: 69 items (e.g., *bebung<u>en</u>* ← *Bebungen* (sg. *Bebung*), *Abiturient<u>en</u>* ← *Abiturienten* (sg. *Abiturient*), *Lied<u>er</u>* ← *Lieder* (sg. *Lied*))

b. items having both the original plural inflections and the English plural inflections: 37 items (e.g., *B<u>ü</u>nd<u>e</u>/bund<u>s</u>* ← *Bünde* (sg. *Bund*), *Frau<u>en</u>/Frau<u>s</u>* ← *Frauen* (sg. *Frau*))

c. items shifted to have the English plural inflections (-*s*, -*es*) (e.g., *dummkopf<u>s</u>* ← *Dummköpfe* (sg. *Dummkopf*), *doppelgänger<u>s</u>* ← *Doppelgänger* (sg. *Doppelgänger*)

As can be seen from Table 4.3, more than 25% of German loanwords have irregular plural inflection, and this percentage is greater than that of Japanese loanwords. This indicates that it is easier for Japanese loanwords to acquire the regular English plural inflections than German loanwords. This can be explained by the fact that Japanese loanwords do not have a plural inflection ending in their origin, so they can simply acquire the English plural ending, while German loanwords have their own plural inflection system, so there can be more resistance to drop the German plural ending and acquire the new plural inflection from English. Then, some questions may arise. What makes one noun to acquire the regular English plural inflection and the other to retain the German inflection? Can it be considered as evidence of the early stages of the assimilation process unlike the case with Japanese loanwords?

Looking into the nouns with irregular plural inflection, I have noticed that they have a common characteristic. Most of them have not completed the pronunciation and/or orthographic adaptations. For example, K_uchen retains the non-anglicized phoneme [x], A_ufklärer, [aʊ] and [ɛː], Lie_d [t], Z_wieba_ck [ts], [v], and [a], Ursp_ra_che [ʃp] and [x], and K_lippe is spelled with 'k' at the beginning not with 'c', so does k_ondi_tor_ei, also including foreign phonemes [i] and [ai].[5] Therefore, it can be assumed that the foreign features of pronunciation and/or spelling prevents the nouns from having the regular English plural inflection.

However, there are some exceptions, but these can be explained. One group of exception consists of the items with Greek origin, borrowed into English by way of German (e.g., *noumenon, schema*). These words have lost the German characteristics of pronunciation and/or spelling, and still retain irregular inflection, but their irregularity is not derived from German but from Greek (i.e., *noumena_, schemata_*). It is usual in English to retain the Greek plural inflection, so it does not affect our assumption about German loanwords. The other exception is *autobahn*, whose pronunciation has been modified to fit the English orthography rules, but it has both German *-en* and English *-s* inflections. This will be explained by the corpus research in Section 4.3. Briefly stated, the corpus data show that its *-en* plural form is no longer in use in English, and only *-s* is used as a plural inflection. Thus, the description of the dictionary is not current enough to show that it has lost its German inflection after finishing pronunciation adaptation. The relationship between irregularity and the degree of assimilation will be discussed in Section 4.2.9.

4.2.6 Attributive Use

Table 4.2 shows that the attributive use was observed in only 6.6% of German loanwords dated after 1940 (cf. Japanese 19.1%). Even if one turns to the German loanwords of all periods, the percentage of attributive use remains low, as shown in Table 4.3, with only 21 items (e.g., *föhn* wind, *Abiturient* pupils, *Abitur* examination, *firn* snow, *landau* carriage, *schiller* rock). This shows that the attributive use in German loanwords do not appear at any stage of the assimilation process to help clarify the meanings of the unfamiliar words

---

[5] The diphthong [ai] does not even exist in German. The German equivalent is [aɪ], the same as English.

as Japanese loanwords do. In addition, unlike Japanese loanwords, most of the attributive use of German loanwords is not repetitive, appearing only once or a few times in quotations, also suggesting its little establishment. Therefore, the attributive use of German loanwords is not considered as one stage of the assimilation process.

4.2.7 Acquisition of Productivity

As for the productivity of German loanwords, I have shown in Table 4.3, the total number of items with productivity and the number of items with each kind of word-formation process: compounding, functional shifts, and suffixation. As a result, a total of 121 items were revealed to have the productivity; this is incomparable to the case with Japanese loanwords. Compounding was by far the most frequent method of producing new vocabulary. This coincides with the result of Japanese loanwords. The percentage of suffixation is not as high as that of Table 4.2, because the technical terms that are used only in the specific sense and field have been excluded, and therefore many of the scientists' names with suffixes are not included in the data. Thus, it is obvious that the productivity of the German loanwords far greatly outnumber that of Japanese loanwords. Some examples of the productivity are shown below:

(91) a. Compounding: *Alp-horn melodies, buhl-saw, Herrenvolk attitude, kitsch culture, lager laut, lieder singer, loden cloak, poltergeist activity, schiller-plane, Wehmacht commander, Zollverein-Department* etc.;

  b. Suffixation: *Bundist, flugelhornist, gneissic, firnification, abseiler, anlauting, Gesellschaft-like, angst-ridden*;

  c. Functional shift: *ersatz* (adj.), *bauhaus* (adj.), *abseil* (n.) *blitz* (adj.) (v.), *zugzwang* (v.).

4.2.8 Semantic Shift

Semantic shift was observed in 90 items; it corresponds to 21.5% of German loanwords. It is apparent that German loanwords provide more new senses than Japanese loanwords, whose semantic shift accounts for only 14 items. In Section

3.2.6, I introduced three kinds of semantic shift including 'Metaphorical use,' 'Expansion,' and 'Transfer.' Here, I add another kind, 'Transfer by ellipsis.' It can be considered as a kind of 'Transfer,' but I have established it as a separate category here since the way it transfers meaning is distinctive from others, and German loanwords provide enough number of items to form a separate category. In the case of Japanese loanwords, *soy* would be included in this category. Some examples of the semantic shift are shown in (92). (Underlines supplied in the examples hereafter.)

(92) a. **Metaphorical use:** *blitzkrieg, Götterdämmerung, katzenjammer, poltergeist, schmierkäse, spurlos, Totentantz, Umwelt* etc.

- 1941 Wyndham Lewis *Let.* 16 Apr. (1963) 288 At the time I was going through a minor economic <u>Blitz</u> of my own.
- 1959 *Listener* 1 Oct. 525/1 A totalitarian régime must either prevail absolutely or else it heads straight for some kind of <u>Götterdämmerung</u>.
- 1955 H. Kurnitz Let. Dec. in G. Marx *Groucho Lett.* (1967) 249, I am..whipping up a <u>schmierkase</u> about light love and dark doings.

b. **Expansion of meaning:** *automat, blitz, Fasching, diktat, fühler, leitmotiv, schema, shaman, Übermensch, zollverein* etc.

- 1909 Webster, <u>*Automat*</u>, a café or restaurant in which orders are automatically delivered to customers, who place coins or tokens in slots. ('a vending machine' → 'a cafeteria where in which food is obtained from a vending machine')
- 1963 *Times* 27 May 13/4 Naked aggression against any state in Africa which does not accept the <u>diktat</u> of himself and his friends. ('A severe settlement or decision with reference to the Treaty of Versailles' → 'a categorical assertion')
- 1963 *Economist* 13 July 103/1 Doctor and detective <u>übermenschen</u>. ('an ideal superior man conceived by Nietzsche' → 'a great/prestigious man')

c. **Transfer of meaning:** *Gestapo, junker, kraut, kitsch, lebensraum, realpolitik. schuss, wedeln, wunderkind* etc.

- 1966 L. P. Davies *Psychogeist* xii. 109 My private Gestapo has already brought the news. ('German secret police' to 'a bodyguard')
- 1966 T. Pynchon *Crying of Lot 49* i. 15 Maybe..he should have been in a war, Japs in trees, Krauts in Tiger tanks. ('a cabbage' → 'a German')
- 1960 *Times* 30 May 13/6 Lebensraum for the Japanese. ('territory which the Germans believed was needed for their natural development' to 'living space')

d. **Transfer by ellipsis:** *delicatessen, flügel, frankfurt, gestalt, lager, lumpen, meerschaum, wiener.*

- 1954 *Grove's Dict. Mus.* (ed. 5) III. 166/1 In English brass bands..a 'flugel' (as it is usually called) is an essential constituent. (= 'flügelhorn')
- 1858 *N.Y. Express* June (Bartlett), The German drinks his lager, and drinks it apparently in indefinite quantities. (= 'lager beer')
- 1974 *Black Panther* 27 Apr. 13/2 The outlaw and the lumpen will make the revolution. The people, the workers, will adopt it. (= the lumpenproletariat)

Apart from the advantage of German loanwords in number, they also differ from Japanese loanwords in that they do not follow the same tendency of the assimilation process as Japanese loanwords do. That is, the semantic shift in German loanwords does not necessarily follow the stage of gaining productivity, while the semantic shift in Japanese loanwords mostly occur after they have gained productivity. This will be discussed further in Section 4.2.9 in determining which words are the most assimilated.

4.2.9 Assimilated German Loanwords

So far, we have observed the changes German loanwords go through in detail, and compared them with those of Japanese loanwords. Here, I would finally like to determine which of the German loanwords are assimilated ones and which are not. First, I extracted the German loanwords that are registered in all of the dictionaries listed in (93) to guarantee their frequency and wide prevalence in English. Appendix F shows which word is registered in which dictionary/ies.

(93) a. *The Oxford Dictionary of Foreign Words and Phrases* (1997)[6]

   b. *The Oxford English Dictionary 2nd ed. ver.3* (2001) or *the Shorter OED 5th ed.* (2002) for newer items.

   c. *Webster's Third* (1999)

   d. *The Random House* (2000)

As a result, 179 items among 418 items were extracted. Then, I investigated their productivity and senses by checking each item in the following points:

(94) a. whether the dictionaries provide compounds, suffixation, functional shift, and labels, such as *Comp.* and *Attrib.* in the definition section.

   b. whether compounds, suffixation, and/or functional shift other than the ones already mentioned in the definition section appear in the quotations.

   c. whether there are labels, such as *fig.*, *transf.*, *gen.*, and *ellipt.* or mention of other senses such as, "extended use" and "wider sense."

   d. whether the dictionaries provide more than one sense; if so, whether the second sense has been developed from the first sense in English (*i.e.*, semantic shift) or borrowed again from German (*i.e.*, doublets).

   e. whether there are the instances of a new sense or a metaphorical use in quotations.

---

[6] All the items clear this condition as our data was originally retrieved from this.

As a result, it is revealed that 59 out of 179 items have developed new senses, while 46 have gained productivity. It is remarkable that the number of the items which have acquired productivity is smaller than that of the items which have gone through the semantic shift. In addition, of the 59 items with multiple senses, as many as 33 items do not have productivity. This result is significant when I compare it with the case of Japanese loanwords because most of the Stage 4 items (*i.e.*, items that have gone through the semantic shift) of Japanese loanwords have produced new vocabulary by compounding, suffixation, and/or functional shifts. This shows that it is not necessary for German loanwords to gain productivity before they go though the semantic shift. These facts clearly show that the German loanwords have a different process of assimilation from Japanese loanwords. That is, German loanwords do not follow the stages in the same order as Japanese loanwords do, but they start their assimilation from various aspects, depending on the form and/or the pronunciation of the items. Some need no pronunciation modification, but first gain productivity, and then go through a semantic shift, while others obtain new senses soon after borrowing and produce compounds at almost the same time, and in the meantime the pronunciation becomes modified gradually.

The following are some examples of transition of German loanwords:

(95) a. *abseil*:

> **1933** First attested (German verb *abseilen* borrowed as a noun).
> **1940** Functional shift to verb.
> **1956** Produced a noun *abseiling* by suffixation.

b. *blitzkrieg*:

> **1939** First attested.
> Metaphorical use.
> Clipping and Functional shift *blitz* (v.).
> **1940** Compound *blitzkrieg method*.
> Produced a noun *blitzing* by suffixation.
> Attributive use *Blitz bombing*.
> Metaphorical use.

1955 Produced an adjective *blitzed* by suffixation.

1963 Technical term for American football (n.).

1965 Functional shift to verb as a technical term for American football.

1968 Suffixation *blitzer*.

c. *giro*:[7]

1896 First attested. Compound *giro account*,

1930 Attributive use *giro transfer*.

1961 *giro system*, 1963, *giro number*, 1972 *giro check*.

1975 Ellipsis *giro* (=giro check).

1976 Semantic shift (a cheque or money order for social security payments) *giro order*.

d. *polka*:

1844 First attested. Compound *polka step*.

1845 Suffixation *polkamania, polkery*.

1846 Suffixation *polkist(e)*.
Functional shift to verb.
Semantic shift ('something popular and pleasant').
More compounds follow.

1884 Suffixation *polkaic* (a.).
Compound *polka-dots*

1908 Suffixation *polka-dotted* (a.).

1969 Back-formation *polka-dot* (v.).

Finally, from the investigation mentioned above, I can determine the assimilated items as in (96). Refer to Appendix E for the complete list of the observed productive forms.

---

[7] Here, I give the example of *giro* because it shows a variety of changes, though it is not included in the 179 items mentioned above since *Random House* failed to enter this word.

(96) a. items with both strong productivity and (a) new sense(s): *blitz(krieg)*, *ersatz, gestalt, Hanse, junker, kindergarten, kitsch, kraut, lager, loden, lumpen(proletariat), panzer, polka, poltergeist, putsch, shaman, sinter, wedeln*

b. items with some productivity and (a) new sense(s): *bund, deli (catessen), Führer, Herrenvolk, jäger, katzenjammer, pretzel, sauerkraut, schiller, schuss, zollverein*

c. items with (a) new sense(s) but little or no productivity: *Anschauung, automat, diktat, föhn, flügelhorn, Fräulein, Gestapo, Götterdämmerung, kaput, Landwehr, lebensraum, leitmotiv, maar, meerschaum, putz, rackett, rinderpest, schema, schmierkäse, sitzkrieg, Sprechstimme, stoss, Sturm und Drang, Volkslied, wiener(wurst), wunderkind, wurst, zugzwang*

d. items with strong productivity but no semantic variation: *Kaiser, umlaut*

e. items with some productivity but no semantic variation: *ablaut, abseil, angst, anschluss, barouche, fest, firn, Jugendstil, ländler, langlauf, schappe, schottische, wanderlust*

Here, I have divided the productivity into three levels; 'strong' productivity, 'some' productivity, and 'little or no' productivity. A word is considered to have strong productivity when it has multiple kinds of productivity among compounding, suffixation, and functional shifts and provides more than one pattern in one or more kind(s) of productivity (*e.g.*, the word *gestalt* is considered to have 'strong productivity' since it has four patterns of compounding and two patterns of suffixation), or when it has one kind of productivity but the patterns are numerous compared to the standard number of patterns which that kind of productivity provides (*e.g.*, ten different patterns of compounding in *kraut* qualifies it as having 'strong productivity.'). I consider the word to have some productivity when it is not as productive as the one above but has one or more kind(s) of productivity and provides multiple patterns in total. Others are considered to have little or no productivity (*e.g.*, *Gestapo* is considered to have little productivity since it has only one pattern of compounding.).

106   I   Assimilation Process of Loanwords

(96a) is considered to be the group whose members achieve the highest assimilation stage, followed by the items (96b) because they fulfill all the conditions that are considered to be the criteria of assimilation, though the German loanwords do not share the same order of change as Japanese loanwords. If we focus on the pronunciation of the items in (96a) and (96b), we can also notice that most of them have finished their adaptation of pronunciation. Some of them have gone through rather drastic changes while others need no modification at all. The following are some of the changed and unchanged parts of pronunciation.[8]

(97)   a. Changed: *ers*a*tz* ([ɛr] → [ɜː], [a] → [æ]),
   *H*a*nse* ([a] → [æ], [zə] → [s]),
   *k*i*nde*r*ga*r*ten* ([i] → [ɪ], [ər] → [ə], [ar] → [ɑː]),
   kriegspiel ([k] → [g], [ʃp] → [sp]),
   *l*u*mpen(pr*o*le*tariat) ([u] → [ʌ], [o] → [əʊ], [e] → [ɪ]),
   *p*a*n*z*er* ([a] → [æ], [ts] → [z]),
   *p*o*lka* ([ɔ] → [əʊ]),
   *sh*a*m*a*n* ([a] → [ˈɑː, ˈæ], [ˈaː] → [ə]),
   *s*i*nter* ([z] → [s])

   b. Unchanged: consonants bound tightly with German orthography rules.
   bund ([t]), *gestalt* ([ʃt]), *junker* ([j]), *wedeln* ([v]), *Herrenvolk* ([f]), *vorlage* ([f]), *zollverein* ([ts], [f])

(97) shows that pronunciation adaptation is mostly completed by the time an item obtains power to produce new vocabulary both morphologically and semantically, though some phonemes, especially consonants bound tightly with German orthography rules, are likely to remain unchanged. As for inflection, no item in (97) has retained a German plural form. This suggests that regularization of a plural inflection is also completed by the time an item obtains power to produce new vocabulary. This supports the assumption in Section 4.2.5 that the German loanwords lose their irregularity around the time they finish their assimilation of pronunciation.

---
[8] Underlined letters are the modified parts, and the bold-faced letters are the parts where foreign features remain.

4.2.10 Other Characteristics

There are many more characteristics to be mentioned about German loanwords. First, it is revealed that there is high percentage of technical terms (22.8%) in German loanwords. More remarkable is that though a language generally borrows an item from another language when it does not have a single word that corresponds to the new concept or object coming into the country where the language is spoken, about half of the German loanwords are not new in concepts and have the equivalent terms in English, meaning they are used to rephrase or alternate the existing terms, or adding a new, more specific sense to the equivalent terms (e.g., *Dirndle, giro, Eiswein* vs. *Anschauung* (≒ *Intuition*), *Erlebnis* (≒ *experience*), *Frau* (≒ *woman*), *wurst* (≒ *sausage*)). In addition, many instances of loan translation and partial translation can be observed, and 43 of them also have the equivalent primary loanwords (e.g., *blutwurst/blood sausage, doppelgänger/double-ganger, entscheidungsproblem/decision problem, durchkomponiert/through composed, Grenzbegriff/limit-conception*). This double borrowing results in more pairs of words/phrases with German lexical items and those consisting of English lexical items.

None of these characteristics are observed in Japanese loanwords, indicating that loanwords from the two languages have respective functions in English. That is, Japanese contributes vocabulary to English by what Bloomfield (1933) called 'cultural borrowing'; it is lexical borrowing from foreign languages as a result of 'cultural diffusion,' while German provides more technical terms to English in many fields of science, including terms in philosophy and psychology as well as chemistry, physics, and mineralogy. As for loan translation, it only started to increase in Japanese loanwords in recent years, while German has provided translated items constantly throughout the history of borrowing, and many are coexisting with the equivalent primary loanwords. Some of these contrasts will be verified and analyzed in more detail using a corpus which contains both written and spoken data of actual English in Chapter 7.

4.2.11 Summary

In this section, I have discussed the changes the German loanwords go through in the process of assimilation in English. As a result, it has been made clear that German loanwords do not follow the same four-stage process of assimilation as

Japanese loanwords. They start several aspects of adaptation simultaneously or in random order instead, and shift toward the highly assimilated state, where all the adaptations are completed and the items fully exert the word-formation power and have multiple senses. As for each of the aspects of the assimilation, I have made clear the following points about German loanwords:

(98) a. There are some phonemes which become assimilated earlier than others, while others are more likely to remain unchanged even after other changes have been completed.

b. The number of the irregular plural inflections in German loanwords is larger than Japanese loanwords.

c. There is a close relation between the foreign features of pronunciation and the irregularity of pluralization.

d. The attributive use of nouns is not a dominant way to explain rather unfamiliar words; it is not considered as one stage of assimilation.

e. The acquisition of productivity is not as frequent as semantic shift.

f. German loanwords have an incomparable word-formation capability to Japanese.

g. The words do not necessarily go through the acquisition of productivity before gaining a new sense.

h. Semantic shifts in German loanwords outnumber those in Japanese loanwords.

i. German loanwords have a respective function in English from Japanese loanwords.

j. Technical terms and loan translations are very frequent in German loanwords.

In the next section, I will verify the characteristics of German loanwords retrieved from the major dictionaries, and update their usage using a large corpus which contains abundant data of both spoken and written Present-day English. As we have already seen in Chapter 3, this process is very important because the dictionaries do not tell everything about the words, especially concerning the frequency and the current usages. I will also deal with the question of context, as was done with Japanese in Section 3.5 to search for other factors that contribute to the assimilation process of loanwords.

4.3 Corpus-based Approach

In this section, I investigate German loanwords further using a corpus. While dictionaries are useful in that they show us the information on the words in a very systematic way, the corpus, though not as systematic as the dictionaries, consists of plenty of raw sentences from various texts in many fields, and gives us more information as to the frequency of the words and their current usages. I will verify the results of the dictionary-based research in Section 4.2, and search for new usages and the context in which they are used.

4.3.1 Procedure

I used the *British National Corpus World Edition* (henceforth the *BNC*) as a source. The *BNC* is an enormous collection of part-of-speech tagged texts collected from both written and spoken British English mainly during 1984-1994,[9] containing 100 million words. The software used here is called BNCweb; it is a web-browser-based client program to access the server called SARA. The server runs on UNIX/Linux machine and can manage SGML-formatted corpora such as the *BNC*. BNCweb enables one to search for and retrieve lexical, grammatical, and textual data from the *BNC* through the network. It provides a whole range of features for corpus analyses, such as concordance display, sorting, collocations, and distribution analysis.[10]

I searched for the words in (99) and excluded any unwanted items, such as proper nouns and the occurrences in German phrases or sentences, by checking each of the resulting texts manually.

(99) a. items which are determined as assimilated items shown in (96)

---

[9] The *BNC* also contains some data from 1960 to 1983.
[10] Refer to the web-site of BNCweb (URL: http://homepage.mac.com/bncweb/home.html) for more detailed information.

b. unassimilated items (items in Section 4.2.9 other than in (96)).

I analyze the data from the following aspects:

(100) a. Frequency: how often the words are used. Unrelated proper nouns, such as the name of a person or a place are excluded.

b. Form: how they appear in the sentence. Capitalization, hyphenation, quoted, glossed *etc.*

c. Context: in what context they are used. Original (*i.e.*, German) or apart from the original.

d. Usage: what the typical usages are. Compounding, suffixation, part of speech, phrase *etc.*

e. Sense: in what sense they are used. Original, extended, transferred, metaphorical *etc.*

In searching the corpus for German loanwords, I encountered the following difficulty due to the nature of the German loanwords and/or to the defects of the search software.

(101) a. The software distinguishes a letter with an umlaut and one without an umlaut, so it is usually the case that a regular expression is used to search for both forms simultaneously (e.g., *Aufklarung* and *Aufklärung*), but some regular expression searches do not work properly (*e.g.*, the query {aufkl[aä]rung} is supposed to pick up both *Aufklarung* and *Aufklärung*, but does not give a proper result.). Thus, one needs some modification to get the results successfully (*e.g.*, {aufkl.rung}, where "." (period) indicates one of any letters).

b. The search using some regular expressions does not work properly in Word-lookup with the "Regular Expression" entry type option (neither of the two entries in (101a) produce any result). One has to carry out searches with the "Beginning of Word" entry type option (*e.g.*, *aufkl* to get both *Aufklarung* and *Aufklärung*); this returns all the words that start with the given sequence. However, this sometimes causes a huge list of results full of unwanted data.

c. Even if I successfully obtain the result in Word-lookup, the matched text for the items with an umlaut cannot be browsed by clicking the item, which results in an error message. One needs to go back and carry out the same search again in Standard query to browse the text.

d. There are other characters (*e.g.*, "/" slash, "( )" parentheses) that the Word-lookup cannot deal with properly, giving the error message mentioned in (101c), and for some unknown reason the first item in the result list of *schnitzel* (schnitzel = NN1) had the same problem.

e. Though the *BNC* is a part-of-speech tagged corpus, enabling search by the tags, it is sometimes inaccurate especially for German loanwords, for the initial letters of German nouns are often spelled with capital letters in texts, resulting in them being categorized as proper nouns when they are actually common nouns.

4.3.2 Unassimilated Loanwords

Table 4.5 shows the frequency distribution of German loanwords which were determined as unassimilated in Section 4.2.9. Only the items with ten or more occurrences are listed.

Looking at Table 4.5, one can soon notice that there are items frequently occurring in the *BNC* even among the items considered to be unassimilated as the result of the dictionary-based investigation. However, the frequency does not always mean their prevalence among English speakers. Some items occur mostly in guide books for traveling in Germany, Switzerland, or Austria (e.g., *gasthaus, lederhosen*), while others almost always appear in specialized books (e.g., *gneiss, loess, Singspiel, Umwelt, verstehen*), and still others do have many occurrences but they come from one or a small number of texts (e.g., *bergschrund, schwa*). Looking from the aspect of context, some items are used almost always in a historical context, designating the person(s) or event(s) in history (e.g., *Wehrmacht* = German army in WWII), others are always bound to the German context without extending the range of designation (e.g., *Frau, Lied*). Items with all those characteristics mentioned above

Table 4.5: Frequency of Unassimilated German Loanwords in the *BNC*

Word	Occurrence[a]		Word[b]	Occurrence	
autobahn	70	(70)	noumenon	13	(13)
bauhaus	37	(39)	realpolitik	32	(32)
bergschrund	13	(13)	schadenfreude	13	(13)
doppelgänger	31	(37)	schnapps	29	(30)
frankfurt	13	(604)	schwa	10	(10)
Frau	12	(320)	singspiel	15	(15)
gasthaus	14	(19)	spritzer	14	(14)
gesellschaft	17	(25)	Strudel	13	(13)
glockenspiel	11	(22)	Wehmacht	51	(51)
gneiss	43	(44)	weltanschauung	21	(21)
Kirsch	28	(31)	zeitgeist	27	(30)
kohlrabi	16	(16)	giro	91	(155)
landau	24	(95)	hamburger	175	(184)
lederhosen	10	(10)	Umwelt	13	(18)
lied	37	(56)	verstehen	12	(14)
loess	33	(35)			

a. The numbers in parentheses are the result given by the *BNC* search before excluding unwanted items.
b. The items below the horizontal line (i.e., *giro, hamburger, Umwelt,* and *verstehen*) were listed though they are not included in the target since they are known to have certain frequencies.

limit their range of usage in some way or other. Therefore, they cannot be considered as fully accepted as general English vocabulary unless they otherwise show their productivity or semantic shift. They also share the same characteristics of unassimilated Japanese loanwords mentioned in Section 3.3.2. There, I introduced various ways of glossing unassimilated items. The same ways are observed with German loanwords as in (102).[11]

(102) a. Explanatory sentence embedded:

- ... *and vernacular opera, usually farcical in nature, with spoken dialogue in the appropriate country's tongue – in Germany and Austria, this was known as* Singspiel. (CEW)
- *Since the environmental rhythm is giving a time-cue to the organism it is called a* zeitgeber *(from the German, Zeit – time; geber – to give)*. (A75)

[11] Three letters in parentheses following an example indicate the text ID in the *BNC*.

b. Apposition of gloss with or without *or* or parentheses or quotation marks:

- They are not always malicious towards mankind, being known as "*kobold*" or "demons of the mines" in Germany, and ... (CAC)
- It is because no institution or individual is proof against the third essential ingredient that makes us what we are – the *Zeitgeist*, the spirit of the times. (AKM)
- In short, modernity itself creates the scientific/rational *Weltanschauung* (world-view) of modern men and women. (CCE)

c. Attributive use, followed by the explanatory words:

- *Bratwurst* sausage (CEK)
- *gneiss* rock (AML)
- *langdau* carriage (ALY)
- *loess* soils (APN)
- *pumpernickel* bread (G2F)
- "*schwa*" vowel (K93)

In Section 4.2.6, I concluded from the dictionary-based research that attributive use is not a very frequent way to explain unassimilated words, but as is shown in (102c), more items have attributive use than the dictionaries mention and some of them are used repeatedly, though it is still a small range of phenomena compared to that of Japanese loanwords.

On the other hand, as a result of corpus-based research, some items revealed their new usages or senses. Some examples are shown below:

(103) a. Productivity:

Compound: *Bauhaus* furniture/chair/building/museum etc.,
gneiss outcrops/peaks/zone/landscape etc.,
loess lands/bluffs/plateau/cover etc.,
noumenon world/realm/things/gardens/level etc.,
wehrmacht officers/troops/unit/helmet etc.,

giro account/cheque/day/credit/transfer etc.,
hamburger restaurant/chain/stall/joint/bar/stand etc.;

Suffixation: *Bauhaus*-inspired, *frankfurter*-coloured, *gneissic*, *hamburger*-shaped, *loess*-covered, *schnapps*-crazed, *Strudel*-like, etc.;

Functional Shift: very *Bauhaus* (adj.), very *hausfrau* (adj.).

b. Semantic variety:

Metaphorical use:

- "Compared with roads back home, Kielder is like an *autobahn*," he said. (CEP)
- "I was about to become *hamburger* on the rocks", he admits. (ASV)
- ...the narrator's unloved Aunt Mildred "had a powdered look, like her own *strudel*"; (A36)
- There was a series of brilliant dialogues with his own stomach, which acquired a separate, living, suffering identity as Tum, his gastric *doppelgänger*. (GSX)
- It says the company's marketing of Cisco is dangerously deceptive; it induces unsuspecting teenagers to guzzle it as if it were a standard *spritzer*. (ABH)

Expansion of meaning:

- *autobahn* (other than the German express way, such as Italian). "...From Vienna it's *autobahn* all the way." (HTJ)
- *realpolitik* (politics in countries other than Germany, such as China, the U.S.A., and Poland). "Operation Just Cause," yesterday's surprise invasion of Panama, will certainly wipe any lingering concern about the White House's Chinese *Realpolitik* from the front pages. (AAF)

Transfer by Ellipsis:

- *hamburger* (← Hamburger steak) *A picture of the American family began to be glimpsed as a super-mobile group that could get together to grill a hamburger only if it drove to the appointment.* (ACS)

The plural forms of the noun loanwords from German found in the *BNC* were regular except for *Lied* (pl. *-er* (32 times)), *noumenon* (pl. *noumena* (five times)), *Umwelt* (pl. *-en* (three times)), and *Weltanschauung* (pl. *-en* (once)). As was mentioned in Section 4.2.5, the plural form of *noumenon* (*noumena*) is not originally German but Greek, and Greek has provided many items with irregular plural endings in English. The number of irregular occurrences of *Lied* is also significant (32 times), as there is only one instance of a regular plural ending *-s*, but this appears in the sentence, *"A singer of German songs will sing Lieds rather than Lieder;"* (ABD), suggesting that the plural form of *Lied* is not *Lieds* but *Lieder*. This may be because the word was borrowed in the plural form first, just as *delicatessen* was, and later *-er* was recognized as a German plural ending.[12] One can claim so because there are many titles of collections of German songs which contain the word *"Lieder"* in the *BNC*, and those were the probable source of the borrowing. Another evidence is that the *BNC* gives an instance which contains a phrase like 'Lieder writers' (ED6); in this case *Lieder* is used as a singular noun as one says 'song writers' not 'songs writers.' As for *Autobahn*, though the *OED2* describes as having two plural forms (i.e., *-en* and *-s*), it appeared in the *BNC* 70 times, nine of which were plural, but all the plural forms were with the regular ending *-s*, showing that the plural form of *Autobahn* has been anglicized, and now the English plural ending *-s* is the dominant, if not the only, plural form.

Thus, irregular inflection of nouns is rare even in the unassimilated words, if they are frequent enough to appear more than ten times in a 100 million-corpus. Only some of the words with low frequencies which are sometimes called 'mere dictionary words' retain irregularity of plural inflections. I can conclude here that irregular inflection cannot be considered as a criterion of a low degree of the assimilation process of German loanwords in actual use in English.

---

[12] Its original German is *delikatesse* + plural ending *-n*. However, the ending *-n* in *delicatessen* has never been recognized as a plural inflection. Instead, it has acquired the clipped form *deli*, and its plural is *delis*.

4.3.3 Assimilated Loanwords

Next, I would like to focus on the items that I determined to be assimilated. I searched for the items in (96), and their frequency is summarized in Table 4.6. Only the items with ten or more frequency in the *BNC* are listed.

Table 4.6: Frequency of Assimilated German Loanwords in the *BNC*

Word	Occurrence[a]		Word	Occurrence	
abseil	230	(234)	kraut	18	(20)
angst	133	(136)	lager	646	(657)
anschluss	13	(13)	langlauf	12	(12)
blitz(krieg)	367	(379)	lebensraum	14	(14)
bund	35	(41)	leitmotiv	15	(15)
delicatessen	185	(197)	lumpen	36	(38)
diktat	32	(32)	panzer	26	(27)
ersatz	31	(31)	polka	47	(51)
Fräulein	59	(186)	poltergeist	37	(41)
Führer	336	(340)	pretzel	10	(10)
gestalt	49	(52)	putsch	35	(35)
Gestapo	95	(96)	sauerkraut	10	(10)
Götterdämmerung	10	(10)	schema	460	(744)
Hanse	32	(45)	shaman	286	(288)
junker	94	(112)	sinter	31	(31)
Kaiser	92	(157)	wanderlust	15	(17)
kindergarten	102	(102)	wunderkind	12	(12)
kitsch	87	(89)			

a. The figures in parentheses are the results given by the *BNC* search before excluding unwanted items.

Among the 75 items in (96), 35 are in Table 4.6. As was the case with Japanese loanwords, some items do not appear in the corpus even though they showed the productivity and/or multiple senses in the dictionary description. Of the 35 items shown in Table 4.6, some show strong productivity, multiple senses, and/or high frequency, while others almost always appear unchanged with relatively low frequencies. The characteristics of those will be discussed below.

Some of the items share the same characteristics of unassimilated loanwords. For example, *Fräulein*, *Führer* and *Kaiser* are used almost always as a title or a prefix followed by the name of a person, just as *Frau* in Section 4.3.2, or designating a certain person (i.e., *Führer* ≈ Hitler and *Kaiser* ≈ Wilhelm).

The technical terms, such as *gesellschaft, gestalt, shaman,* and *sinter*, are almost always used in the text of the specialized field, just as *bergschrund, gneiss, loess,* and *schwa* in Section 4.3.2. The terms, such as *bund, Gestapo, junker, Hanse,* and *Panzer*, which designate historical German social/martial groups or classes are strongly bound to the German context with the original senses, appearing in the books about German society or history, just as *Wehrmacht* in Section 4.3.2. All these items mentioned above are limited in usage in some way or other, and therefore cannot be considered as common vocabulary in English.

Glossing is observed only for a few items:

(104) a. *bürgeriche* Gessellschaft *or civil society* (GW4)

b. ... *And the alternative to this is* wanderlust. *The person who wants to explore, keep on the move <pause> and typified by some form of touring holiday.* (F88)

c. *Re-arranged, the parts make up a different whole which has a different form or* gestalt.[13] (H0Y)

d. *To him, independence was not something achieved: it was a* leitmotiv, *a mode of existence.* (FAN)

Attributive use, shown in (105), is not very frequent either, and it does not appear repeatedly. This fact, together with the finding in Section 4.3.2, revealed that some of the German loanwords have attributive use, though it is not a significant stage of the assimilation process, as was the case with Japanese loanwords. This supports the result of the dictionary-based research.

(105) wanderlust *urge,* abseil *descent,* panzer *tank,* kindergarten *school,* junker *land-owners/lord/aristocracy,* blitzkrieg *attack*

Irregular inflection was observed in *schema* (*schemata* (101 times), *schemas* (84 times)), *Gestapo* (collective), and *wunderkind* (*wunderkinder* (twice)). The plural form of *schema*, as was already mentioned in Section 4.2.5, is not derived from German but from Greek, whose irregular plural forms are usual in English.

---

[13] Strictly speaking, this is not a glossing of *gestalt* but a rephrasing of *form* with a more technical vocabulary.

118   I   Assimilation Process of Loanwords

Gestapo ('German secret police') is sometimes used collectively without adding a plural ending, but this does not contradict the English rule as the English word 'police' is also used collectively. As for the plural form of *wunderkind* (*wunderkinder*), though it cannot be said decisively due to its low frequency, it might be affected by the famous word with a German origin 'kindergarten.' Other than these three, the irregular inflection was not observed, suggesting that the irregular inflection is also rare at a relatively advanced stage of the assimilation process.

Compounding was observed in the following items:

(106)   a. *abseil: rope, point(s), equipment, anchor, retreat, inspection,* etc.;

b. *angst: film, sexuality, life, outsiders, quality, impression,* etc.;

c. *blitz(krieg): bombing, victory, triumph, blackout, game, start,* etc.;

d. *delicatessen: business, food, meats, shelves, stores, meal,* etc.;

e. *polka: dot, standard, dress, tie, material, handkerchief,* etc.;

f. *panzer: division, Corps, convoy, Army, regiment*;

g. *lager: pilsner, lout(s), pint(s), can(s), beer(s), alchohol(-free),* etc.;

h. *kitsch: value, fashion, stool, rubbish, atomosphere, object, taste,* etc.;

i. *kindergarten: teachers, children, time, days, kids, facilities, fees,* etc.;

j. *junker: resistance, class, tradition, status, estate, families,* etc.;

k. *gestalt: psychology, therapy, school, mind, quality, principles,* etc.;

l. *gestapo: agent, officer, unit, prison, torture, jail, commander* etc.

Suffixing is less popular, but some are new that were not included in the dictionary research:

(107)   a. *abseil: abseiler, abseiling, abseiled*;

b. *angst: angst-filled, angst-free, angst-ridden, angst-struck, angsty* etc.;

c. *blitz: blitzed, blitzer, blitzing, blitz-torn*;

d. *delicatessen: delicatessen-cum-drinking, deli-dinner, deli-restaurant*;

e. *poltergeist:* poltergeist-like;

f. *polka:* polka-dot(ted);

g. *lager:* lager-brewing, lager(-)laut(s), lager-swilling, lager-type, lagered;

h. *kraut:* krautish, krautrockers;

i. *junker:* junker-dominated, junker-middle-class;

j. *schema:* -based, -consistent etc.;

k. *shaman:* shamanesque, shamanic, shamanism, shamanist, shamanistic.

Functional shift was the least frequent, observed only with *abseil* (n. to v.), *blitz* (n. to v.), *lumpen* (a. to n.), and *ersatz* (a. to n.). There was no item that showed little or no productivity in (96) but showed some or great productivity in the corpus.

Semantic variation was observed the most frequently among the changes:

(108) a. **Metaphorical use**: *Gestapo, gotterdammerung, polka*;

- *I imagine it's a legacy of the war: centralised personal data sounds too much like the Gestapo – though mind you, it would be a hell of a storage problem if you hid [sic] start collecting copies of all these.* (H86)
- *His pulse was a distant polka retreating into the unknown.* (FP0)

b. **Expansion of meaning**: *blitz(krieg), diktat, ersatz, lebensraum, leitmotiv, kitsch, putsch, schema, wunderkind*;

- *European union is his leitmotiv.* (A83) 'a theme associated throughout the work of Wagner musical drama' → 'a theme, or goal'
- *The 1989 by-election result, when even a split centre vote got within 2,650 of defeating Tory wunderkind Mr William Hague, was proved to be a midterm aberration.* (K4W) 'a child prodigy in music' → 'a talented young man'

c. **Transfer of meaning**: *bund, kraut, polka, blitz*;

- *It then had the good fortune of lengthy bureaucratic delays in setting up the DTB in Frankfurt, which enabled LIFFE to establish a very liquid <u>Bund</u> contract market.* (HY2) 'the confederation of German states' → 'bond'
- *He capitalised on the TV ban with a press <u>blitz</u> through McCann-Erickson which put ICBINB into the top five dairy spreads.* (BNH) 'sudden air-raids made on London' → 'massive campaigns'

d. **Transfer by Ellipsis**: *delicatessen, lager.*

- *Many continental fresh cheeses have now found their way to the supermarket shelves and to the specialist <u>delicatessen</u>.* (ABB) = 'delicatessen store'
- *Twenty years ago <u>lager</u> accounted for less than 10 per cent of total beer sales.* (A0A) = 'lager beer'

Three items revealed newly expanded senses:

(109) a. *abseil* (descent from a building or a wall, not from the steep face of a mountain, a kind of sports);

- *Phil, who graduated in Physics in 1987, invited fellow students and staff to take part in the sponsored <u>abseil</u> and received such a positive response that he had to take down the posters advertising the idea after 48 people volunteered.* (EE6)

b. *angst* (anxiety of a nation or a society, not of a person);

- *THE main focus of British <u>angst</u> at the Strasbourg Summit is likely to be the Social Charter.* (A8U)

c. *anschluss* (annexation of organizations, not of nations).

- *Unix System Labs president Roel Pieper, a member of the COSE <u>anschluss</u>, predicted USL's partnership with OpenVision will "be*

*able to drive the COSE effort in systems management forward"
by establishing common tools and technologies.* (CMY)

The following is the description of two of the most frequent and productive items:

(110) • *blitzkrieg*

Frequency 367 times

Context war, politics, sports, media, business

Form *Blitzkrieg, britzkrieg, Blitz, blitz (n., v.), blitzed, blitzer, blitzing*

Usage often co-occurs with *on* (e.g., *had a <u>blitz</u> on the cleaning, the <u>blitz</u> on London, BR <u>blitz</u> on fare cheats, Watchdog <u>blitz</u> on car sales cowboys, a bin-bag <u>blitz</u> on residents*)

Sense (Germany's or other countries') sudden air-raid (original), to attack aggressively (soccer), blistering approach by media, extensive political campaign, massive sales campaign *etc.*

• *abseil*

Frequency 230 times

Context mountaineering, others (*<u>abseiling</u> into terrorist-held embassies, <u>abseiling</u> down the side of the building*)

Form *abseil* (n., v.), *abseiling, abseiler(s), abseiled*

Usage *abseil* (n.) *descent/rope/equipment/line/anchor* etc., *abseil* (v.) *down/off/from/across/onto/the steep*

Sense to descend by means of abseil, to descend using rope.

The search in this section supports the result of the dictionary-based analyses of the degree of assimilation. In the dictionary-based analysis, I have concluded that the items in (96a) are the items of highest assimilation. The corpus search shows that all except one ski-related items (i.e., *weldeln*) appeared in the *BNC* ten times or more. On the other hand, from the group with productivity but no semantic variation, (96d) and (96e), as few as six items out of 16 appeared in the *BNC* ten times or more, and three (i.e., *abseil, angst,* and *anschluss*) of them showed a new sense in the *BNC*. This suggests that there is a strong correlation between the occurrence in a corpus and the multiple senses. In addition to that, as I view from (96c) 'no productivity' to (96a) 'strong productivity,' I see that the percentage of the items with ten or more occurrences rises (from 25.9% to 94.4%). This suggests that the productivity also contributes to the frequency.

4.3.4 Summary

In this part of the study, I have searched the *BNC* for German loanwords to unveil their actual usage. I proved that some items which were considered to be unassimilated have active use in English texts, while some items which were considered to be assimilated have little or no frequency and productivity in the corpus. I can now revise the list of the assimilated items (96) as follows:[14]

(111) a. items with both strong productivity and (a) new sense(s): *abseil*, *angst*, *blitz(krieg)*, *delicatessen*, ersatz, *Führer*, gestalt, **hamburger**, Hanse, junker, kindergarten, kitsch, kraut, lager, lumpen(proletariat), panzer, polka, poltergeist, shaman, sinter

b. items with some productivity and new sense(s): **autobahn**, **bund**, *schema*, **strudel**

c. items with new sense(s) but little or no productivity: *anschluss*, diktat, **doppelgänger**, Fräulein, Gestapo, Götterdämmerung, lebensraum, leitmotiv, *putsch*, **realpolitik**, **spritzer**, wunderkind

d. items with strong productivity but no semantic variation: **Bauhaus**, **giro**, **gneiss**, **loess**, **noumenon**, **wehrmacht**

e. items with some productivity but no semantic variation: langlauf, **lied**, **schnapps**

I have also shown that the attributive use cannot be considered as a criterion of unassimilated items of German origin. This supports the results of the dictionary-based research. As for the irregular plural form, it can be observed mostly with low-frequency words that appear only in large dictionaries, and it rarely occurs in the *BNC*. Thus, it may be safe to conclude that irregularity

---

[14] The items in bold face are new from the unassimilated group, and the underlined items are ones that have moved within the list.

disappears as the item gains frequency in actual English. I have mentioned the effect of foreign phonemes on the irregularity of plural forms in Section 4.2.5, but it cannot be verified with the corpus because the corpus does not provide the information as to how the words are pronounced. However, as the dictionary-based research showed, it is highly likely that most of the foreign features in the assimilated items have already been anglicized, or it may be the case that the assimilated items that are actually used in English texts have even less foreign features than described in English dictionaries. Finally, I have shown that the assimilated items are certain to have a substantial number of frequencies in a corpus, depending on the existence of semantic variation and the degree of productivity.

Chapter 5 Comparison of Assimilation Processes of Japanese and German Loanwords

In Part I, I have examined the assimilation process of Japanese and German loanwords in English based on English dictionaries and have attempted to verify the degree of assimilation of each word using electronic corpora.

In each chapter of Japanese and German loanwords (Chapter 3 and 4), I have established the assimilation process and showed that the processes of loanwords from the two languages differ from each other significantly. That is, Japanese loanwords go through a stage-by-stage process from pronunciation/orthographical adaptation to semantic shift, while German loanwords do not necessarily finish one stage of assimilation before starting another stage, but some kinds of adaptation go on simultaneously, and they do not always start their process from the same point. I can now visualize the assimilation process of Japanese loanwords and German loanwords as in Figure 5.1 and 5.2, respectively.

The same types of changes were observed for loanwords from both of the languages, but differ in the following points:

(112) a. the percentage of the items which go through each of the changes.

   b. the point at which each of the changes occurs.

   c. the characteristics which are likely to remain unchanged or to disappear in a short time.

The number of items that have acquired productivity or a new sense is larger in German loanwords than in Japanese loanwords. These changes are observed in relatively early years after the borrowing of German loanwords, while

126   I   Assimilation Process of Loanwords

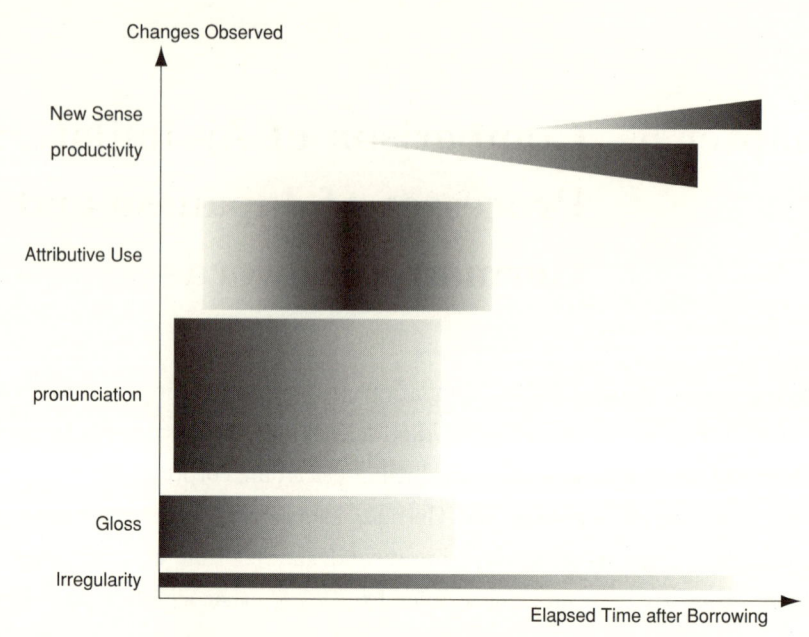

Figure 5.1: Japanese Assimilation Process

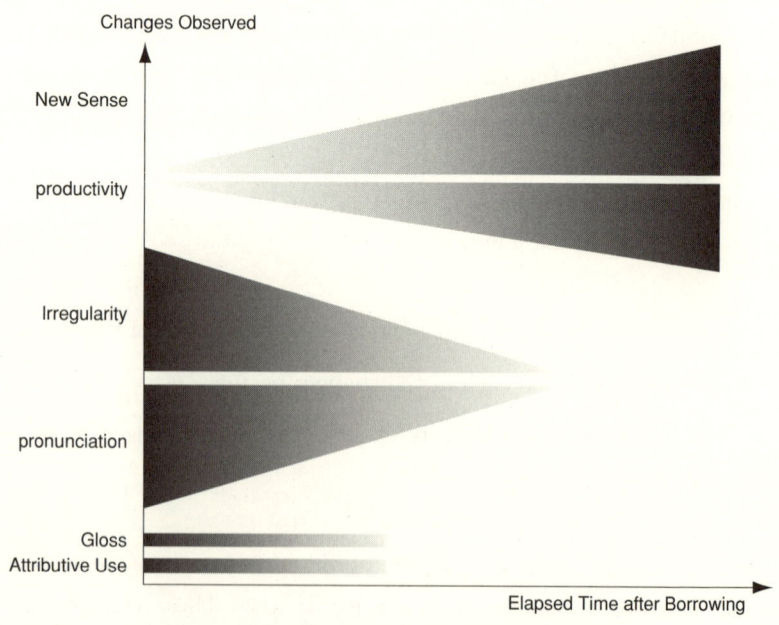

Figure 5.2: German Assimilation Process

5 Comparison of Assimilation Processes of Japanese and German Loanwords

Japanese loanwords go through these kinds of changes only after the other changes in the earlier stages have been completed. German loanwords have experienced semantic shift more often than a gain in productivity, but Japanese loanwords have the opposite tendency. Irregular inflections (*i.e.*, ϕ plural form) of some of the nouns from Japanese are retained even after they have achieved high assimilation, though the nouns from German tend to lose their irregular plural endings in the course of assimilation. Frequent use in actual English texts and anglicization of foreign phonemes seem to play a role in the regularization of inflection. The frequent and repeated use of nouns as attributives that can be considered as an early stage of assimilation is unique to Japanese. The ways of pronunciation adaptation are distinctive between Japanese and German loanwords; stress assignments and the lengthening and weakening of vowels are almost always observed in an early stage of Japanese loanwords, while the phonological adaptations of German loanwords do not include the same changes as Japanese loanwords, and the process tends to last longer than Japanese loanwords with some phonemes remaining foreign until later in the assimilation process than others. The same kinds of glossing of unassimilated items are observed in loanwords from both languages.

At the same time as the loanwords change themselves in the course of assimilation, they also exercise an influence on the vocabulary that has existed in English by simply expanding the number of lexical items, by providing irregularity of spellings or inflections, and by causing conflicts between synonymous expressions. In Part II, I will cast a spotlight on the other side of the loanwords; the way they affect the existing lexical system, focusing on the conflicts between the synonymous loanwords and the existing lexical items.

Part II

Impact of Loanwords on the Existing Lexical System

Chapter 6 Introduction and Previous Studies

6.1 Introduction

There are many ways in which loanwords can make an impact on the existing lexical system. They include the expansion of vocabulary, the increase of irregularity, and the conflict between synonyms. In Part II, those points of impact will be examined using English dictionaries and corpora. The focus will be made especially on the conflict between synonyms. In Section 6.2 and 6.3, the previous studies will be reviewed on the related subjects. Then in Chapter 7, I will focus on the coexistence patterns of synonymous pairs of an existing word and a newer loanword, and reveal the differences in collocation and distribution of the seemingly synonymous pair. In Chapter 8, I will deal with a pair of synonyms as a case study, and the coexistence pattern will be discussed in detail.

6.2 Studies on Vocabulary Expansion

Loanwords have regularly added lexical items to the English lexicon, and the English lexicon has kept expanding to this day. There are many books and articles that introduce new vocabulary in English borrowed from other languages. Among them, one of the earliest studies of the loanwords is Serjeantson's *A History of Foreign Words in English* (1961), which overviews the influx of the loanwords chronologically by the languages of their origin. Emphasis has been laid throughout on 'the *first* introduction from individual languages and the *first* appearances of individual words.' Naturally, the greatest amount of space has been devoted to early loans from Latin, French, and Scandinavian, but loanwords from many other languages have been made mention of, including 19 Japanese loanwords with some historical explanations.

132   II   Impact of Loanwords on the Existing Lexical System

6.2.1   Studies by Finkenstaedt *et al.*

Finkenstaedt *et al.* (1969) is a statistical study of English lexicon with the full use of computer-based calculation. They show the increase of the English vocabulary by constructing the distribution chart of the number of the lexical items in the *Shorter Oxford English Dictionary* (3rd ed., 1964) and two other sources by hundred-year periods (Figure 6.1[1]). They also capture the distribution of each part of speech, of the initial letter of the words, and of the language of the word origin.

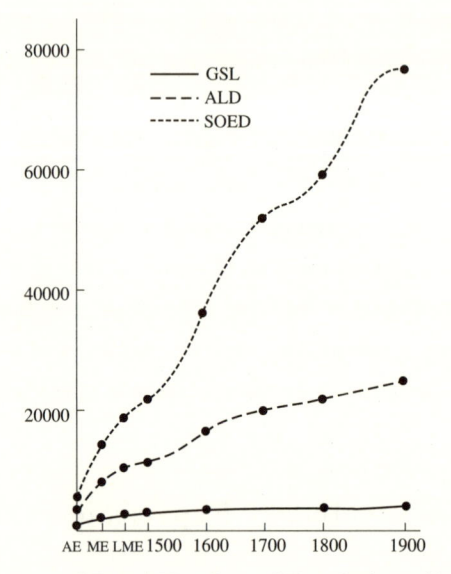

Figure 6.1: Distribution of Total Number of Vocabulary (from Finkenstaedt *et al.* 1969)

Finkenstaedt *et al.* (1970) is the first chronological dictionary whose headwords are arranged not in alphabetical order but in chronological order, and it is compiled and statistically analyzed with the great help of computers, which is remarkable for that time. The aim of this work is to give a clearer idea of the history of the English vocabulary, so that it can answer such questions as follows:

---

[1] SOED, ALD, GSL in the figure stand for *The Shorter Oxford English Dictionary* (3rd ed., repr. 1964, including *Addenda*), *An Advanced Learner's Dictionary of Current English* (A. S. Hornby, OUP 1963), *A General Service List of English Words* (M. West, London 1953)

(113) a. Which words were modern when Shakespeare started to write?

b. Which types of word-formation predominated around 1700?

c. Which foreign languages were most influential around 1650?

It contains all the words listed as main entries in the *SOED* and more from other sources. They antedate 1771 items in the *SOED*, which equals to about 2.2% of all the words in the *SOED*, but it is concluded that the reliability of the *SOED* is 'considerable' since the differences between the earliest dates from the *SOED* and his corrected dates are relatively small (one-third: under eleven years, two-thirds: under 31 years).

Finkenstaedt *et al.* (1973) is a collection of studies on English lexicon, based on the analysis techniques of Finkenstaedt *et al.* (1969) and the chronological data of Finkenstaedt *et al.* (1970). In addition to the analyses done in Finkenstaedt *et al.* (1969), they present more growth curves of vocabulary from many aspects, and show the vocabulary growth of English in comparison with Shakespeare's vocabulary (Figure 6.2). The figure shows the rapid expansion of

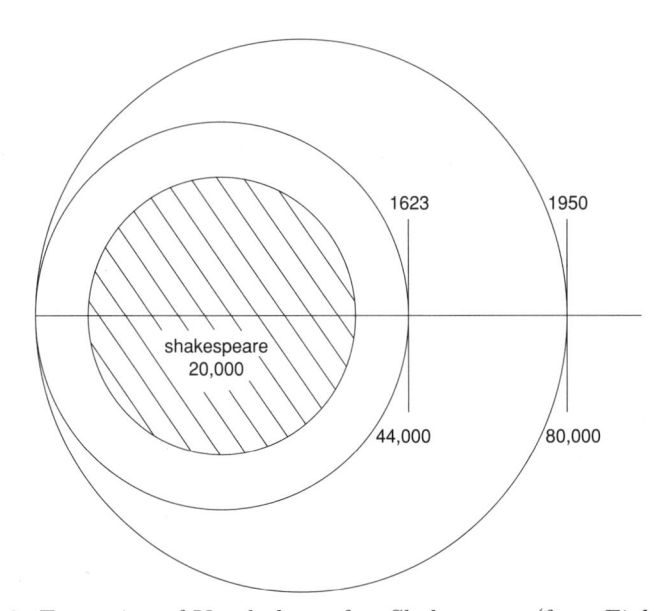

Figure 6.2: Expansion of Vocabulary after Shakespeare (from Finkenstaedt *et al.* 1970)

English vocabulary during the 300-year period.

They also deal with the word labels, such as 'rare,' 'obsolete,' and '[i]n the English of the USA,' the semantic fields, such as 'Chemistry,' 'Botany,' and 'Zoology,' and word length and its relation to the age of the word. The large chapter of 'Etymology' discusses the etymological distribution of English vocabulary, and lists the loanwords by the languages of their origin. It includes 30 Japanese loanwords.

6.2.2 Studies by Cannon

Various studies by Cannon were introduced in Part I with regard to the loanwords from specific languages. Here, I review some of his works on new vocabulary including loanwords. Cannon (1978) is a statistical study of the etymology of new words in American English. He uses Merriam-Webster's *6,000 Words* (1976) as a source, and establishes 16 categories to group all the entries in respect of the etymologies:

(114) a. 869 new meanings;

b. 1443 affixations;

c. 1365 compounds;

d. **249 borrowings**;

e. 48 Briticisms and Old English;

f. 246 proper-noun derivatives;

g. 179 shortenings;

h. 166 initialisms (and combinations);

i. 97 functional shifts;

j. 36 abbreviations (and combinations);

k. 35 blends;

l. 26 back-formations;

m. 19 trademarks and coinings;

n. 11 imitations;

o. 28 spelling alternates;

p. 37 others (23 origin unknown, 14 miscellany).

The borrowings (*i.e.*, loanwords) are not a major supplier of new vocabulary in his list, and he mentions the fact and the future perspective of borrowings as in (115):

(115) The 249 borrowings ... may seem surprisingly small until we recall that English morphemic resources were rich enough to provide 2,808 Affixations — Compounds of the total 3,985 new words. The percentage of future borrowings may well not rise and may diminish further, considering the near-automatic creations of the International Scientific Vocabulary.

In Cannon (1979), he analyzes the combined 473 borrowings in *6,000 Words* mentioned above, and *The Barnhart Dictionary of New English since 1963*

Table 6.1: Etymology of New Vocabulary (from Cannon 1987, abbreviated)

			Total	
Shifts	new meanings		1,968	14.4%
	functional shifts		558	4.1%
	remaining shifts		158	1.2%
Borrowings			**1,029**	**7.5%**
Shortenings	abbreviations		460	3.4%
	acronyms		153	1.1%
	unabbreviated shortenings		628	4.6%
	back-formations		151	1.1%
	shortenings + bound morpheme(s)		405	2.9%
	shortenings + word(s)		552	4.0%
	blends		131	1.0%
Additions	free morphemes		85	0.6%
	bound-morpheme items		268	2.0%
	initial affixations		1,648	12.0%
	terminal affixations		1,313	9.6%
	remaining affixations		84	0.6%
	noun compounds		3,591	26.3%
	adjective compounds		290	2.1%
	verb compounds		135	1.0%
	remaining compounds		24	0.2%
Remaining items			52	0.4%
Totals			13,683	100.0%

(1973). Refer to Section 2.1.3 for details.

Cannon (1987) further expands the source material to *The Second Barnhart Dictionary of New English* (1980) and G. & C. Merriam's 1981 Addenda Section to *Webster's Third*. He concludes that 7.5% of the etymologies of new vocabulary is borrowings (Table 6.1).

As was mentioned in Section 2.1.3, Cannon (1984) refers to the increase of irregularity by Japanese loanwords.

6.2.3 Jucker (1994)

Jucker (1994) outlines three ways of exploring the *OED2* on CD-ROM:

(116) a. the number of new words from six major contributing languages to the word stock of English;

b. the origin of all new words;

c. the semantic field of vocabulary.

As for (116a), he shows that Latin is by far the most important contributing language, followed by French, but both influences diminish considerably in recent centuries, while the influence of German remains fairly stable.

As for (116b), he points out that the rate of borrowing fell off sharply in the twentieth century. Nowadays, most new words in English are not borrowed from other languages, but formed from language-internal resources. He also shows the transition of productivity of suffixes in English, *-ment* being no longer productive, *-ism* being considerably more popular in the last two hundred years, and *-ity* being quite stable in its productivity through out the centuries.

I will refer to (116c) in the next section because it is closely related to the study of synonyms.

He also points out some problems with carrying out the search in the *OED2*, and concludes that the computerized version of the *OED2* is an indispensable research tool but at the same time dangerous. One should always bear in mind that the interpretation of the results is up to researchers, as is always the case with other computer tools.

6.2.4 From the Introduction Section of Recent Dictionaries

As we have seen in the previous studies above, the vocabulary keeps expanding, and the dictionaries keep collecting the new words. If we turn to the introduction section of the dictionaries, the struggle of the editors with vocabulary growth can be often observed. Some of the editors' comments worth mentioning are introduced here.

12,000 words (1986) is a supplemental dictionary of *Webster's Third New International Dictionary*, and there the editor describes the growth of the English vocabulary as follows:

(117) The vocabulary of English, like that of every other living language, is constantly growing. This growth is certainly not new. Always, as people have met with new objects and new experiences and have developed new ideas, they have needed new words to describe them.

He explains that the recent vocabulary is derived from the following fields:

(118) science and technology, political and social ferment, the drug subculture, minorities, the changing attitude of Americans toward sexual matters and materials, entertainment, and cooking.

He also gives various ways of forming new words (an underline supplied):

(119) old words given new meanings (*i.e.*, semantic shift), functional shift, compounding, blends, affixes, shortening (*i.e.*, clippings), back-formation, borrowing from other languages, loan translation, the names of people or places, trademarks, and onomatopoeia.

Thus, he acknowledges borrowing as one source of new vocabulary, but no statistics are shown as to which word-formation process is dominant and in what proportion they are distributed.

Fifty Years in Among the New Words (Algeo, 1991) is a dictionary of neologisms dated from 1941 to 1991. "Among the New Words" is a long-running serial column in *American Speech*, to which a band of volunteer workers contribute. In the introduction to this dictionary, the editor gives 'six basic etymological sources for new words,' which include 'creating, borrowing, combining, shortening, blending, and shifting.' He further divides loanwords into three subtypes: simple loanwords, adapted loanwords, loan translations. Simple loanwords and loan translations are straightforward, but adapted loanwords need some explanation. Adapted loanwords involve morphological changes by replacing the endings to adapt from their foreign word patterns so that they fit to the English indigenous patterns. They are observed in loanwords from European languages, including Latin, Greek, French, and Spanish. He provides one table of the distribution of etymological sources, borrowing occupying only 2% of the new words (Table 6.2, left). The other table shows the decline of borrowing as a source of new words (Table 6.2, right). He concludes that 'the types of word making that introduce new word elements (morphemes),' including borrowing, blending, and shortening, are 'minor processes' and that 'the English vocabulary seems to follow what Otto Jespersen called the Principle of Efficiency.'

Table 6.2: The Distribution of Etymological Sources (from Algeo 1991)

Combining	68
(Compounds 40)	
(Suffixes 20)	
(Prefixes 8)	
Shifting	17
(Semantic 11)	
(Grammatical 6)	
Shortening	8
Blending	5
Borrowing	2
Creating (below .5)	
Unknown (below .5)	
Total	100%

	ANW	BDNE	LRNW
Combining	68.3	63.9	54.3
(Compound forms	40.3	29.8	36.3)
(Affixed forms	28.0	34.1	18.0)
Shifting	17.4	14.2	19.4
Shortening	7.6	9.7	10.0
Blending	4.6	4.8	9.8
Borrowing	1.6	6.9	4.3
Unknown	.3	.5	2.2
Creating	.2		

ANW = "Among the New Words," 1941–1991
BDNE = Barnhart Dictionary of New English since 1963
LRNW = Longman Register of New Words, Vol. 1

In the introduction of *Twentieth Century Words* (1999), it is mentioned that the '*Oxford English Dictionary* and its supplementary volumes record about 90,000 new words and new meanings of old words, that have come into the English language in this [20th] century,' which 'represents approximately a 25% increase in the total vocabulary of the language as it had evolved in the thousand and more years up to 1900.' Borrowing is also referred to here along with other word formation processes, and it is concluded that it occupies 5%

of the 20th century words, mostly as a result of some novel cultural influence.

As is discussed by the editors of the dictionaries above, borrowing is not a major process of adding new vocabulary to English today. Nevertheless, there is no doubt that a considerable number of loanwords have come into English until today and will continue to do so from now on as long as English speakers have contact with speakers of other languages and cultures.

6.3 Previous Studies on Synonyms and Collocations

In this section, I will review major studies on synonyms to clarify their nature. I will also refer to the studies on collocations, for they play an important role in a corpus-based study on synonyms, and then establish the methodology of researching the synonym pairs of a loanword and an existing lexical item.

6.3.1 Konishi (1976)

Konishi (1976) classifies a pair of synonyms as two words with:

(120) a. an overlapped semantic realm;

b. the same <u>sense</u> and <u>implication</u> but with a different <u>usage</u>;

c. the same <u>sense</u>, but with a different <u>implication</u> and <u>usage</u>.

He further defines the term 'sense' in detail. What is referred to as the 'sense' in (120) is called 'cognitive sense,' and there are three patterns in 'cognitive sense.' As opposed to the 'cognitive sense,' what is referred to as the 'implication' in (120) is called 'emotive sense,' and there are 18 patterns. Finally, he states that what is called 'usage' in (120) can be identified with 'collocable lexical items,' which is a collection of lexical items that collocate with synonyms. The details are summarized in (121).

(121) a. Cognitive sense ⇐ 'Sense'

- the two have almost the same (e.g., *till, until; strike, hit*);
- one includes the other(s) (e.g., *hit, punch; understand, comprehend*);

- some part of the two is overlapped (e.g., *punch, slap*);

b. Emotive sense ⇐ 'Implication'

1. one is more intensifying than the other(s) (e.g., *repudiate, refuse*);
2. one is more emotive than the other(s) (e.g., *repudiate, reject, decline*);
3. one contains moral admiration or reproach while the other(s) is/are neutral (e.g., *thrifty, economical; eavesdrop, listen*);
4. one is more technical than the other(s) (e.g., *decease, death; domicile, house*);
5. one is more literary than the other(s) (e.g., *passing, death*);
6. one is more colloquial than the other(s) (e.g., *turn down, refuse*);
7. one is more dialectal than the other(s) (e.g., *flesher (Scott.), butcher*);
8. one belongs to the vocabulary of nursery language (e.g., *teeny, tiny*);
9. one is more formal or informal than the other(s) (e.g., *garments, cloth, duds*);
10. one gives more old-fashioned or fresh impressions than the other(s) (e.g., *befall, chance happen; finalize, complete*);
11. one gives more elegant impressions than the other(s) (e.g., *stout, fat*);
12. one is more euphemistic than the other(s) (e.g., *disable, cripple*);
13. one is more reserved than the other(s) (e.g., *not bad, good*);
14. one contains contempt (e.g., *whore, prostitute*);
15. one can contain irony (e.g., *kindly, please*);
16. one is jocular (e.g., *better half, wife*);
17. one is recognized as a loanword or a native word (e.g., *conflagration, fire; oeuver, work*);
18. one is more toward American English or British (e.g., *sick, ill*).

c. Usage: identified with collocable lexical items.

6.3.2 Firth (1951)

Firth (1951) also considers that some lexical items are more likely to co-occur than others, and he calls this co-occurring relations as 'meaning by collocation' and 'collocability.' However, he does not consider them as a means of defining word-meaning, stating that '[m]eaning by collocation is an abstraction at the syntagmatic level and is not directly concerned with the conceptual or idea approach to the meaning of words.'

6.3.3 Jucker (1994)

In recent years, as the dictionaries and corpora are available on electric-basis, the analyses of sense and usage by collocation have become more effective. Now, it is established as a standard method to look for collocations using electric data in dictionary-making and many other fields of linguistic studies.

As for (116c) in Section 6.2.3, he proposes the way to search for candidates for vocabulary of the same semantic field, using the definition search of the *OED2*. He uses *throw* as an example, and compares the search results with the entries in the *Oxford Thesaurus*. He then categorizes the items in the search results which are not registered in the *Oxford Thesaurus* as follows:

(122) a. words which are obsolete;

b. entries in which *throw* is used in a metaphorical sense in the definition text;

c. entries in which *throw* is used as a phrasal verb in the definition text;

d. entries which do not belong to the word field of *throw* at all;

e. entries which describe a special way of throwing but which are perhaps too specific for inclusion in a general purpose thesaurus;

f. entries which are close synonyms of *throw* but which are dialectal or slang.

Although the proposed method and the categorization are useful and on target, he only deals with the definition section of the *OED2* and does not go into the discussion of how those synonyms are used differently in quotations and in actual English sentences.

6.3.4 Biber (1996)

Biber (1996) mentions the potential usefulness of finding collocations based on corpora in a study of synonyms as follows:

(123) "Corpus-based investigation of association patterns show that there are important, patterned differences in the ways that native speakers use seemingly synonymous words."

What he calls 'association patterns' here is a notion that extends Firth's concept of collocation mentioned in Section 6.3.2. He maintains that association patterns should be identified empirically from analysis of a representative corpus, and they must be analyzed in quantitative terms. In this way, one can avoid the stereotypical collocations that do not in fact represent strong association patterns, and discover unanticipated collocations.

6.3.5 Inoue (2001)

A corpus-based study of synonyms by collocation is done by Inoue (2001) using *Cobuild Direct* [currently called *Wordbanks* online], in which he analyzes the synonym pair, *happen* and *take place*. He analyses the collocation of these two lexical items by calculating two statistics: t-score and MI-score. These are the indices to measure the strength of two words that co-occur close to each other in a sentence. He investigates the words with high scores of these statistics, and discusses the differences in the usage of *happen* and *take place* from three aspects:

(124) a. abstractedness and concreteness;

b. mental certainty of the speaker;

c. situational explanation of causality.

He maintains that the word *happen* co-occurs with such abstract words as *what*, *something*, *anything*, and *things*, while *take place* co-occurs with more concrete terms (e.g., *change*, *event*, *meeting*, a relative pronoun *which*, etc.). It is also proved that the semantic feature of *take place* contains readiness of the event, the certainty of the speaker, and the objective judgment of the cause of the event.

This study represents well how the collocation and the related statistics can reveal the differences between synonyms. However, the statistics utilized here, t-score and MI-score, are suitable for the analyses of *happen* and *take place*, but they may not be appropriate for the study of loanwords. One must be careful of which statistics to apply to his/her study since some indices, including t-score and MI-score are known not to give a proper value if the target word has a low frequency, and it is often the case that loanwords have relatively low frequencies.

6.3.6 Stubbs (2001)

In Chapter 8 "Words in Culture 2: Case Studies of Loan Words in English" of Stubbs (2001), the etymology of loanwords and the changes in meaning which accompany the process of borrowing are discussed.

As corpora, Stabbs uses the 50-million-word section of the Bank of English, which has been designed specifically for linguistic study, *The Times and the Sunday Times for 1995* on CD-ROM to study for examples of contemporary usage, *Cobuild English Dictionary* (1995), which is based on a 200-million-word corpus of contemporary English, and the *OED2* on CD-ROM, which can be searched in many ways with the search software.

It is noteworthy that he emphasizes that words should be studied in the collocations and the text types in which they typically occur. He shows that there are intimate connections between the etymology of words, the social class of the speakers, and the text-types in which words of different origins are used. He examines the connotation of German loanwords, taking three German loanwords, *flak*, *blitz*, and *angst* as examples, and points out the differences in their uses in German and English.

6.4 Purpose of Part II of the Study

The aim of this part of the study is not to estimate the size of the current English vocabulary or to measure the speed of the vocabulary expansion, as was done by Finkenstaedt *et al.*. Nor is it aimed to calculate the proportion of loanwords among the etymologies of new vocabulary, as was done by Cannon and other dictionary makers. I rather analyze the relationship between the existing lexical items and newer loanwords by studying synonym pairs, one of which is a lexical item long existing in English and the other of which is a newer loanword. I investigate synonyms with the aid of a corpus of sufficient size (the *BNC*), not only from the aspect of collocations but also from the aspect of the domains and media in which they are used, in order to describe the differences in usage of the synonym pairs. The recent development of the large scale corpora such as the *BNC* has made it possible to study the synonyms used in actual English in a systematic and effective way. Thus, in the following chapters (Chapters 7 and 8), one of the effects that the newer loanwords have on the existing English lexicon will be revealed.

As was mentioned in (121), three patterns of cognitive sense in synonyms are claimed to exist: almost the same, one includes the other, some parts overlapped. However, in dealing with the synonym pairs of the existing vocabulary and newer loanwords in English, it is often the case that the existing vocabulary has a wider range of cognitive sense. It is natural for those words to have a different usage and emotive sense if they are compared in a different cognitive sense, and therefore I exclude the instances from the target of analyses if they are used in different cognitive senses, and only deal with the instances of synonyms with the same cognitive sense. In this way, I can look for the differences in the emotive sense and usage when the two expressions are used in the same cognitive sense.

Chapter 7 Coexistence of Old Vocabulary with Newer Loanwords

7.1 Introduction

In this chapter, I will discuss the distributions and the usage differences of synonym pairs, one being a lexical item which has long-existed in English, and the other being an item which is relatively new in English. I will define the terminology used in this chapter, and introduce the purpose and methodology of this chapter of the study, then state the results and analyses, with a detailed discussion with examples, followed by a summary.

7.2 Definition and Purpose of This Chapter

I use the phrases 'existing lexical items' and 'newer loanwords' in this section to observe old and new vocabulary in contrast with each other. 'Existing lexical items' include the vocabulary of English origin and old loanwords from Latin, Greek, French, or other languages in English that have long been in English and are accepted as general English vocabulary. 'Newer loanwords' designate the loanwords that have been borrowed into English in relatively recent years. As a matter of convenience, loanwords in the 19th or 20th century are studied as 'newer loanwords.'

When the meanings of these two kinds of vocabulary overlap, a conflict between them occurs. It can be observed in the following cases:

(125) a. when loanwords go through a semantics shift, and acquire a wider, more general sense.

b. when English borrows words whose concepts are not new.

c. when English borrows a concept in both a direct and a translated form.

English generally borrows words from other languages when it does not have a proper word to describe a concept that is newly introduced to English. However, the loanwords sometimes go through a semantic shift and gain a new sense in the course of assimilation, as we have seen in Part I. When they acquire a wider, more general sense, the conflict of (125a) occurs. An example of this type is *kamikaze*. According to the *Oxford English Dictionary* 2nd ed. (*OED2*), *kamikaze* was originally borrowed to designate 'one of the Japanese airmen who in the war of 1939–45 made deliberate suicidal crashes into enemy targets,' but when it developed a new sense and began to be used in the sense, 'reckless' or 'self-destructive,' conflicts with these words occurred.

(125b) is the case when English borrows a word from other languages even though it already has the equivalent English term. This can be observed often with German loanwords. In this case, the conflict occurs right after borrowing. For example, the word *realpolitik* was borrowed into English though there had been an English expression *practical politics* to designate the same concept.

Finally, I include (125c) in this research though it is different in nature from the others. That is, a conflict between direct loanwords, which retain literal forms of the original words, and their equivalent loan translations, of which the original forms are replaced by English words with the same meanings. I regard this type as a conflict between existing lexical items and newer loanwords, for the loan translations are composed of English vocabulary. Though the concepts may be new, the forms are often phrases that consist of existing lexical items, or the old English words to which a new sense is added. The example of this type is *kanban*, which means, according to the *OED2*, 'a manufacturing system in which parts etc. are ordered on cards' and *just-in-time*, which is loose translation of *kanban*.

When these three types of loanwords are added to the English lexicon, conflicts can arise. In this section, I aim to clarify the actual use of those conflicting lexical items by analyzing the words that co-occur with them, and the domains and media in which they are used. I seek the differences in usage between the existing lexical items and the newer loanwords.

7.3 Materials and Methodology

The sources used in this section are as follows:

(126) a. *The Oxford Dictionary of Foreign Words and Phrases* (*ODFWP*)

b. *The Oxford English Dictionary* 2nd ed. (*OED2*)

c. *The British National Corpus* (*BNC*)

(126a) is used to choose the target words, (126b) is used to refer to the definition and usage of the word, and (126c) is used to search for the target words.

I determine the target words by the following criteria:

(127) a. the words registered in the *ODFWP* that were borrowed from Japanese or German during the 19th or 20th century.

b. the word used in a general sense, not limited to 'Japanese ...' or 'German ...,' according to the *OED2*.

c. the words whose synonym is registered in the *OED2* (e.g., *kohlrabi*: included, *poltergeist*: excluded)

To collect data, I used the *BNC* and BNCweb as was done in Section 4.3.[1] The search in this chapter was carried out as follows:

(128) a. I used the regular expression, ".*" in Standard Query to pick up the inflected forms and the derivatives.

b. The items providing ten or more instances after excluding the instances with a different sense or as a proper noun were determined as target words.

c. I used the available menus in BNCweb for efficient analyses: 'Distribution,' 'Collocation,' and 'Delete hits....'

---
[1] The search of this chapter was carried out by connecting to the SARA server at the Faculty of Language and Culture, Osaka University. Refer to Section 4.3.1 for the detailed information on the *BNC* and BNCweb.

The statistics used for analyses are frequency per million and log-likelihood. Frequency per million is the normalized value of frequency, indicating how many times the target word occurs in a one-million-word text. This value is useful in comparing the frequencies among the domains or media because each domain or medium has different sizes (*i.e.*, word counts), and it enables the comparison between groups of texts with different sizes.

A log-likelihood statistic is a ratio that indicates the collocation strength between the two words. This statistic fits the purpose here from the viewpoint of the frequencies of the target words, as it is known to be applicable to low frequency items, while other statistics to measure the collocation strength such as MI-score and Z-score are known not to give proper value for the items with low frequencies, and loanwords are mostly classified as low frequency words. This value is automatically calculated by choosing 'Collocation' from the pulldown menu in BNCweb.

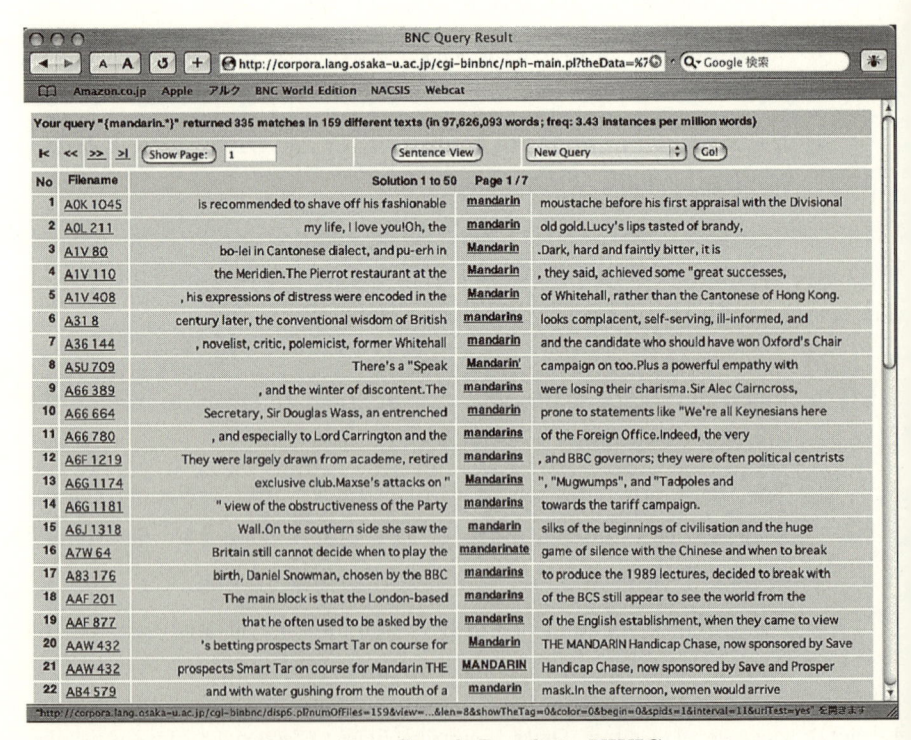

Figure 7.1: Search Result in KWIC

Here, I demonstrate the procedure using *mandarin* as an example. Figure 7.1 is a screenshot of browsing the search result of {mandarin.*} in KWIC format in BNCweb. One can see that the original form *mandarin* and its derivatives (plural form and *-nate*) are retrieved.

From this search result screen, I operated various options. First, I excluded unwanted items with the 'Delete hits...' option. In this case, I was looking for *mandarin* only with the sense of 'an important official in an organization or government' to find out about the conflict with *tycoon*. Therefore, *mandarin* with other senses (*e.g.*, 'a type of small orange' and 'the official language of China') should be excluded by this option. However, choosing items in terms of their sense can never be automatic, and I needed to determine by interpreting each instance, in which sense the target word was used in the instance and which items should be excluded. Then, I went to the next step of inquiring further options: 'Distribution' to capture the distribution of the word by domain and medium, or 'Collocation' to find the typical collocates of the word.

Text type:			
Category	No. of words	No. of hits	Frequency per million words
Written books and periodicals	78,588,761	83	1.06
Written miscellaneous	7,373,675	4	0.54
Spoken demographic	4,206,058	0	0
Spoken context-governed	6,135,671	0	0
Written-to-be-spoken	1,321,928	0	0
total	97,626,093	87	0.89
Text Domain (written):			
Category	No. of words	No. of hits	Frequency per million words
Commerce and finance	7,257,529	20	2.76
World affairs	17,132,004	28	1.63
Natural and pure sciences	3,784,273	5	1.32
Arts	6,520,625	7	1.07
Social science	13,906,177	11	0.79
Leisure	12,185,390	7	0.57
Applied science	7,104,636	3	0.42
Imaginative	16,386,486	6	0.37
Belief and thought	3,007,244	0	0
total	87,284,364	87	1

Figure 7.2: Distribution Option

150   II Impact of Loanwords on the Existing Lexical System

Figure 7.2 is a screenshot of the 'Distribution' result. Categories and the frequencies in the categories are listed in the order of frequency per million counts. In the case of *mandarin*, the 'world affairs' domain has a higher raw frequency (28 hits) than the 'commerce and finance' domain (20 hits), but 'commerce and finance' has a higher value of frequency per million after normalizing (2.76 *vs.* 1.63) because of the different size of the texts in these domains.

Figure 7.3 is a screenshot of the 'Collocation' result. There are several indices that show the collocation strength of the two words, and one can choose other statistics from the top pulldown menu on the right. Here, 'Log-likelihood' is chosen. The words that co-occur with the target within a designated distance are listed in the order of the index values. The figure shows that the political terms, including *whitehall*, *treasury*, and *ministers* have strong collocative relations with *mandarin*.

Collocation parameters:

Information:	collocations	Statistics:	Log-likelihood
Window span:	-3 - 3	Basis:	whole BNC
F(n,c) at least:	3	F(c) at least:	3
Filter results by:	Specific collocate:	and/or tag: no restrictions	Submit changed parameters Go!

There are 361 different types in your collocation database for "{mandarin.'}". (Your query "{mandarin.'}" returned 335 matches in 159 different texts, manually deleted 232 hits (remaining solution set: 103 hits), manually deleted 16 hits (remaining solution set: 87 hits))

No.	Word	Total No. in the whole BNC	As collocate	In No. of texts	Log-likelihood value
1	the	6054237	68	45	306.695898
2	of	3049275	32	24	118.801468
3	whitehall	892	7	7	115.628482
4	treasury	2621	6	6	84.222827
5	.	5026136	31	23	83.876970
6	ministers	6747	6	3	72.873923
7	and	2621932	19	15	54.335454
8	former	16845	4	4	37.939587
9	to	2599307	15	13	36.113200
10	bbc	4251	3	3	34.943531
11	decided	14614	3	3	27.548726
12	office	24794	3	3	24.392119
13	"	770315	7	6	22.028699
14	that	1120748	8	8	21.739772
15	have	461430	5	5	17.261789
16	by	513387	5	5	16.271719
17	"	752604	5	5	12.801283

Figure 7.3: Collocation Option

As was pointed out in Section 4.3.1, due to some defects in BNCweb, several searches cannot be carried out straightforwardly. In addition to the ones listed in (101) in Section 4.3.1, more defects were found in carrying out the search for this chapter.

(129) a. Some instances were doubly-listed in the 'Word lookup' result.

b. Some queries cannot be used with a regular expression in the 'Standard Query,' including a phrase (*i.e.*, multiple words),[2] and a word with an umlaut.

c. Instances cannot be deleted by the 'Delete hits...' option when one tries to delete too many instances (probably more than half of the result).

7.4 Results and Analyses

As a result of the searches as was mentioned in Section 7.3, it was revealed that the following words have potentially conflicting synonyms:

(130) *hara(-)kiri* = *disembowel oneself*; *honcho* = *leader*; *kamikaze* = *reckless*; *kanban* = *just-in-time*; *shiatsu* = *acupressure*; *tsunami* = *tidal wave*; *tycoon* = *magnate* (and other synonyms); *angst* = *anxiety*; *bergschrund* = *crevasse*; *doppelgänger* = *wraith*; *ersatz* = *substitution*; *gesellschaft* = *association*; *gestalt* = *configuration*; *glockenspiel* = *carillon*; *kohlrabi* = *turnip cabbage*; *realpolitik* = *practical politics*; *umwelt* = *environment*; *verstehen* = *understand*; *wunderkind* = *prodigy*.

As a result of the analyses described in Section 7.3, the synonym pairs in (130) can be divided into four patterns of conflict/coexistence.

(131) a. Newer loanwords have a restricted range of use.

b. Newer loanwords have a wider range of use.

---

[2] To obtain the search result of both *tidal wave* and *tidal waves* in one result sheet, one must first carry out the search {wave.*}, and then look for the instances that co-occur with *tidal* in the -1 position (*i.e.*, right before the target word) using the 'Collocation' option.

c. Newer loanwords and the equivalent existing lexical items coexist and have overlapped use.

d. Newer loanwords and the equivalent existing lexical items have exclusive use.

Each of the patterns will be discussed in the following sections.

7.4.1 Restricted Range of Use of Newer Loanwords

The first pattern is the one in which newer loanwords have a smaller range of use than the existing lexical items. The great number of synonym pairs have been categorized in this group. The relationship between the newer loanwords and the equivalent existing items can be demonstrated as Figure 7.4.

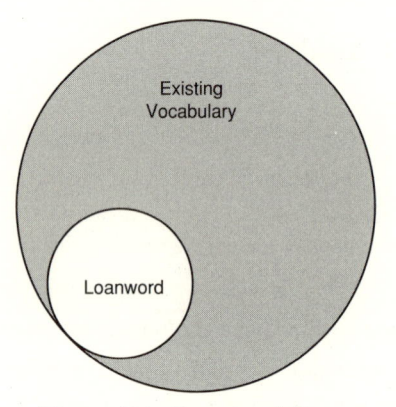

Figure 7.4: Restricted Range

The following items belong to this group:

(132) a. honcho < boss, leader;

b. kamikaze < reckless, self-destructive;

c. tsunami < tidal wave;

d. bergschrund < crevasse;

e. ersatz < substitute;

f. gesellschaft < association;

7 Coexistence of Old Vocabulary with Newer Loanwords   153

g. umwelt < environment;

h. verstehen < understanding;

i. kanban < just-in-time, JIT;

j. gestalt < configuration.

Here, let us take *tsunami* as an example. Originally, the huge wave that occurs in an earthquake or similar underwater disturbance was called a *tidal wave* in English because it was believed that the wave was caused by the ebb and flow of the tide. In recent years, it has been scientifically proved that what was called a *tidal wave* has nothing to with the regular tides in the sea, and the wave began to be called *tsunami*. The distribution by domain is summarized in Table 7.1.

Table 7.1: Distribution of *Tsunami* and *Tidal Wave* in Frequency per Million

Domains	tidal wave (113 occs.) (86 texts)	tsunami (29 occs.) (14 texts)
Natural and pure sciences	2.11 (17.6%)	3.44 (77.5%)
World affairs	1.98 (16.5%)	0.47 (10.6%)
Leisure	1.97 (16.4%)	0 (0.0%)
Arts	1.38 (11.5%)	0 (0.0%)
Belief and thought	1.33 (11.1%)	0.16 (3.6%)
Imaginative	1.16 (9.7%)	0.37 (8.6%)
Spoken demographic	0.95 (7.9%)	0 (0.0%)
Social science	0.43 (3.6%)	0 (0.0%)
Applied science	0.42 (3.5%)	0 (0.0%)
Commerce and finance	0.28 (2.3%)	0 (0.0%)

Nearly 80 percent of the instances of *tsunami* are used in the 'natural and pure sciences' domain. This is by far the most frequent domain of *tsunami* followed by 'world affairs' and 'imaginative,' while *tidal wave* is also used in such domains as 'leisure,' 'arts,' and 'belief and thought,' in addition to the domains where *tsunami* appears. Looking into the actual sentences from the search result, I discovered that this difference in the range of use between *tsunami* and *tidal wave* is attributed to the ways these two words are used.

In the 'natural and pure sciences' domain, *tsunami* is used in the articles on geography. In the 'world affairs' domain, it is also used in weather-related or geographical articles or books that describe the tsunami in the past from the various places in the world. All the occurrences (six times) in the 'imaginative' domain are from one source, which is a novel whose locale is a volcanic island, where a tsunami often happens. Some examples of *tsunami* are shown in (133). (Underlines supplied in the examples hereafter.)

(133) a. Natural and pure sciences

- Slowly, life returned to something like normal in the Straits, and the bewildered survivors were able to bury their dead, and salvage what they could of homes in towns and villages that had been swept by tsunamis and showered with ash. (ASR)
- Each seismic shock produced a tsunami, which swept shallow water sediments and fauna (including reef corals) down the fault scarp to settle among the boulders. (H7K)

b. World affairs

- The infamous Chilean case, in May 1960, began with an earthquake deep in the subduction zone between the Nazca and the South American Plates: scores of people died near the town of Puerto Montt. But it was the resulting tsunami that did the greater damage: ...(CJD)
- The coastal geomorphologist therefore focused upon the processes ...of wave activity in relation to the swash, nearshore and offshore zones, and to the less-studied influence of tides and of impulsive events such as tsunamis. (GVW)

c. Imaginative

- "...And lastly, but by no means least, are the tsunami effects, vast tidal waves usually generated by undersea earthquakes: those tsunami have been responsible for the deaths of tens of thousands of people at a time when they struck low-lying coastal areas." (CKC)

In the meantime, it was revealed that *tidal wave* is used differently in the other domains (*i.e.*, 'leisure,' 'arts,' 'belief and thought'). That is, *tidal wave* is used metaphorically to express the large movement of something such as emotion and changes. Some examples are given in (134). This usage to designate something other than the real wave contributes to the occurrence in the wider range of domains.

(134) a. "Body Exit Mind" is the sound of a band sticking to their guns, no matter the tidal wave of opposition. (CK5: Art)

b. The "seventies saw a tidal wave of supernatural horrors featuring demonic possession, poltergeists, and various manifestations of the Great Beast. (B1J: Belief and thought)

c. One could be tempted to say that this evening was no exception but that would be a little harsh. It was more a tidal wave in a punch bowl. (HCV: Commerce and finance)

d. make ordinary people even more dependent upon the state for protection against "lawlessness" and the rising tidal wave of crime, even though it is the state and its agents who are often directly and indirectly victimizing ordinary people. (CHL: Social science)

In the 'natural and pure sciences' domain, *tidal wave* is always used with *tsunami* before or after the word to explain it. These facts tell us that *tidal wave* is currently a more common expression to designate the phenomenon, and *tsunami* began to be used as a technical term in meteorology, but is not well-known, and therefore it still needs to be accompanied by the explanatory words as seen in (135).[3]

(135) a. Much the most destructive effects of the explosions, however, were a series of tsunamis (often wrongly called tidal waves) which swept up and down the shores of the Sunda Straits. (ASR)

---

[3] The Sumatra-Andaman Islands Earthquake that occurred on December 26, 2004 made the term *tsunami* and its serious danger known to the world. The expansion of usage and sense can be expected in the near future.

b. Thousands of inhabitants reeled from a double disaster as tremors from the quake also created a <u>Tsunami tidal wave</u> that destroyed whole areas of land and villages. (GX6)

If we turn to the collocation of these words, it is revealed that the words that co-occur with them support the result of analyses in the distribution above.[4] The strongest collocate of *tsunami* is *earthquake*, followed by *tidal*, and all the others ranked in the result of calculation are such functional words as *the* and *or*. This shows that *tsunami(s)* is mentioned in relation to earthquake and rephrased by *tidal wave*. As for *tidal wave(s)*, the strongest collocation is *tsunami*, which again indicates that *tidal wave* is used as a rephrasing of *tsunami* or vice versa, followed by the words that describe the wave and effect of the wave such as *swept*, *destroyed*, and *huge*. The remarkable difference is that words that have nothing to do with the tidal wave as a natural phenomenon are ranked in the result of the calculation. These are *crime* and *like*. *Tidal wave* is used metaphorically with both of these words. *Crime* is used in the phrase as 'a tidal wave of crime' to describe the rapidly increasing number of crimes, and *like* is used in the phrase as 'like a tidal wave' to describe the fierce emotion or movement. Some examples of co-occurring words are given in (136):

(136) a. The subterranean manifestation of Poseidon was in the form of <u>earthquakes</u> and <u>tsunamis</u>; the terrestrial aspect was seen in the form or a bull; the celestial was the sun and moon. (CM9)

b. There is <u>a tidal wave of crime</u> in this country, and it does no good to the people of Cardiff, Sandwell and Westminster to say there is not as much crime there as in Chicago or Sydney. (HHX)

c. The mood spread backward, rolling down the room <u>like a tidal wave of</u> hostility, the sound of slamming beer mugs following in its wake. (CA9)

---

[4] Here, the collocation calculation was carried out with the span of -3 to +3 (*i.e.*, three words before the target word and three words after the words) and the least collocate number of 3 (*i.e.*, the items that co-occur less than three times were excluded from the result list). However, as for *tidal wave(s)*, the span was set to -4 to +3 because *tidal* is counted as -1.

A similar situation can be observed in the contrast between *bergschrund* and *cravasse*. *Bergschrund* is used only in the periodicals of mountaineering, while *crevasse* is used in a wider range of domains as shown in (137).

(137) a. At the very last abseil, which crossed a small, then large bergschrund, the abseil snowstake came out and Dave Lister, the third man down, fell past the two crevasses onto an open slope, miraculously stopping after about 50 feet. (CG2: Leisure, *Climber and Hill Walker*)

　　b. If the wind blows and snow fills your footprints the safe way between the crevasses will be lost. (A6T: Leisure)

　　c. State Trooper Lamica concluded: "We just hope he hasn't gone onto the glacier. It is filled with 400 ft deep crevasses, and is extremely dangerous." (K3C: World Affair)

　　d. Two hot-water bottles slumped against each other in the crevasse that Nannie had left in her mattress. (H7H: Imaginative, metaphorical use)

7.4.2　Wider Range of Use of Newer Loanwords

The second pattern is the one in which newer loanwords a have wider range of use than the equivalent existing lexical items. This pattern can be illustrated in Figure 7.5.

The items in (138)[5] have this kind of relationship.

(138) a. hara(-)kiri (11) > disembowel oneself (3);

　　　(**Imaginative**, Natural and pure sciences, Leisure, Applied science, **Commerce and finance, Social science**)

　　　　• A MAN who threatened to commit harakiri with a 3ft sword after a row with his mother surrendered to police at Seaview, Isle of Wight. (CH2: Leisure)

　　　　• Yorick had disembowelled himself, messily but effectively, with his samurai sword. (GUU: Imaginative)

---

[5] The numbers in parentheses are raw frequencies, and the domains in boldface are common to the pair. Underlines are supplied to examples for emphasis.

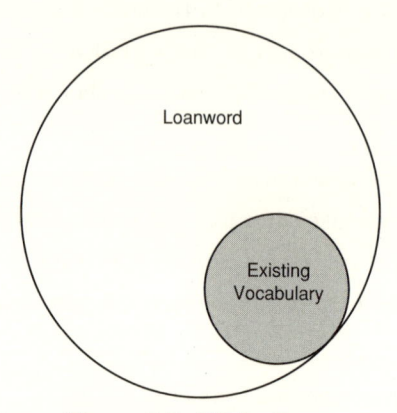

Figure 7.5: Wider Range

b. glockenspiel (11) > carillon (5);
   (**Belief and thoughts**, Arts, **Imaginative**)

   - In another letter he describes how he impishly tried to put Schikaneder's nose out of joint by playing the glockenspiel out of time from the wings. (CEW: Arts)
   - There were charming carillons on the Continent, but something dreadful seemed to happen to Catholic bells when they crossed the Channel. (ABW: Imaginative)

c. shiatsu (18) > acupressure (4) (**Leisure**, Belief and thoughts, Arts, Applied science, **Social science**, **Imaginative**);

   - From shiatsu in hairdressers to inflight beauty therapy on planes. (CD5: Arts)
   - Doctors describe how people with bad headaches can get relief by using simple techniques including exercise, relaxation, acupressure and even a visit to the dentist! (K40: Social science)

d. (tycoon > king).[6]

---

[6] This will be discussed in association with other synonymous items of *tycoon* and *magnate* in Section 8.4.9.

The characteristics of this group is that the newer loanwords have higher frequencies than the existing lexical items. However, the frequencies of the newer loanwords themselves are also relatively low. Therefore, it can be considered that the concepts/objects the words designate do not have a great magnitude in the country where the language is spoken (*i.e.*, England).

7.4.3 Overlapped Range of Use

The third pattern is the one in which the synonym pair has an overlapped as well as a different range of use, though the degree of overlap is different from one pair to another. One characteristic common to the items in this group is that the main part of their use overlaps. It can be illustrated as in Figure 7.6.

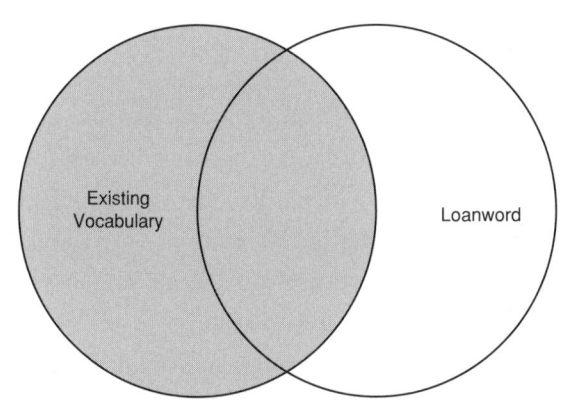

Figure 7.6: Overlapped Range

The items included in this group are shown in (139):[7]

(139) a. *doppelgänger* ⇔ *wraith* (belief, imaginative, arts, leisure);

b. *tycoon* ⇔ *magnate* (world affairs, art, leisure, commerce and finance);

c. *realpolitik* ⇔ *practical politics* (world affairs);

d. *wunderkind* ⇔ *prodigy* (art).

The pairs of *doppelgänger–wraith* and *tycoon–magnate* overlaps in all the top four domains, though the orders of the dominance in each item are different. On

---
[7] Domains in parentheses are major overlapped domains.

the contrary, the pairs of *realpolitik–practical politics* and *wunderkind–prodigy* share only one of the main domains. In this way, each item can have a different degree of overlap as shown in 7.7. I will discuss the distribution of *tycoon* and *magnate* in association with their other synonyms in Chapter 8 in detail.

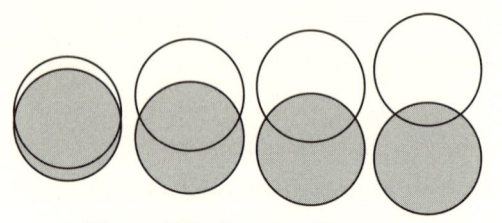

Figure 7.7: Overlap Patterns

7.4.4 Exclusive Range of Use

The final pattern is the one in which the synonym pair has an exclusive range of use. The use of the words in the pair may not be totally exclusive, with some parts overlapping, but their main domains have a different range. The number of the items which belong to this group is very small, with only two pairs extracted from this search (*angst* vs. *anxiety*, *tycoon* vs. *prince*). This relationship is illustrated in Figure 7.8.

As I will discuss *tycoon* and its synonyms in Section 8.4.9, here I show the distribution of *angst* and *anxiety* only (Table 7.2). One can see that the fourth domain is the same for both words, but the first three domains are different.

The difference between *angst* and *anxiety* can also be observed in collocation. The top ten collocates of both *angst* and *anxiety* are listed in Table 7.3.

The table shows that the words that come before or after *angst* are the ones that express that someone is affected by *angst* (e.g., *ridden* and *disturbed*), or the ones that indicate the kind of angst in more specific ways (e.g., *metaphysical* and *adolescent*). In contrast, many of the words that come before or after *anxiety* are the words that express a mental burden similar to *anxiety* (e.g., *depression*, *stress*, and *fear*), and the words that indicate the cause of the emotion or the way it is expressed (e.g., *cause*, *symptoms*, and *source*).

When the actual instances of these words were investigated, I observed further differences. The term *angst* often indicates the anguish or struggle that movie

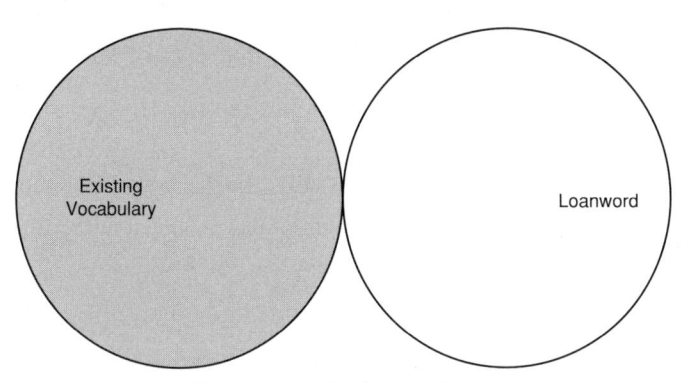

Figure 7.8: Exclusive Range

Table 7.2: Domains of *Angst* and *Anxiety*

angst (136)	anxiety (2612)
Art	Social science
Leisure	Applied science
World affairs	Belief and thought
Imaginative	Imaginative

Table 7.3: Collocations of *Angst* and *Anxiety*

angst	anxiety
1. -ridden, ridden	1. depression
2. metaphysical	2. stress
3. existential	3. fear, fears
4. recriminations	4. cause, caused
5. angst	5. symptoms
6. teen, adolescent	6. expressed
7. travels, meets	7. guilt
8. endless	8. acute
9. disturbed	9. neurosis
10. geographical	10. source

directors, musicians, or painters are trying to express in their works. Another point is that the names of nations or the adjective derived from them often co-occur with *angst*, including *USSR*, *British*, and *German*, though names of these nations do not appear in the collocation list. This shows that *angst* is also used to indicate the fear or apprehension that nations have. Examples of *angst* are shown in (140).

(140) a. By starting from the premise that the historical moment had arrived to sweep away not only the nihilistic, angst-ridden literature of modernism but also the crass simplicity of Stalinist socialist realism, ...(FTW: Art)

b. The second thing was all the teenage angst ; very disturbed letters. (K5F: Art)

c. German angst over the issue prompted Turkish President Turgut Özal to assert on German television on Jan. 24 that "Germany had become so rich that it has completely lost its fighting spirit". (HL3: World affairs)

On the contrary, *anxiety* is used in scientific journals often as one of the technical terms for mental disorders. It is also used in the 'belief and thought' domain to indicate the emotion of worry individuals have.

(141) a. The most common are anxiety and depression, but many more serious illnesses, including psychosis and schizophrenia, have also been attributed to food. (BM1: Social science)

b. Let us imagine that you are studying this in your room and you read verse 6: "Have no anxiety about anything, but in everything by prayer and supplication with thanksgiving let your requests be made known to God." (ABV: Belief and thought)

Taking all these things into consideration, I can now sum up the coexistence pattern of *angst* and *anxiety* as (142):

(142) a. angst:

- used mainly in the 'art' domain.

- use to designate a philosophical theme or an emotion shared by a generation (e.g., *teens, adolescent*).
- expressed by artists in music or movies.
- also used as the apprehension of nations.

b. anxiety:

- used mainly in the 'social/applied science' domains as a technical term.
- used to express an emotion the individual feels in his/her social life.
- co-occurring with other words of mental burdens (e.g., *stress, depression, fear, guilt*).

7.5 Summary

In this chapter, I have compared and contrasted the synonym pairs of existing lexical items and newer loanwords, and shown that they have differences in the domains in which they are used and their co-occurring words. I categorized their range of use into four patterns as in (143) and demonstrated the characteristics of each pattern with examples.

(143) a. Newer loanwords have a restricted range of use.

b. Newer loanwords have a wider range of use.

c. Newer loanwords and the equivalent existing lexical items coexist and have overlapped use.

d. Newer loanwords and the equivalent existing lexical items have exclusive use.

(143a) is the largest group among the four, where newer loanwords are used only in some specialized fields, while the existing vocabulary has a wider and more general use. Though the number in this group is relatively large, the effect of loanwords on the existing lexical system is scarcely greater than just adding new vocabulary to English because of their limited use as technical terms. (143b) is the second largest group, where newer loanwords have a wider range of use than the existing lexical items. However, the influence of this group is not very great either, since the concepts that most of the items in this group designate are rather uncommon in English-speaking countries, and both of the synonyms in the pairs have low frequencies in the corpus.

(143c) and (143d) consist of small groups, but their impact on the English language is large. They have established their positions in English in spite of the existence of their equivalent lexical items. Their designating concepts are more general, and the frequencies are higher than the items in (143b). They have various degrees of overlapping usage ranges as well as an exclusive range of their own. As a result of these kinds of conflict, the lexical items which once had an overall usage in a certain meaning have been eroded by the newer loanwords, and their usage has been narrowed.

The number of the pairs dealt with in this chapter was rather limited, but the overview of the conflict or coexisting situation could be observed along with some examples of the synonymous pairs. Furthermore, it will be interesting to observe the shifts that may come about in the future, from the less influential patterns of (143a) and (143b) to the more influential ones of (143c) or (143d), as the items gain a wider acceptance as general English vocabulary.

In the next chapter (Chapter 8), I will take a group of words synonymous with *tycoon* as a case study and discuss the distribution and usage differences in detail.

Chapter 8 A Case Study of Synonym Pair: *Magnate* and *Tycoon*

8.1 Introduction

The aim of this chapter is to demonstrate the similarities and the differences in the use of synonymous words in English as a case study: a relatively new loan-word *tycoon* and a long-existing word *magnate*. The word *tycoon* was originally borrowed to designate Japanese *shogun* when the Westerners encountered the Japanese social hierarchy in Edo period, which was new to them. After being borrowed into English, the word went through a semantic shift and obtained a new sense, 'a successful man in business, a man of wealth.' On the other hand, before *tycoon* developed the new sense, there had been another word in English, *magnate*, whose meaning was synonymous with *tycoon*. Today, we often see these two words in newspapers and magazines used in a similar way.

Through the analyses of the *OED2*, the origins and the developments of these words are revealed. The characteristics derived from the *OED2* are then verified using the *BNC*, and further detailed analyses are carried out. I clarify the distinctions between these words by comparing and analyzing them in the following aspects: sense, frequencies, domains and media of texts in which they are used, co-occurring words in context, number (singular/plural), usage patterns, connotation, referents, and so on. This reveals the nature of these words and the similarities and differences between them, and shows how these two words, which seem synonymous, though one is a long-existing word in English and the other is a relatively new loanword, are distinct from each other.

In Section 8.2, the dictionary and the corpus used in this chapter and the procedure are briefly introduced. In Section 8.3, the description of *magnate* and *tycoon* in the *OED2* are summarized, and the characteristics extracted from the dictionary description are stated. In Section 8.4, the result of Section 8.3

is verified and the characteristics of *magnate* and *tycoon* are analyzed in more detail using the *BNC*. The inconsistency and insufficiency of the descriptions of the *OED2* are also pointed out. In Section 8.4.9, I also deal with the other synonymous words of *tycoon* and *magnate*, including *mogul*, *baron*, *bigwig*, and so on. Finally, Section 8.5 presents a summary.

8.2 Methodology

8.2.1 Materials

In this chapter, the *OED2* on CD-ROM ver. 3 was used to investigate the origin of *tycoon* and *magnate* and their development from their first appearance in the English language to the current usage. A corpus is a strong tool for the investigation of distinction between synonyms, as Biber (1996) stated (cf. Section 6.3.4). The *BNC* was used in this part of the study to verify the description in the *OED2* and to analyze the current use of these two synonymous words in more detail. I also searched for *tycoon* and *magnate* in the two corpora of Present-day American English, the *BROWN* and the *FROWN* to investigate the American usages. However, because of their limited size (one million words each), the number of cases of *tycoon* and *magnate* retrieved from them were not large enough for analyses (*tycoon*: one instance in the *BROWN*, two in the *FROWN*, *magnate*: two instances in the *BROWN*, one in the *FROWN*). In addition to it, I also searched *ARCHER*[1] corpus to find out about the historical change, but the size of this corpus was not large enough either, only to provide one instance of *magnate* in 1975 and two instances of *tycoon* in 1961.

8.2.2 Procedure

To search in the *OED2*, both a headword search and a full text search were carried out using the software attached to the *OED2* data CD-ROM. By a full text search, one can find more information and quotations of the target words because it collects all the instances of the target words in the *OED2* in the definition and quotation section of other headwords as well as of the target word.

---

[1] *ARCHER* stands for 'A Representative Corpus of Historical English Registers,' which is a 1.7 million-word corpus of English text samples dating between 1650 and 1990.

To search for words in the *BNC*, one can use the attached software called SARA, but as the data of the *BNC* consist of SGML formatted texts, a researcher can carry out a more flexible search by writing scripts using such a programming language as Perl to meet his/her own needs. Another benefit of using self-made scripts is that it is easier to access the results and to format them into a more comprehensive display, for the data can be dealt in plain text format rather than in the software-specific format. In this research, the author wrote Perl scripts to search for *magnate* and *tycoon* and their derivatives, and to process the results so that they could be displayed in KWIC format. As shown in Table 8.1, each search result has text information derived from the header of each text in the beginning of the line as "serial number | text ID | source | medium | domain |" followed by KWIC-formatted data. Fifty characters before and after the keyword are taken as context.

Based on the KWIC formatted results, the data were sorted and classified, and the frequencies of co-occurring words and the distribution in each domain and medium were calculated to analyze the data quantitatively. As for qualitative analyses, I interpreted each target word in the paragraph or the whole text and determined the sense of the word used in a text, identified the referents the word designates, and compared the connotation of *magnate* and *tycoon* within the same text.

8.3 Usage of *Magnate* and *Tycoon* as Seen in the *OED2*

8.3.1 *Tycoon* in the *OED2*

According to the *OED2*, *tycoon* is originally 'the title by which the shogun of Japan was described to foreigners.'[2] It first appeared in English in 1857, and the last quotation of *tycoon* in the sense of 'shogun' is in 1887. It went through a semantic shift soon after borrowing, and obtained a new sense, '[a]n important or dominant person esp. in business or politics; a magnate.' The first quotation of the shifted sense is recorded in 1861, as in (144). (Underlines supplied in the examples hereafter.)

---

[2] The word is originally spelled as 'taikun.'

Table 8.1: Example of KWIC-formatted Results

tycoon

#	Code	Source	Type	Domain	Left context	Node	Right context
1	A2S	Independent,	periodical	leisure	e of a shy, reclusive, multi-millionaire property	tycoon	and that of a terrace tearaway was too sudden to
2	A2S	Independent,	periodical	belief	irectors Amer Midani and Nigel Burrows, the media	tycoon	Eddie Shah, and the former estate agent and local
3	A44	Independent,	periodical	belief	d Americanism on his pictures, but he did so as a	tycoon	, in competition with writers, directors and stars
4	A6L	Advice from t	book	commerce	of Tamwood.There were also rumours that newspaper	tycoon	Robert Maxwell was showing more than a passing in
5	A8U	The Guardian,	periodical	commerce	Publishing	tycoon	Robert Maxwell, and his family plan to buy out t
6	A9D	The Guardian,	periodical	commerce	e.By Lisa BuckinghanTHE KEY company in Australian	tycoon	Alan Bond's crumbling empire was yesterday threat
7	AAS	The Guardian,	periodical	commerce	courtroom drama follows a year of struggle by the	tycoon	— owner of Castlemaine XXXX lager — t
8	AAU	The Guardian,	periodical	world affa	the brewing businesses of the Australian yachting	tycoon	, Mr Alan Bond, in what may prove to be the first
9	ABE	The Economist	periodical	commerce	nister, some of his economic advisers and Chinese	tycoons	who control four-fifths of the country's private
10	ABE	The Economist	periodical	commerce	o displace Hong Kong as the Hollywood of Asia.The	tycoon	Deacon Chiu is building three film studios at his
11	ABK	The Economist	periodical	commerce	Of course, modern	tycoons	have yachts and private aircraft and tropical isl
12	ABK	The Economist	periodical	commerce	nnedy newspaper advertisement sponsored by an oil	tycoon	, H.L. Hunt, and other prominent Dallas businessme
13	ABK	The Economist	periodical	commerce	WARSAWCONTRARY to popular belief, not all Poles	tycoonski	
14	ACN	The Face.	periodical	arts	the Thirties movie mogul Monroe Stahr in The Last	tycoon	, the film version of F. Scott Fitzgerald's last,
15	ACN	The Face.	periodical	arts	nes, but De Niro certainly doesn't come on like a	tycoon	, talking about his company as not so much a busin
16	ACV	The forest of	book	imaginativ	Emily giggled.&bquo;I think it's &bquo;	tycoons	&equo; Lil. &equo;
17	ACV	The forest of	book	imaginativ	&equo; &bquo; typhoons &equo; ; they're all full of		
18	ADR	Kylie Minogue	book	leisure	imated at more than £10 million, a property	tycoon	in Australia where she was spending a fortune ren
19	AE8	Roads that mo	book	leisure	His patrons, the Fuggers, the Wall Street	tycoons	of the sixteenth century, were a similarly ruthle
20	AHF	Daily Telegra	periodical	world affa	The husband is described as a yacht-sailing	tycoon	who is the darling of the New York tabloid newspa

magnate

#	Code	Source	Type	Domain	Left context	Node	Right context
1	AON	King Cameron.	book	imaginativ	il — he only wanted it for himself.He was a	magnate	, Angus.like his son today.They coin money at Bolf
2	A8F	The Guardian,	periodical	arts	y.Thus the joke about Boss Mangan, the industrial	magnate	and political adviser, is that he is frock-coated
3	A8X	The Guardian,	periodical	world affa	y chairman of the Conservative Party, to shipping	magnates	at the London Hilton, told them: &bquo; I am proud
4	A90	The Guardian,	periodical	leisure	ht the team this year from the Swiss slot-machine	magnate	Walter Brun, who had bought it from Bernie Eccles
5	A9D	The Guardian,	periodical	commerce	Germany's Bertelsmann and interests controlled by	magnates	such as Silvio Berlusconi and Carlo de Benedetti
6	ABD	The Economist	periodical	commerce	my! &equo; This cry, uttered in 1908 by a property	magnate	called Toad, marked the beginnings of the British
7	ABH	The Economist	periodical	commerce	h &bquo; Chickengate &equo; .A wealthy Texan chicken	magnate	, Lonnie &bquo; Bo &equo; Pilgrim, walked on to the
8	AC2	Man at the sh	book	imaginativ	enry's magnificent $ 590,000 gift.The motor	magnate	was furious and rang the Editor to say so, whereu
9	AC2	Man at the sh	book	imaginativ	ears later, on completion of the social club, the	magnate	was asked if he would like something suitable ins
10	AC2	Man at the sh	book	imaginativ		magnate	placed the phone back on the receiver … slo
11	ACH	Britain on th	book	social sci	, publishers, duchesses and Labour MPs marching ar	magnates	
12	ADB	Friends in hi	book	world affa	cleuch, the biggest landowner in Europe, the beef	magnate	Lord Vestey, another of the richest men in Britai
13	ADB	Friends in hi	book	world affa	n there were what you might call the &bquo; county	magnates	&equo; , who were important in their counties.They
14	ADC	The Oxford il	book	belief and	rful men in their societies — rulers, great	magnates	— towards the churches of which they consid
15	ADC	The Oxford il	book	belief and	id, were transferred from semi-autonomous secular	magnates	to wealthy and disciplined ecclesiastical corpora
16	ADC	The Oxford il	book	belief and	en kings and at least a proportion of the secular	magnates	.Tenth-century kings tried to achieve a balance be
17	AE4	Mary Queen of	book	social sci	kes us very far from the idea of lawless Scottish	magnates	.The evidence is that the magnates infinitely pref
18	AE4	Mary Queen of	book	social sci	awless Scottish magnates.The evidence is that the	magnates	infinitely preferred strong royal rule to lack of
19	AE4	Mary Queen of	book	social sci	over the legitimacy of heirs.There were no great	magnate	coalitions, such as the League of the Commonwealt
20	AE4	Mary Queen of	book	social sci	happened was that individual kings and individual	magnates	or magnate families sometimes came into collision

(144) 1861 J. Hay *Diary* 25 Apr. in *Lincoln & Civil War* (1939) 12 Gen. Butler has sent an imploring request to the President to be allowed to bag the whole nest of traitorous Maryland Legislators. This the Tycoon. .forbade.

It follows that a new sense of the word was developed in just four short years. However, this usage was limited to American English for the time being. It was first used as a nickname of Abraham Lincoln, the president of the United States at that time. In 1886, it was used in the phrase, 'the tycoon of the baggage car' in American English, and it was the first quotation of *tycoon* with the meaning of 'a dominant person in business.'

(145) 1886 *Outing* (U.S.) IX. 164/1 The tycoon of the baggage car objected to handling the boat.

It was not until 1926 that the first quotation in the shifted sense appeared in British English as in 'hair-tonic tycoon.'

(146) 1926 *Time* 14 June 32/3 *Married.* Fred W. Fitch, 56, rich hair-tonic tycoon.

After this, the quotations similar to what we often see in newspapers and magazines follow: 'oil and aviation tycoon,' 'stores tycoon,' and so on. The last quotation, recorded as recently as 1982, shows that this usage is still current in Present-day English.

(147) 1982 M. Russell *Rainblast* iii. 21 She has a thing going with Marcus Hicks, the stores tycoon.

It was observed that while the sense of 'a dominant person in business' is commonly used, the sense of 'a dominant person in politics' did not appear except for the first quotation about Lincoln in 1861. All the quotations but one in 1952 appeared in the singular form.

In addition to the chronological quotations, the *OED2* supplies more information about the word (*i.e.*, its attributive uses and derivatives). *Tycoon* was found to have the following derivatives: *tycoonate, tycoonery, tycooness, tycoonish, tycoonism, tycoonship*. Quotations are given for each derivative from 1863 to 1983. In all the quotations given for these derivatives except the early quotations in 1863 and 1876, *tycoon* is used in the sense of 'a dominant person in business.'

(148) 1983 *Listener* 27 Oct. 34/3 He was busy trying to set up a rival consortium to buy the Sunday Times, competing with (and losing to) Murdoch in tycoonery.

To collect further instances from the entire *OED2*, a full text search was carried out using the *OED2* as a huge corpus. This enabled me to search for *tycoon* used in the definition and quotation sections of other headwords. As a result, 54 more instances were retrieved. Twenty-three of them were used in the sense of 'shogun,' but 21 of the 23 were excluded from the result for the following reasons: 19 were a part of the title of the book, *The Capital of the Tycoon*, as the source of the quotations, another was used in the definition section of 'shogun', and the other was used under the headword of *taikun*, which is registered in the *OED2* as a spelling variation of *tycoon*. Thus, only two of the 54 results, one in 1871 and the other in 1875, were used in the sense of 'shogun' in actual quotations to rephrase it.

(149) 1871 A. B. Mitford *Tales of Old Japan* I. 95 *Hatamoto*. This word means 'under the flag'. The Hatamotos were men who..rallied round the standard of the Shogun, or Tycoon, in war-time.

(150) 1875 *N. Amer. Rev.* CXX. 281 The fall of the shogun's (tycoon's) government.

Thirty-one instances of *tycoon* appeared in the sense of 'a dominant person in business,' but 15 of the 31 were excluded from the result as they were a part of the title of the book, *The Last Tycoon*, indicating the source of the quotations. Thus, 16 were actually used in quotations from 1935 to 1977.

(151) 1977 *Daily Tel.* 13 Jan. 17/3 I'm not playing the role of the hard-headed tycoon who thinks all philanthropoids are Socialists and all university professors are Communists.

Thus, it can be assumed that *tycoon* was used in its original sense from 1857 to 1887, and that the frequent use of the shifted sense of 'a dominant person in business' began in British English after 1929.

8.3.2   *Magnate* in the *OED2*

As the *OED2* mentioned 'a magnate' in the definition section of the shifted sense of *tycoon*, the entry for *magnate* was also consulted. In the *OED2*, it is described as follows: *magnate* is adapted from *magnāt-*, *magnās* in Latin, first appeared in English in 1430–40, and is chiefly used in the plural. However, as the *OED2* mentioned, "it is possible that all the instances before the 19th century represent the Latin plural *magnātēs*," so there are only six quotations of the English *magnate* for sure, starting from the one in 1814.

(152) 1814 Byron *Lara* i. vii, Born of high lineage. .He mingled with the Magnates of his land.

No quotation is recorded after 1883.[3] In the definition section, the word is defined as follows: 'A great man; a noble; a man of wealth or eminence in any sphere.' This shows that *magnate* is used similarly to *tycoon* in the sense of 'a man of wealth.' However, in the quotation section, *magnate* is used in the sense of 'a noble' or 'a local influential' in all the quotations but one in 1874, and this exception was a case of 'a man of eminence in literature.'

(153) 1874 L. Stephen *Hours in Library* (1892) I. iv. 167 Unlike the irritable race of literary magnates. .[Scott] never lost a friend.

---

[3] The quotations are basically supposed to be listed in chronological order in the *OED2*, but the quotation in 1883 comes before the quotation in 1853 in the entry of *magnate* for an unknown reason. However, if one searches for *magnate* in the older version of the *OED2*, the quotation in 1853 is listed separately, and labeled as 'transformed.' This label is deleted from the current version of the *OED2*, but the reason is unknown.

Unlike *tycoon*, no quotation of *magnate* in the sense of 'a man of wealth' is given. *Magnate* in quotations co-occurs with such words as 'ruler of the toun,' 'Nobilitie,' 'the kingdom,' 'his land,' 'patrician,' 'territorial,' and 'country.' This also suggests the sense of *magnate* as 'a noble' or 'a local influential.'

There was no description of derivatives in the entry, but two words derived from *magnate* were listed as separate headwords: *magnateship* and *magnatical*. Since *magnatical* is labeled as '*Obsolete*,' it is not in use any more, but *magnateship* gives two quotations, one of which is recorded in 1937 in the sense of 'a dominant person in business' as in 'glass jar magnateship.' This is the only quotation of *magnate* in the sense similar to *tycoon* thus far.

However, the full text search of the entire *OED2*, as was done with *tycoon*, gives us more instances of *magnate*.[4] Sixty-four instances of *magnate* were obtained from the definition and quotation section of other headwords. While more than half of the results were used in the sense of 'a noble' or 'a local influential,' some cases of *magnate* in the sense of 'a dominant person in business' were found, which could not be retrieved by just examining the entry of *magnate*. As a result, 13 more quotations from 1888 to 1948 in which *magnate* was apparently used in the sense of 'a dominant person in business' were found.

(154) 1888 Bryce *Amer. Commw.* iii. lxiii. II. 458 Some discontented magnate objects and threatens to withdraw. ... If such a 'sore-head' persists, a schism may follow.

(155) 1948 *Time* 29 Nov. 24/1 In many ways he seemed a throwback to the lumber barons, the cattle kings and the mining magnates who had ruled the West before him.

In addition to that, *magnate* was used 16 times in the definition section of headwords other than *magnate* that have the same meaning as 'a dominant person in business' (*baron, boursocrat, captain, lord, prince, robber, tycoon, Vanderbilt*), and of the headword of the name of the industries (*cotton, fund,*

---

[4] In the actual search, to obtain the cases of the derivational forms (e.g., *magnatical*), the words starting with 'magnat-' were searched for and the cases which are not considered to be a derivational form of *magnate* were excluded.

money, oil, pork, press, rum) to define or explain such phrases as 'cotton lord' and 'oil king.'

(156) **baron**: b. A magnate in commerce, finance, or the like; a great merchant in a certain commodity, usu. defined by a qualifying word, as *beef baron, coal baron.* (Cf. king *n.* 6 a.) orig. *U.S.*

(157) **cotton lord**: A wealthy cotton-manufacturer; a magnate of the cotton trade.

Through the full text search, not only were more instances discovered, but also it was made clear that *magnate* in the sense of 'a dominant person in business' is so commonly known that it can be used to define the synonymous words. However, since the occurrence of this sense could only be observed until 1948, it is not certain from the *OED2* if the word is still used frequently in this sense. More discussion will be given about *lord, baron,* and other words that are described to have the same sense as *magnate* in the *OED2* in Section 8.4.9.

8.3.3 Differences between *Tycoon* and *Magnate* Derived from *OED2*

As a result of the investigation of the *OED2*, the differences between *tycoon* and *magnate* can be summarized as follows. The word *magnate* is mainly used in the plural form and in the sense of 'a noble' or 'a local influential,' and has a limited number of derivational forms. It developed the sense of 'a man of wealth' or 'a dominant person in business' in the middle of the 19th century. However, the frequency of its use is not high, especially after 1950. On the other hand, *tycoon* was used in the sense of 'shogun' only for 30 years after borrowing, and it is not in common use in this sense any more. The word went through a semantic shift soon after borrowing in American English first, and then in British English in later years and acquired a new sense, 'a dominant person in business,' and is in common use to this day. The word is usually used in the singular form, and has productivity in English with many derivatives. The characteristics of these words are summarized in Table 8.2.

In this section, we have seen the characteristics of *magnate* and *tycoon* observed in the *OED2*. However, the dictionary cannot tell fully how these words

Table 8.2: Characteristics of *Magnate* and *Tycoon* as Seen in the *OED2*

	magnate	tycoon
First recorded	in 1814 (1430-40 from Latin)	in 1857 (from Japanese)
Semantic shift	in 1874, 1888	in 1926 (in 1861 in AE)
Last quoted	in 1948, (1883 under *magnate*)	in 1983
Present use	not in use	in use
Sg./pl.	chiefly in plural	chiefly in singular
Productivity	limited, a few derivatives	many attributives, derivatives
Sense	a noble, a local influential, (an eminent person in a sphere) (a dominant person in business)	shogun, (a dominant person in politics) a dominant person in business

are used in Present-day English. In the next section, the description of the *OED2* will be verified, and the actual use of these words will be revealed by searching for them in the *BNC* and by analyzing the data from various aspects.

8.4 Verification and Detailed Analyses Using the *BNC*

As a result of searching for *magnate* and *tycoon* in the *BNC*, *magnate* occurred 369 times, and *tycoon* 243 times. One can at once notice that *magnate* is still used in English.

Plural forms were observed in 213 (57.7%) of 369 instances of *magnate* and in 35 (14.4%) of 243 instances of *tycoon*. The percentage of the plural form of *magnate* is about four times higher than that of *tycoon*, but this is not high enough to be described as 'chiefly in plural' as in the *OED2*. The plurality of *magnate* will be discussed further in Section 8.4.7.

Since derivatives or compounds of both *magnate* and *tycoon* appeared in the corpus only a few times (*magnate* twice, *tycoon* three times), it is safe to say that the productivity is not detected from the data.

Each of the retrieved cases was interpreted, and the meaning of the target word was determined from the context. It was found that *magnate* was used in the sense of 'a noble' or 'a local influential' in 249 of 369 instances, in the sense of 'a dominant person in business' in 117 instances, and in other senses ('a man of eminence,' 'a leader') in three instances. From these figures, one can tell that the major sense of *magnate* is 'a noble' or 'a local influential' but 'a dominant person in business' is also common, while the sense of 'a man of eminence in a sphere (*e.g.*, art and literature)' is rarely used. On the other hand, *tycoon* is never used in the sense of 'shogun' in the corpus. In all the instances but six (the title of a book or the name of a racehorse), it was used in the sense of 'a dominant person in business.' The frequency of *magnate* in the sense of 'a dominant person in business' is about half of that of *tycoon*. The frequencies of *tycoon* and *magnate* in each sense are summarized in Table 8.3. As a result of the search in the *BNC*, the characteristics of *tycoon* and *magnate* can be summarized as in Table 8.4. Underlined items show modification of Table 8.2.

As can be seen here, *magnate* is still widely used in Present-day English, unlike the description in the *OED2*. One can conclude here that the data in the *OED2* are not sufficiently updated, giving us a false impression that the word is not in common use any more. Moreover, one has to admit that the description in the *OED2* is not totally consistent on the ground that in the section of *tycoon* and some other synonymous words such as *lord* and *baron* in the sense of 'a dominant person in business,' the word *magnate* is used to give definitions and explanations of those words, yet no instance of *magnate* in that sense is shown in the quotation section of *magnate*. Sufficient update and a

Table 8.3: Frequencies of *Tycoon* and *Magnate* in Each Sense

	magnate (369)	*tycoon* (243)
original sense	(a noble) 249	(shogun) 0
'a dominant person in business'	117	238
other senses	3	5

$\chi 2=276.54;\ p<0.001^{a}$

a. These equations show that the difference in figures in the table is statistically significant at 0.1% significance level.

Table 8.4: Characteristics of *Tycoon* and *Magnate* as Seen in the *BNC*

	magnate	*tycoon*
Present	still in use	in use
Sg./pl.	in plural in many cases (57.7%)	chiefly in singular (pl.:14.4%)
Productivity	not detected	not detected
Sense	a noble, a local influential, a dominant person in business	~~shogun~~ ~~a dominant person in politics~~ a dominant person in business

more consistent description are desired in the next edition of the *OED*.

8.4.1 *Magnate*: Diachronic Shift in Sense

Looking into the cases of *magnate* retrieved from the *BNC* in more detail, one should notice that even though all the texts were written in Present-day English, the contents of the texts are varied in time period. Thus, the time period about which each text containing *magnate* was written was determined by interpreting through the context, and the texts were sorted in chronological order. In this way, it became clear that the meaning of *magnate* differs greatly, in terms of whether the text deals with event before or after the 19th century. Eighty-five percent of the texts written about events before the 19th century are taken from books about the history of some countries and religions, and in 240 out of the 242 instances, *magnate* is used in the sense of 'a noble' or 'a local influential.' In the meantime, the texts written about events in the 20th century are taken more from periodicals than books. In 108 out of the 111 instances, *magnate* appears with the sense of 'a dominant person in business.' In the texts written about the time period in between, which is the 19th century, both senses were equally observed. This shows that the 19th century was the transitional era for the major sense of *magnate* to develop from 'a noble' to 'a dominant person in business,' as the structure of the society changed from the early modern period to the contemporary one.[5] This transition is summarized in Table 8.5.

Table 8.5: Transition of the Sense of *Magnate*

sense	before 19th c.	19th c.	20th c.
a noble, a local influential	240	8	1
a dominant person in business	2	7	108
others	0	1	2

χ^2=342.91; p<0.001

---

[5] As for the society change in the 19th century, refer to Cain and Hopkins (1993) for more detail. This use of *magnate* can be said to be similar to the use of *Ronin* in Japanese in that they both have historical and modern meanings. *Ronin* is used in the texts written about the medieval era in the sense of 'a lordless wandering samurai in feudal Japan; an outlaw,' while in modern use it means, 'a Japanese student who has failed and is permitted to retake a university (entrance) examination.' The definitions are cited from the *OED2*.

8 A Case Study of Synonym Pair: *Magnate* and *Tycoon* 177

KWIC-formatted results of *magnate* show clearly that the co-occurring words differ greatly between the texts written about events before and after the 19th century. In the cases before the 19th century, such words as 'local,' 'great,' 'king,' 'territorial,' and 'lay (as opposed to ecclesiastical)' are observed many times, while in the cases of the 20th century, the names of industries and businesses including 'property,' 'media,' 'shipping,' 'oil,' and the names of the persons who are considered to be magnates are often observed. Examples are shown in (158) and (159). (The letters in parentheses at the end of the lines are text IDs in the *BNC*.)

(158) Examples of *magnate* before the 19th century:

rful men in their societies --- <u>rulers</u>, <u>great</u>	magnates	--- towards the churches of which they consid (ADC)
and the lack of a firm response by corrupt <u>local</u>	magnates	were to have a violent sequel to which we shall r (CB6)
owed the king as one of the greatest <u>territorial</u>	magnates	of the kingdom, and it was a third <u>territorial</u> di (CKR)
|ety --- <u>pope</u>, <u>king</u>, <u>royal family</u>, <u>clergy</u>, <u>lay</u>	magnates	and warriors'. This litany served to keep ali (EA7)

(159) Examples of *magnate* in the 20th century:

last year and chairman John Devaney, a <u>property</u>	magnates	and ex-Oxford director, will sell if the price is (HAE)
4 kidnapped Hétor Delgado Parker, a <u>media</u>	magnates	and a friend and former aide of Garća, fr (HKU)
onair, and Mr. Adam Polemos, a Greek <u>shipping</u>	magnates	, contributed to the funds of the Conservative p (HHV)
campaign re-election committee with a Texan <u>oil</u>	magnates	, Bobby Hold, as finance chairman. (HLC)

This difference becomes more distinctive when the co-occurring words in the context before and after *magnate* within a 50-character distance are ordered according to their frequencies. The sentences written about events before and after the 19th century differ in words frequently occurring around *magnate*. In the frequency list of the co-occurring words for the pre-19th century context, the words that designate the persons in power or authority at that time (*e.g.*, 'king,' 'royal,' 'bishop,' and 'prelates'), or the area in which they had power or authority at that time (*e.g.*, 'local,' 'northern,' and 'territorial'), are ranked high, while in the frequency list for the 20th century, the words that indicate the names of industries or businesses (*e.g.*, 'property,' 'media,' and 'shipping'), or the names of the persons regarded as magnates in those areas (*e.g.*, 'Berlusconi')

178   II Impact of Loanwords on the Existing Lexical System

are ranked high (Table 8.6[6]). From here on, the uses of *magnate* in the pre-19th and 20th century contexts are dealt with separately and called 'the old use' and 'the modern use' of *magnate*, respectively. Since eight of the 19th century instances show the old use and seven the modern use, the instances from the 19th century are divided into two groups and included in the group of either the old or the modern use.

Table 8.6: Co-occurring Words of *Magnate* in the *BNC*

| before 19th century || 20th century ||
pre-keyword	post-keyword	pre-keyword	post-keyword
25 great	6 local	10 property	7 Berlusconi
17 king	6 commons	10 media	5 Sir
11 northern	5 royal	8 shipping	5 Silvio
11 leading	5 court	8 oil	4 years
10 local	4 war	5 owned	4 recently
8 powerful	4 support	5 industrial	4 later
8 lay	4 military	4 newspaper	4 collection
6 support	4 like	4 italian	3 Peter
5 scottish	4 later	4 Greek	2 young
5 prelates	4 king	4 cotton	2 yesterday
5 individual	4 great	3 turned	2 wife
5 bishops	4 France	3 steel	2 take
4 territorial	4 Edward	3 press	2 son
4 power	3 Thomas	3 million	2 sold
4 parliament	3 terms	3 married	2 political
4 joined	3 Sir	3 London	2 Olsen
3 substantial	3 serve	3 financial	2 new
3 secular	3 Robert	3 chocolate	2 money
3 royal	3 power	2 York	2 Mark
3 response	3 parliament	2 wealthy	2 Ludwig

---

[6] To make the list more comprehensive, the function words are eliminated from the frequency table. To count the frequencies regardless of upper and lower case, all the capital letters are once replaced to lower cases before counting. Then, as for the proper nouns and adjectives, the first letters are replaced back to upper case for the comprehensibility of the list. However, the words which were used as both proper nouns and common nouns remain in lower case.

8.4.2 *Tycoon*: Similarities to the Modern Use of *Magnate*

Now, let us examine the search result of *tycoon*. This word is never used in the original sense of 'shogun' in the *BNC*, and unlike *magnate*, it is rarely (only five times) used in the texts written about events before the 19th century. The examples in (160) and Table 8.7 show that *tycoon* has a tendency similar to the modern use of *magnate* with regard to the co-occurring words. The words frequently appearing around *tycoon* are the names of industries or businesses, including 'media,' 'property,' 'business,' and 'newspaper,' and the names of the persons who are considered to be tycoons, including 'Murdoch,' 'Branson,' and 'Maxwell.'

(160) Examples of *tycoon* in the *BNC*:

e visitTHE man once described as Australian media	tycoon	Rupert Murdoch's 'chief pornographer' w (HJ3)
Top view on state FALLEN property	tycoon	Michael Kelly is having his £307,000 mortga (CBF)
AIRLINE	tycoon	Richard Branson has asked his 3,000 staff to sh (CEM)
of Tamwood.There were also rumours that newspaper	tycoon	Robert Maxwell was showing more than a passing in (A6L)

The examinations thus far have made clear the differences between *magnate* and *tycoon* in the time period they cover. That is, *magnate* is used more often in texts written about events before the 19th century than in texts about the 20th century, and the old use and the modern use of this word differ in meaning and co-occurring words. Furthermore, the modern use of *magnate* is similar to the use of *tycoon*, though the frequency of the modern use of *magnate* is about half as low as that of *tycoon*. In the following sections, I will consider the differences between *tycoon* and the modern use of *magnate* in more detail with regard to their collocations, connotations, the nature of the texts in which they appear, their usages, the persons they designate, and number (singular/plural).

In the following sections, I use the word *magnate* to refer to the modern use of *magnate* unless otherwise specified.

8.4.3 The Difference in Collocation

If we investigate Tables 8.6 and 8.7 to compare the frequently co-occurring words of *magnate* and *tycoon* in more detail, one can point out the differences in co-occurring words that are seemingly similar to each other. Such words

Table 8.7: Co-occurring Words of *Tycoon* in the *BNC*

pre-keyword	post-keyword
11 media	15 Robert
9 property	13 Maxwell
8 disgraced	13 Alan
8 business	12 yesterday
8 Australian	12 Richard
7 newspaper	9 Branson
7 Maxwell	8 Bond
7 American	6 owner
5 publishing	5 new
5 fallen	5 Asil
4 Virgin	4 wife
4 romantic	4 tycoon
4 role	4 Sugar
4 oil	4 private
4 late	4 Nadir
4 film	4 Lord
3 crooked	4 how
3 yacht	4 asked
3 racehorse	3 used
3 plundered	3 son

as *property*, *media*, and *newspaper* are common to both words, but *magnate* co-occurs often with *shipping*, *oil*, *industrial*, and *cotton*, while *tycoon* co-occurs with *business*, *publishing*, and *film* more often than *magnate*. This leads us to realize that *magnate* is more often used in the context of industry or manufacturing, while *tycoon* has more frequency in the context of business or commerce. The expressions *industrial magnate* and *business tycoon* are ranked fifth and fourth in Table 8.6 and 8.7, respectively, but the other combinations *industrial tycoon* and *business magnate* are uncommon as each appears only once in the *BNC*. Further discussion regarding the collocations of *tycoon* and *magnate* will be carried out in Section 8.4.9 in association with other synonymous items.

8.4.4 The Difference in Connotation of *Tycoon*

If we look into Table 8.6 and Table 8.7 once again, with a focus on a different aspect, another characteristic can be observed. That is, there are some words in the list of the co-occurring words of *tycoon* that do not appear in the list of the co-occurring words of *magnate*. Those words are 'disgraced,' 'fallen,' 'crooked,' and 'plundered,' which suggest that the *tycoon* has lost his status, dignity, or property. Moreover, words related to death (*e.g.*, 'die,' 'dead,' 'death,' 'kill,' 'late (referring to the person recently deceased),' and 'suicide') occur ten times in all, though each word is not ranked high in the list. These death-related words hardly appear in the list of the frequently co-occurring words of *magnate*.[7]

Then, a further search was carried out to find cases which contain both *tycoon* and *magnate* in the same texts, so that one can see the in-depth differences in the way these two words are used. As a result of the search, 23 texts in which both *tycoon* and *magnate* occurred were obtained. The difference could not be observed in most of them (17 texts) as they consisted of a collection of the articles from newspapers or magazines, and these two words were used in different articles designating different persons. However, a tendency could be observed that either *tycoon* or *magnate* was mainly used, depending on the referent person (cf. Section 8.4.6). There were also some cases of rephrasing *magnate* with *tycoon* or vice versa, which is a stylistic feature typical of English. In two cases, there was a clear difference in the sense, *tycoon* meaning 'a dominant person in business,' and *magnate* 'a noble.'

From the cases above, the differences in the connotation of the two words can not be observed, but there are some texts from newspapers and magazines, each of which is written by a single reporter and contains both of these words within the same article close to each other. In these texts, a clear distinction in connotation between the two words can be observed. The following examples (161)–(163) show the distinction that *tycoon* is used with a negative connotation, while *magnate* is used in a neutral way:

(161) DONALD TRUMP, the much-troubled New York property magnate, has

---

[7] *Die* and *late* appeared in the context of *magnate* only once respectively, and the other death-related words did not occur at all.

a new problem, his lawyer said yesterday — a steamy book written by Ivana, his ex-wife. In a novel called For Love Alone, described by the publishers as a sexy sizzler, she tells how a Czech woman loses her husband to a leggy honey blonde with a soft Southern drawl. The husband is described as a yacht-sailing tycoon who is the darling of the New York tabloid newspapers. (AHF)

(162) TYCOON Tiny Rowland is selling shares in his troubled Lonrho conglomerate for the first time, it was revealed last night. The sell-off paves the way for 75-year-old Rowland to retire within three years. A £300 million rescue package will virtually hand control of the company to German property magnate Dieter Bock. (CBF)

(163) FALLEN tycoon Alan Bond was freed from a 2 1/2-year jail sentence yesterday to await a retrial on dishonesty charges. His voice breaking with emotion, the 54-year-old Australian businessman said outside prison near Perth: 'I was innocent in the first place. I am going to spend some time with my family.' He was released on £40,000 bail after serving three months. An appeal court said fresh evidence presented last month could have had a bearing on the jury's original verdict. The former brewing, media and property magnate went bankrupt in April owing millions of pounds. (CH6)

In (161), *tycoon* is used by the divorced wife describing the ex-husband in her tell-all book, while the writer of this article uses *magnate*. (162) is about two businessmen; the one whose business is in a financially critical situation is called a *tycoon*, while the one called a *magnate* is powerful enough to buy off the *tycoon*. In (163), *tycoon* and *magnate* designate the same person, but he is called *magnate* before the bankruptcy and *tycoon* after coming out of prison. In this way, when the two words are used in contrast, it is often the case that *tycoon* is situated in a dishonorable position. Therefore, it can be inferred from the examples above that *tycoon* possibly has a negative connotation, while *magnate* is relatively neutral.[8] The use of *tycoon* with negative connotation

---

[8] On the contrary, unlike what was observed in the *BNC*, in some dictionaries, such as *Readers+Plus*, *magnate* is labeled as 'sometimes derogatory,' while *tycoon* is only labeled as 'spoken.'

first appeared in the *BNC* in the texts written in 1991 to refer to Robert Maxwell, the owner of the Mirror group, when his criminal frauds were revealed after his mysterious death. After that, it began to be used to refer to other dishonorable dominant persons in business, such as John de Lorean, Trevon Deaves, Asil Nadir *etc.*. However, the *BNC* does not provide enough data to reach a conclusion since it contains data only until 1994. This usage remains for further analyses.

8.4.5 The Difference in Usage: Apposition Patterns *etc.*

Next, the differences between *tycoon* and *magnate* in usages and apposition patterns will be examined. Today, we often see *tycoon* in newspapers and magazines in the following pattern: "place name + industry/business name + *tycoon*, + person's name," as in 'Greek shipping tycoon, Aristotle Onassis,' or 'Australian media tycoon, Rupert Murdoch.' This order also holds true of the search result in the *BNC*, where 80 instances follow this order, though in some cases either the place name or the industry name is missing. This shows that this pattern is the most typical usage of *tycoon*. The investigation of the *BNC* reveals that *tycoon* has the following three kinds of usages as shown in (164): apposition, designation, and general use. The use of apposition (164a) can further be divided into two types: one is *tycoon* followed by a person's name as has already been mentioned above [I], and the other is a person's name followed by *tycoon* [II]: "person's name, place and/or industry name + *tycoon* ... " as in 'Walker, the Jersey-based ex-steel tycoon.'

(164) a. Apposition: *tycoon* accompanies a person's name either before or after it.

  [I] *tycoon* followed by a person's name
  [II] a person's name followed by *tycoon*

  b. Designation: *tycoon* is not an appositive of a person's name, but one can tell from the context that it designates a specific referent.

  c. General use: *tycoon* does not designate a specific referent but is used in a general sense.

184 II Impact of Loanwords on the Existing Lexical System

The use of apposition (164a) was observed 96 times ([I]: 80 times and [II]: 16 times). Seventy-five instances fall under the use of designation (164b), and 67 instances under general use (164c). *Magnate* in the *BNC* follows similar usage patterns, but the frequency of each use is distinctively different: (164a-[I]) 36 instances, (164a-[II]) 26 instances, (164b) 18 instances, and (164c) 31 instances. Table 8.8 shows the relative frequencies of the usage of *tycoon* and *magnate*.

Table 8.8: Three Types of Use of *Tycoon* and *Magnate*

Usage Type	tycoon	magnate
(a) Apposition	96 (40.3%)	62 (55.9%)
[I] ···, person's name	80 (83.3%)	36 (58.1%)
[II] person's name, ···	16 (16.7%)	26 (41.9%)
(b) Designation of a certain person	75 (31.5%)	18 (16.2%)
(c) General use	67 (28.2%)	31 (27.9%)

$\chi^2 = 24.22$; $p<0.001$

Table 8.8 tells us the following points. Both *tycoon* and *magnate* are the most frequently used in (a) appositive use, but the frequency is higher with *magnate* than *tycoon*. *Tycoon* is also used in (b) designative use at a similar frequency to (a), while *magnate* has a low frequency of (b). Within the appositive use, the percentages of (a-[I]) and (a-[II]) of *magnate* do not differ greatly, while the major use of *tycoon* is obviously (a-[I]). Both are used in (c) general use at almost the same frequency (about 28%). Here, it is shown that these two words appear to be similar in usage but have different tendencies in the frequency of each usage and apposition pattern.

8.4.6 The Difference in Referents

Now, let us go back to Tables 8.6 and 8.7 to clarify the different tendencies regarding the referents of *tycoon* and *magnate*. In those tables, place names and industry/business names, as well as the names of persons that are referred to as tycoons or magnates can be seen. When we compare the words appearing in Tables 8.6 and 8.7, it appears that they tend to designate different persons. *Tycoon* designates 'Robert Maxwell' the most frequently (29 times), followed by 'Richard Branson' (nine times), 'Alan Bond' (eight times), 'Alan Sugar' (four times), 'Asil Nadir' (four times), 'John de Lorean' (three times), 'Gerald Ranter' (three times), 'Rupert Murdoch' (three times). The place and industry/business names ranked high in the list correspond to the names of tycoons: *media* (first rank), *newspaper* (sixth), and *publishing* (ninth) *tycoon* refer to 'Robert Maxwell' (media tycoon also includes two cases of Murdoch), *Australian* (fifth) *tycoon* refers to 'Alan Bond' (one case of Murdoch is included), *Virgin* (eleventh) *tycoon* refers to 'Richard Branson.'

As for *magnate*, 'Silvio Berlusconi' is the most frequent referent, appearing seven times, which makes it first in the rank of *magnate* (Table 8.6, right). Names such as 'Peter Ludwig' (chocolate), 'Fred Olsen' (shipping), 'Carlo Benedetti' (business), and 'Donald Trump' (property) follow after 'Berlusconi,' but they appear only twice. Judging from the fact that 62 instances are revealed to have apposition of person's names as can be seen in Table 8.8, there should be more referents with one or two frequencies, but they appear so far down the list that they are not included in Table 8.6. Here, it can be concluded that *tycoon* and *magnate* tend to designate different persons and that *tycoon* is used frequently to refer to particular persons (*e.g.*, Maxwell, Branson, and Bond), while *magnate* is used more broadly to refer to a larger number of successful persons in business, but each one less frequently.

8.4.7 The Difference in Number: Singular or Plural

Here, the matter of number (singular or plural) of *tycoon* and *magnate* will be discussed. In the beginning of Section 8.3.3, it is stated that *magnate* is not so frequently used in the plural as is suggested by 'chiefly in plural' in the *OED2*. If we divide *magnate* into the old and the modern use and check the number of each occurrence in the *BNC*, a new fact emerges. That is, in the texts about events before the 19th century, *magnate* is used in the plural with very high frequency (178 times, 73.6%). This indicates that the description in the *OED2* is valid. On the other hand, in the texts about events in the 20th century, the plural form of *magnate* appeared only 24 times (21.6%). This percentage does not differ greatly from the plural form of *tycoon* (14.4%). In other words, the description in the *OED2* is about the use of *magnate* before the 19th century and is not applicable any more to the current usage of *magnate*, and the modern use of *magnate* is used more frequently in the singular as is *tycoon*. The *OED2* needs to be updated in this matter as well.

8.4.8 The Different Distribution: Domains and Media

In this section, let us consider the differences in the nature of the texts in which *magnate* and *tycoon* are used. The domains and media of the texts are investigated by referring to the header information of each text. Since *magnate* has different usages in the old and the modern era, it is expected that there are also differences in domains and media in which old and modern usages of *magnate* appear. Thus, investigations of old and modern *magnate* were carried out separately, and the comparison between *tycoon* and the modern use of *magnate* are mainly mentioned here.

As for the domain, the following tendencies were observed (Table 8.9): the two words appeared in the 'world affair' domain at similar frequencies (about 26.75% and 30.77%),[9] while *tycoon* is more frequently used in the 'leisure' domain than *magnate* is, and *magnate* in the 'art' domain more than *tycoon*. The examples are given in (165).

(165) a. *tycoon* in 'leisure' domain:

- Jane, who won the best actress award for her role in Coming Home, recently married media tycoon Ted Turner. (CH6: *The Daily Mirror*)

Table 8.9: *Tycoon* and *Magnate* Used in Different Domains

tycoon (243)		old *magnate* (249)		modern *magnate* (117)	
75 leisure	30.86%	183 world affairs	73.49%	36 world affairs	30.77%
65 world affairs	26.75%	30 belief	12.05%	22 leisure	18.80%
33 imaginative	13.58%	17 social science	6.83%	20 arts	17.09%
26 commerce	10.70%	12 imaginative	4.82%	16 imaginative	13.68%
20 arts	8.23%	6 leisure	2.41%	14 commerce	11.97%
16 social science	6.58%	1 arts	0.40%	7 social science	5.98%
4 applied science	1.65%			2 applied science	1.71%
2 natural science	0.82%				
2 belief	0.82%				

---

[9] The most major domain in which the old usage of *magnate* appeared is 'world affairs.'

8   A Case Study of Synonym Pair: *Magnate* and *Tycoon*   187

- After a 20-minute coach trip to the harbour, they caught the speedboats to the yacht Alexander, on loan from Greek tycoon John Latsis. (CH6: *The Daily Mirror*)

- The gossipy world of New York dealers in convinced that the picture is in the Greek tycoon's Manhattan apartment; or at one of the three villas in St Moritz, probably Villa Marguns. (ED9: *Harpers & Queen*)

- And inside The Maxwell House. Treasures of a tycoon, under the hammer. (K27: [Central television news scripts])

b. *magnate* in 'art' domain:

- The German chocolate magnate Peter Ludwig, gargantuan collector, founder of museums and museum wings and lender to others (The Art Newspaper No.23, December 1992, p.12), wrote his thesis in the 1940s on Picasso and has collected him ever since. (CKT: *The Art Newspaper*)

- The picture was sold by the Earl of Rosebery at Sotheby's London in July 1992 to New York dealer Otto Naumann and his partner Milwaukee chemical magnate Alfred Bader (himself a noted collector of Rembrandt school paintings) for £3.8 million ($6 million) and ...(CKT: *The Art Newspaper*)

- The collection was formed by the late shopping-centre magnate Sir Harold (later Lord) Samuel who, on the advice of dealer Edward Speelman, amassed ...(EBW: *The Art Newspaper*)

The high frequency of *magnate* in the 'art' domain results from the fact that *magnate* often appeared in the news articles related to art that reports the magnate's action as an art collector of buying and selling works of art or contributing them to museums. In the meantime, the occurrence of *tycoon* in the texts of the 'art' domain is mostly as the title of the book or the movie, *The Last Tycoon*. There is only one case of *tycoon* as an art collector. Furthermore, in one text (CKX), *tycoon* is used in a clause of rejected condition: "...if we had had a lot of tremendous tycoons who were interested in the arts, ...,"

188   II   Impact of Loanwords on the Existing Lexical System

presuming that there are not many tycoons who are interested in art. The word *tycoon* in the 'leisure' domain appears mostly in tabloid newspapers, in passages disclosing the tycoon's misdeeds or private life. Thus, from the investigation of the domain of texts, a magnate and a tycoon can be visualized respectively as a person who invests or wastes his property on collecting works of art, and as a person who trifles away his finances on real estate such as mansions and villas, and on gorgeous vacations with yachts and cabin cruisers.

As for the medium, 'periodicals' (*i.e.*, newspapers and magazines) show the highest frequencies for both words, but the difference lies in that *magnate* is used more frequently in books than *tycoon* and not used in spoken media (Table 8.10[10]).

Table 8.10: *Tycoon* and *Magnate* Used in Different Media

tycoon (243)		old *magnate* (249)		new *magnate* (117)	
164 periodical	67.49%	239 book	95.98%	61 periodical	52.14%
65 book	26.75%	10 miscellanea	4.02%	53 book	45.30%
11 spoken	4.53%			3 miscellanea	2.56%
3 miscellanea	1.23%				

8.4.9   Other Synonymous Words of *Tycoon* and *Magnate*

Before concluding, as was mentioned in Section 8.3.2, other synonyms of *tycoon* and *magnate* will also be introduced and the relationship among them with regard to their distribution and collocation will be discussed.

The word *tycoon* was originally borrowed from Japanese to designate Japanese shogun, and later gained a current sense of 'a successful man in business.'[11] There are other words borrowed from foreign languages that have come to have the similar sense as *tycoon*. *Mandarin* is borrowed from Chinese, whose original meaning is 'a generic name for all grades of Chinese officials,' and now means 'a person of much importance, a great man.' *Mogul* was the common designation among Europeans of the emperor of Delhi, but is now used in a sense of 'a great personage; an autocratic ruler.' *Tsar* is historically 'the title

---

[10] The percentage of books on the history of nations or thoughts occupies more than 85% of the sources of the old usage of *magnate*.
[11] All the definitions in this section are taken from the *OED2*.

8   A Case Study of Synonym Pair: *Magnate* and *Tycoon*   189

of the autocrat or emperor of Russia,' but now is used to designate 'a person having great authority or absolute power; a tyrant.' Among the existing lexical items, the words that designate the man in power in a nation, including *king*, *prince*, *lord*, and *baron*, have the same usage as *tycoon* and *magnate*, and the colloquial phrases, including *bigwig*, *big-gun*, *big-shot*, and *big man*, are used in the same sense as *tycoon*. Some examples of those words are shown in (166).

(166)   a. MOVIE boss Barry "Killer" Diller has had a staggering £15 million payoff from media tycoon Rupert Murdoch. (CH6: Leisure)

b. As designed by architect Thomas Jeckyll for the London dining room of shipping magnate Frederick R. Leyland, the 20 x 32-foot compartment was lined with sixteenth-century leather wall hangings, ... (CKX: Art)

c. In their great mock-palazzo in Whitehall, FO ministers and mandarins are brainstorming about a possible Middle East peace conference and a post-war security structure for the region. (ABH: Commerce and finance)

d. At the age of 47, Robert De Niro is coming out of a creative crisis and entering a new phase as a movie mogul. (ACN: Art)

e. IF AMERICA ever needs a banking tsar, Bruce Sundlun is your man. (ABD: Commerce and finance)

f. "Out of my way – I'm king of the road". (A7D: Leisure)

g. At nineteen Shallot was virtuous, a prosperous man soon to be a merchant prince who would show both Master Benjamin and the great Wolsey that he could rise without their help. (HH5: Imaginative)

h. They were supported by the press lord, Beaverbrook, and the combination of the Daily Worker and Daily Express created a unique political movement which still awaits its historian. (CE7: World affairs)

i. Gun battles between rival gangs of inmates had left 18 prisoners dead following an unsuccessful assassination attempt on Olivero Chavez

190 II Impact of Loanwords on the Existing Lexical System

Araujo, a self-styled drug <u>baron</u> serving an eight-year sentence for drug trafficking. (HL8: World affairs)

j. A post-premiere mambo party at Harlem's legendary Roseland dancehall studded with stars and industry <u>bigwigs</u>. (CGB: Arts)

I looked up the domains in which all these words are used in the same sense as *tycoon*.[12] Figure 8.1 shows the domain distribution of the items in this synonym group.

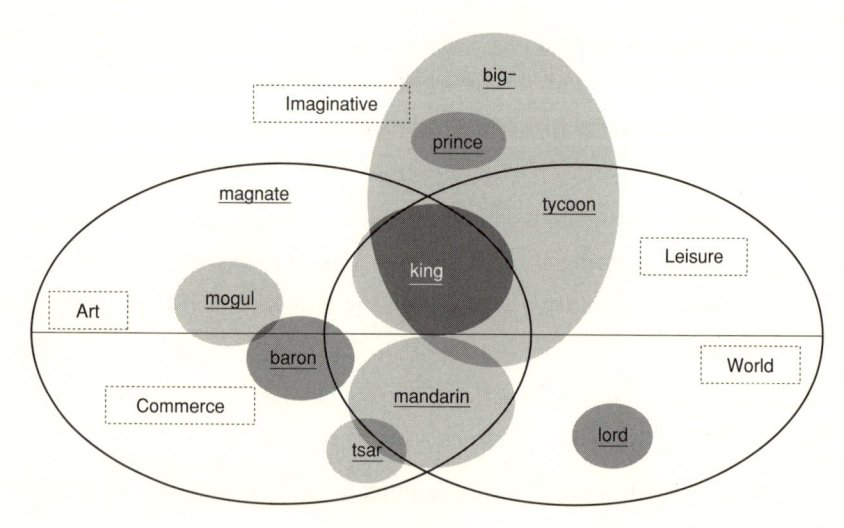

Figure 8.1: Domain of *Tycoon* and its Synonyms

As the differences in distribution between *tycoon* and *magnate* have already been discussed in Section 8.4.8, only their relationship with other synonyms are mentioned here. *Mandarin* and *king* are used in the overlapping region of *tycoon* and *magnate*, but different from each other (*mandarin* in the 'commerce and finance' and 'world affairs' domains, *king* in the 'art' and 'leisure' domains). *Lord* and *mogul* are mainly used in the 'world affairs' and 'art' domains, respectively, while *baron* and *tsar* are often used in the 'commerce and finance'

---

[12] Since it is impossible to determine the sense by reading the thousands of instances one by one for the high frequency words (e.g., *king* and *lord*), I first calculated the collocation, picked up the instances that co-occur with the words that seem to indicate the range of power or authority (e.g., *press, business*, etc.) the persons (i.e., *king, lord*, or others) have, and checked the sense of each instance to see if they really are used in the sense in question.

8 A Case Study of Synonym Pair: *Magnate* and *Tycoon* 191

domain. All the words mentioned above are within the range of *tycoon* and *magnate*, but *prince* and the items starting with *big-* have different range from them (*i.e.*, 'imaginative'). As Figure 8.1 shows, it turns out that the items in a synonymous group have different distribution as to the domains in which they are used.

In Section 8.4.3, we have seen that *tycoon* and *magnate* have different collocates which indicate that they have power or authority in different fields. Here, I extend this idea to the items in the group of synonyms. The words co-occurring with the synonyms and indicating the field of business/industry were picked up from the search result. Figure 8.2 shows the typical collocation of each item and the overlapping areas. The three words (i.e., *tycoon*, *magnate*, and *baron*) that provide many instances of 'a dominant person in business' are placed as the main factors. The collocates common to all three are *newspaper* and *media*, while business-related terms, including *business* itself and *publishing* are unique to *tycoon*, industry-related words, including *oil*, *shipping*, and *industrial* itself are unique to *magnate*, and *drug* is by far the most frequent in *baron*, followed by *cocaine*, *robber*, and *union*. The figure clearly shows the typical field in which each of the three has power or authority. In addition

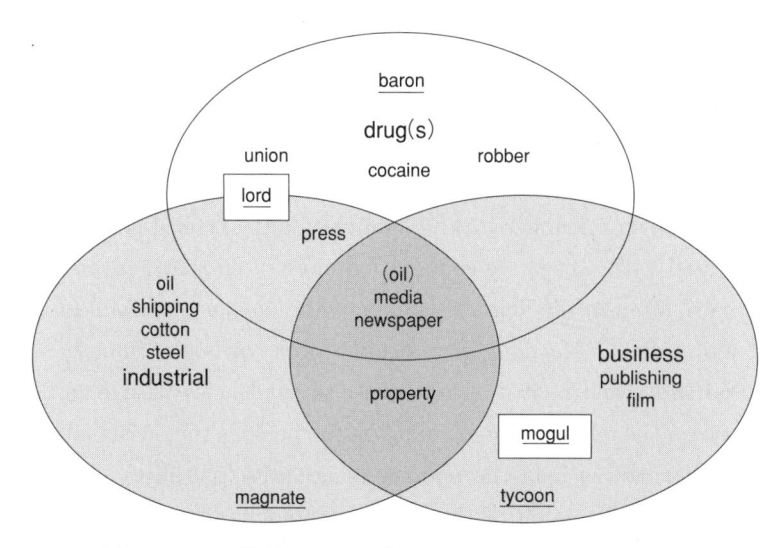

Figure 8.2: Collocation of *Tycoon* and its Synonyms

to the three, *lord* overlaps the collocates of *baron* and *magnate*, co-occurring with *drug*, *press* and *merchant*. The word *mogul* is often used with *media* and *movie*, probably due to the preference of the English speakers for alliteration.[13]

8.5 Summary

To sum up, the differences between the two synonymous words, the long-existing word *magnate* and the newer loanword *tycoon*, were investigated using the *OED2* and the *BNC*. The origin and the development of these words were revealed through the analyses of the *OED2*. *Magnate* is mainly used in the sense of 'a noble' or 'a local influential.' It developed the sense of 'a man of wealth' or 'a dominant person in business' in the middle of the 19th century. However, the frequency of its use is not high. On the other hand, *tycoon* was used in the sense of 'shogun' only for 30 years after borrowing, and it is not in common use in this sense any more. The word went through a semantic shift soon after borrowing, first in American English, and then in British English and acquired a new sense, 'a dominant person in business,' which is in common use to this day.

The descriptions of these words in the *OED2* were then verified using the *BNC*, and it was found that they cover a different range of time period, and that *magnate* has two kinds of usage, the old (before the 19th century) and the modern (in the 20th century). It was also revealed that though, roughly speaking, the usage of *tycoon* and the modern use of *magnate* share similarities in many points, they have different tendencies in detail. The typical field of *tycoon* is business or commerce, while industry is the typical field of *magnate*. *Tycoon* is used with a negative connotation more often than *magnate*. *Tycoon* appears more often in the 'leisure' domain while *magnate* appears in the 'art' domain more often. *Magnate* is used more often in books than *tycoon* and is not used in spoken media. There are also tendencies with regard to the choice between the two words depending on the persons they designate, the use of apposition patterns, and the number (singularity/plurality). The domain distribution and collocation of the related synonyms of *magnate* and *tycoon*

---

[13] This was pointed out by Prof. Hideki Watanabe at Osaka University in the course of developing this study (personal communication).

were also investigated, and the different usage of each word was demonstrated.

In addition to these analyses, it was pointed out in this chapter that the description of the modern use of *magnate* in the *OED2* is insufficient and inconsistent and that the quotations and the definition of *magnate* in the *OED2* need to be updated.

Chapter 9 Concluding Remarks and Future Perspectives

In this study, I have captured the behavior of loanwords with special reference to Japanese and German loanwords from two aspects: the way loanwords change themselves in the course of the assimilation process and the impact of the loanwords on the English lexical system.

In Part I, I have picked up loanwords from two languages: Japanese and German, and have shown that each has a different assimilation process. Japanese loanwords go through the four-stage process of assimilation, from pronunciation and orthographical adaptation to semantic shift, while German loanwords start their assimilation from a certain point arbitrarily or some points simultaneously. Though it is impossible to generalize the assimilation process of loanwords from all languages in English just by comparing the loanwords from only two languages, one can conclude that many factors affect the assimilation process of a specific language: the phonological, orthographical, and morphological characteristics of the words in the source languages. It is also true that other relative factors exist, such as how similar/different the source languages are to English and how familiar the English speakers are with the source languages, though it is beyond the scope of this study to measure the distance between the languages and the familiarity of English speakers to the languages. These are left for future investigation.

I have also dealt with secondary loanwords, such as loan translation and re-borrowings, as well as primary loanwords, and showed the differences in their assimilation processes. Furthermore, the contexts in which the loanwords are used have also been investigated and some relation between the deviate from the original context and the degree of assimilation have been shown.

In Part II, I have dealt with the loanwords from a different aspect from that of Part I. It was aimed to focus on the influence or impact the loanwords have on the existing English vocabulary. As the loanwords get assimilated into

English, they change not only themselves but also the English lexical system by expanding the vocabulary or increasing the number of irregular inflections. However, the change is not limited to just the addition of lexical items or irregularity to the lexical system of English. It includes the replacement of older lexical items or narrowing the semantic range of them when the loanwords come to have an overlapped range of sense and usage with the existing lexical items. This conflicting pair of lexical items is usually called synonyms, and this was the main theme of Part II.

In Chapter 7, I have taken an overview of conflicting vocabulary and introduced four patterns of coexistence. In Chapter 8, *tycoon* and *magnate* are taken as an example of pairs of synonymous existing words and newer loanwords in English. The related synonyms (e.g., *mogul*, *lord*, *king*, *bigwig*, etc.) were also investigated, and the different usage of each word was demonstrated. In addition to the synonymous pairs and groups discussed in Part II, I will extend the target words in the future, to cover a wider view of pairs or groups of synonymous newer loanwords and existing words in English, such as *boss*, *leader* and *honcho*, and *reckless* and *kamikaze*, and investigate them in detail. It will allow us to capture the process by which newer vocabulary affects the existing structure of English lexis. In order to do so, I will develop a tool that can carry out the quantitative analyses and visualize the results automatically so that I can deal with a larger target set and leave more time to carry out qualitative analyses.

In this study, I have derived most of the information on loanwords from the computerized data, including the dictionaries, the *OED2*, *Webster's Third*, the *Random House*, and the *Shorter OED* to obtain the historical transition of loanwords and the definition of the words in English, and the corpora, *TIME*, *The Times*, *Wordbanks* online and the *BNC* to verify and update the information from the dictionaries. I have also developed some tools to search the corpora and format the data in flexible ways, and launched the corpus server for the greater use of it. I am certain that this study has proved that computerized dictionaries and corpora are effective tools to investigate the changes and behaviors of lexical items including loanwords if they are used properly. The defects and inconsistencies of the *OED2* and the *BNC* have been pointed out in the hope that they will be improved when the next versions of their software come out.

Borrowing is not the major source of the increase in the size of vocabulary in Present-day English, but it will continue to exist and new lexical items will continue to be added to English as long as English speakers have contact with the world. Especially, Japanese loanwords are said to be increasing in number even today. It will be interesting to observe what kind of words will be borrowed from Japanese and other languages, which words will proceed to which stage of the assimilation process, and which words will come into conflict and make an impact on the English lexical system.

Bibliography

Agency for Cultural Affairs (Ed.). 1976. *Gairaigo*, Vol. 4 of *Kotoba Shiriizu*. Tokyo: Printing Bureau, Ministry of Finance in Japan. (in Japanese).

Agency for Cultural Affairs (Ed.). 1997. *Jisho*, Vol. 5 of *Shinkotoba Shiriizu*. Tokyo: Printing Bureau, Ministry of Finance in Japan. (in Japanese).

Agency for Cultural Affairs (Ed.). 1999. *Kotoba ni Kansuru Mondooshu — Imi no Nita Kotoba —*, Vol. 10 of *Shinkotoba Shiriizu*. Tokyo: Printing Bureau, Ministry of Finance in Japan. (in Japanese).

Algeo, J. (Ed.). 1991. *Fifty Years Among the New Words; A Dictionary of Neologisms, 1941-1991*. Cambridge: Cambridge University Press.

Aston, G. & Burnard, L. 1998. *The BNC Handbook — Exploring the British National Corpus with SARA —*. Edinburgh Textbooks in Empirical Linguistics. Edinburgh: Edinburgh University Press.

Ayto, J. 1999. *Twentieth Century Words*. Oxford: Oxford University Press.

Baumgardner, R. J. 1997. English in Mexican Spanish. *English Today 52*, 13(4), 27–35.

Bentley, H. W. 1932. *A Dictionary of Spanish Terms in English —With Special Reference to the American Southwest*. New York: Columbia University Press.

Biber, D. 1996. Investigating Language Use through Corpus-based Analyses of Association Patterns. *International Journal of Corpus Linguistics*, *1*(2), 171–197.

Bloomfield, L. 1933. *Language*. New York: Holt.

Brown, C. H. 1998. Spanish Loanwords in Languages of the Southeastern United States. *International Journal of American Linguistics*, *64*(2), 148–167.

Burchfield, R. W. & Smith, V. 1973. Azuki to Gun: Some Japanese Loanwords in English. *The Rising Generation*, *119*, 524–526, 593–595.

Burnard, L. 2000. *Reference Guide for British National Corpus (World Edition)*. HTML or PDF file contained in BNC CD-ROM.

Cain, P. & Hopkins, A. 1993. *British Imperialism —Innovation and Expansion*

1688-1914—. London: Longman.
Cannon, G. 1978. Statistical Etymologies of New Words in American English. *Journal of English Linguistics, 12*, 12–18.
Cannon, G. 1981a. Japanese Borrowings in English. *American Speech, 56*, 190–206.
Cannon, G. 1981b. New Onomastic Item in English. *Names: Journal of the American Name Society, 29*, 101–119.
Cannon, G. 1982a. 698 Japanese Borrowings in English. *Verbatim, 9*(1), 9–10.
Cannon, G. 1982b. Linguistic Analysis of 4520 New Meanings and New Words in English. *Dictionaries, 4*, 97–109.
Cannon, G. 1984. Zero Plurals Among the Japanese Loanwords in English. *American Speech, 59*, 149–158.
Cannon, G. 1985. Functional Shift in English. *Linguistics, 23*, 411–431.
Cannon, G. 1987. *Historical Change and English Word-formation: Recent Vocabulary*. American University Studies IV. New York: Peter Lang Publishing.
Cannon, G. 1988. Review of The Barnhart Dictionary of Etymology. *Dictionaries, 10*, 184–196.
Cannon, G. 1990. Sociolinguistic Implications in Chinese-language Borrowings in English. *International Journal of the Sociology of Language, 86*, 41–55.
Cannon, G. 1992. Malay(sian) Borrowings in English. *American Speech, 67*, 134–162.
Cannon, G. 1993. Recent Spanish-based Items in English, In Crochetier, A., Boulanger, J.-C. & Ouellier, C. (Eds.), *Proceedings of the XVth International Congress of Linguist, Quebec, University Laval, 9-14 August 1992*, Sante-Foy, Quebec: Laval UP. International Congress of Linguists.
Cannon, G. 1994a. Modern Spanish-based Lexical Items in English. *Dictionaries, 15*, 117–31.
Cannon, G. 1994b. Recent Japanese Borrowings into English. *American Speech, 69*(4), 373–397.
Cannon, G. 1995a. Chinese Borrowings in English. *American Speech, 63*(1), 3–33.
Cannon, G. 1995b. Innovative Japanese Borrowings in English. *Dictionaries, 16*, 90–101.
Cannon, G. 1996. Recent Borrowing from Spanish into English. In Rodríguez

González, F. (Ed.), *Spanish Loanwords in the English Language*, pp. 41–60. New York: Mouton de Gruyter.

Cannon, G. 1997. 90 post-1949 Arabic loans in written English. *Word, 48*(2), 171–192.

Cannon, G. 1998a. Persian Loans in the English Language. *International Bulletin of Linguistic Documentation, 40*, 147–178.

Cannon, G. 1998b. Post-1949 German loans in written English. *Word, 49*(1), 19–54.

Cannon, G. 2000. Turkish and Persian Loans in English Literature. *Neophilologus, 84*(2), 285–307.

Cannon, G. & Egle, B. M. 1979. New Borrowings in English. *American Speech, 54*, 23–37.

Cannon, G. & Kaye, A. S. 1994. *The Arabic Contributions to the English Language: An Historical Dictionary*. Wiesbaden: Harrassowitz Verlag.

Cannon, G. & Pfeffer, A. 1994. *German Loanwords in English*. Cambridge: Cambridge University Press.

Cannon, G. & Warren, N. 1996. *The Japanese Contributions to the English Language: An Historical Dictionary*. Wiesbaden: Harrassowitz Verlag.

Carman, C. P. 1991. Japanese Loanwords in English. *Journal of UOEH, 13*(3), 217–226.

Daulton, F. E. 2002. Lexical Assimilation of English into Japanese — Extent, Transformations and Comprehensibility. *Ryukoku Studies in English Language and Literature, 21*, 13–15. (in Japanese).

de Jonge, B. 1993. The Existence of Synonyms in a Language: Two Forms but One, or Rather Two, Meanings? *Linguistics, 31*(3), 521–538.

Duffley, P. & Joubert, J.-F. 1999. The Gerund and the Infinitive with the Verbs *intend*, *mean*, *propose* and Their Close Synonyms. *Canadian Journal of Linguistics, 44*(3), 251–266.

Edmonds, P. & Hirst, G. 2002. Near-Synonymy and Lexical Choice. *Computational Linguistics, 28*(2), 105–144.

Evans, T. M. 1990. *Eigo ni Natta Nihongo — Kotoba ni Miru Saishin Amerika Jouhou —*. Tokyo: Japan Times. (in Japanese).

Finkenstaedt, T., Leisi, E., & Wolff, D. 1970. *A Chronological English Dictionary; Listing 80000 Words in Order of Their Earliest Known Occurrence*. Heidelberg: Carl Winter/Universitätsverlag.

Finkenstaedt, T. & Wolff, D. 1969. Statstische Untersuchungen des englishen Wortschatzes mit Hife eines Computers. *Beiträge zur Linguistik und*

Informationsverarbeitung, 16, 7–34. (in German).

Finkenstaedt, T. & Wolff, D. 1973. *Ordered Profusion; Studies in Dictionaries and the English Lexicon.* Heidelberg: Carl Winter/Universitätsverlag.

Firth, J. R. 1957. Modes of Meaning. In *Papers in Linguistics 1934–1951.* Oxford: Oxford University Press.

Hasegawa, K. 1976. Eigo ni Natta Nihongo. In *The Cultural Background of the Japanese and English Language*, chap. 3, pp. 81–131. Tokyo: Saimaru Shuppankai. (in Japanese).

Hayakawa, I. 2003. The Antedating of Japanese Loanwords in English. *Japanese Linguistics, 13*, 79–108. (in Japanese).

Hoel, P. G. 1981. *Elementary Statistics* (4th edition). Baihukan.

Hudson, R., Holmes, J., & Gisborne, N. 1996. Synonyms and Syntax. *Journal of Linguistics, 32*(2), 439–446.

Inoue, N. 2001. A Corpus-based Study on English Synonyms —A Case of *happen* and *take place*—, *English Grammar and Usage Studies, 8*, 37–53. (in Japanese).

Ishimaru, T. 1990. *Eigo no Naka no Nihongo.* Tokyo: Chukoshinsho. (in Japanese).

Itou, K. 2001. *Umi no Kanata no Nihongo.* Osaka: Osaka Kyoiku Tosho. (in Japanese)

Itou, M. 2002. *Keiryou Gengogaku Nyuumon.* Tokyo: Taishukan. (in Japanese)

Jespersen, O. 1905. *Growth and Structure of the English Language.* Leipzig: B. G. Teubner.

Jucker, A. H. 1994. New Dimensions in Vocabulary Studies: Review article of the Oxford English Dictionary (2nd ed.) on CD-ROM. *Literary and Linguistic Computing, 9*(2), 149–154.

Kabakchi, V. V. 1997. Russianisms in Modern English. *Journal of English Linguistics, 25*(1), 8–49.

Katou, H. & Kumakura, I. 1999. *Gaikokugo ni Natta Nihongo no Jiten.* Tokyo: Iwanami Shoten. (in Japanese)

Kimura, M. 1995. *Japanese Borrowings in OED.* BA thesis, Osaka: Kansai Gaidai University.

Kimura, M. 1996. The Characteristics of Japanese Borrowings in *OED* — A Research Paper Using the *OED2* on CD-ROM—. *English Corpus Studies, 3*, 105–118. (in Japanese).

Kimura, M. 1997a. *The Naturalization Process of Japanese Borrowings in English.* MA thesis, Graduate School of Language and Culture, Osaka:

Osaka University.

Kimura, M. 1997b. Study of Loanwords using OED2 on CD-ROM — A Critical Consideration of the Way OED Reflects the Process of Naturalization of Japanese Loanwords —. In *Proceedings of the Fifth International Symposium of the National Language Research Institute, Session 1: Linguistic Research and Thesaurus*, pp. 4–12. Tokyo: National Language Research Institute. (in Japanese).

Kimura, M. 1998. Japanese Loanwords as Seen in *TIME* and *The Times*. *English Corpus Studies*, 5, 63–79. (in Japanese).

Kimura, M. 2000. The Naturalization Process of Japanese Loanwords as Reflected in English Dictionaries —The Four-Stage Hypothesis and Associated Problems —. In *Lexicographica Series Maior 103, Symposium on Lexicography IX*, pp. 293–303. Tübingen: Max Niemeyer Verlag.

Kimura, M. 2002. Meaning and Context of Loanwords. In *Theoretical Approach to Natural Language: Semantic Section*, pp. 35–45. Collaboration Project in Graduate School of Language and Culture, Osaka University. (in Japanese).

Kimura, M. 2003. Different Usages between Synonymous Words: *magnate* and *tycoon*. *English Corpus Studies*, 10, 25–40. (in Japanese).

Kimura, M. 2004a. Semantic Shift of Loanwords in English —Usages, Prevalence and Image Seen in the Metaphorical Use. In *Methodology and Scope of Metaphor*, pp. 39–46. Collaboration Project in Graduate School of Language and Culture, Osaka University. (in Japanese).

Kimura, M. 2004b. *Magnate* and *Tycoon*: A Case of Rivalry between Existing Vocabulary and Newer Loanwords as Seen in *OED2* and *BNC*. In *English Corpora under Japanese Eyes*, Vol. 51 of *Language and Computer*, pp. 93–113. Rodopi.

Kimura-Kano, M. 2003. A Comparative Study of Assimilation Processes of Japanese and German Loanwords in English. *Bulletin of Bunka Women's University Muroran Junior College*, 26, 45–58. (in Japanese).

Kimura-Kano, M. 2004. *Dynamics of Language Contact —Assimilation Process of New Loanwords and Impact on the Existing Lexical System with Special Reference to Japanese and German Loanwords in English—*. Ph.D dissertation, Graduate School of Language and Culture, Osaka: Osaka University.

Kimura-Kano, M. 2005a. Coexisting Patterns of Existing Vocabulary with Newer Loanwords in British English: A Study of Synonyms Focusing on

Japanese and German Loanwords in *BNC*. *English Corpus Studies, 12*, 1–17.

Kimura-Kano, M. 2005b. Dynamics of Language Contact —Assimilation Process of New Loanwords and Impact on the Existing Lexical System with Special Reference to Japanese and German Loanwords in English—. *Bulletin of Bunka Women's University Muroran Junior College, 28*, 54–70. (A Summary of Ph.D Dissertation in Japanese).

Knowlton, E. C. 1970. Chinese, Japanese, and Korean Loanwords in Webster's Third. *American Speech, 45*, 8–29.

Kokusai Gengo Bunka Kenkyuka Koukai Kouza Iinkai, Faculty of Language and Culture, Nagoya University (Ed.). 2001. *Intanetto to Eigo Gakushu*. Tokyo: Kaibunsha. (in Japanese)

Konishi, T. 1976. *Aspects of English Synonymy*. Tokyo: Kenkyusha. (in Japanese).

Koura, T. 1992. Giapponesismi in italiano —Con speciale riferimento al grado di italianizzazione—. *The Hiroshima University Studies Faculty of Letters, 51*, 411–427. (in Japanese).

Kurtböke, P. & Potter, L. 2000. Co-occurence Tendencies of Loanwords in Corpora. *International Journal of Corpus Linguistics, 5*(1), 83–100.

Matsuda, Y. 1974. History of *Tycoon*. *Kwansei Gakuin University Annual Studies, 23*, 35–39.

Matsuda, Y. 1976a. Soy Gogen Kou. *The English Teacher's Magazine, 24*(2), 47–49. (in Japanese).

Matsuda, Y. 1976b. The Etymology of *Soy*. *Kwansei Gakuin University Annual Studies, 25*, 55–58.

Matsuda, Y. 1979. Zoku Soy Gogen Kou. *The English Teacher's Magazine, 27*(6), 69–70. (in Japanese).

Matsuda, Y. 1991. *Nichi-eigo no Koryu — Ibunka Sesshoku no Asupekuto —*. Tokyo: Kenkyusha. (in Japanese).

Miller, R. A. 1967. *The Japanese Language*. Chicago: University of Chicago Press.

Millward, C. M. 1988. *A Biography of the English Language*. Orlando: Hartcourt Brace Jovanovich College Publishers.

Miwa, N. 1990. Shakuyougo *catch* no Imihenka —Imihenka Kousatsu no Mouhitotsu no Shiten. *The Rising Generation, 135*(11), 541–544. (in Japanese).

Miyajima, T. 1999. Nihongo to Doitsugo no Goishi no Hikaku. *Kokugo to Kokubungaku, 76*(1), 1–12.

Moody, A. J. 1996. Transmission Languages and Source Languages of Chinese Borrowings in English. *American speech, 71*(4), 405–420.

Mugglestone, L. (Ed.). 2000. *Lexicography and the OED — Pioneers in the Untrodden Forest —*. Oxford: Oxford University Press.

Norman, A. M. Z. 1954. Linguistic Aspects of the Mores of U.S. Occupation and Security Forces in Japan. *American Speech, 29*, 301–302.

Norman, A. M. Z. 1955. Bamboo English: The Japanese Influence upon American Speech in Japan. *American Speech, 30*, 44–48.

Owada, S. 1995a. OED no Nakano Nihongo. *Modern English Teaching, July*, 26–28. (in Japanese).

Owada, S. 1995b. A Study of Japanese Words in the *Oxford English Dictionary*. *Bulletin of Tokyo Seitoku College, 28*, 77–103. (in Japanese).

Owada, S. 1996. A Study of Japanese Words in the *Oxford English Dictionary* (2). *Bulletin of Tokyo Seitoku College, 29*, 1–13. (in Japanese).

Owada, S. 1997. A Study of Japanese Words in the *Oxford English Dictionary* (3): With Special Reference to Engelbert Kæmpfer. *Bulletin of Tokyo Seitoku College, 30*, 27–35. (in Japanese).

Owada, S. 1998a. A Study of Japanese Words in the *Oxford English Dictionary* (4): *Additions Series* Vol. 1–3. *Bulletin of Tokyo Seitoku College, 31*, 1–12. (in Japanese).

Owada, S. 1998b. A Study of Japanese Words in the *Oxford English Dictionary* (5): With Special Reference to the Recent Oxford Dictionaries. *Bulletin of Tokyo Seitoku College, 32*, 19–27. (in Japanese).

Owada, S. 2000. A Corpus Study of Japanese Borrowings in English: BROWN & LOB Corpus. *Bulletin of Tokyo Seitoku College, 33*, 61–64. (in Japanese).

Pfeffer, J. A. 1987. *Deutsches Sprachgut im Wortschatz der Amerikaner und Engländer —Vergleichendes Lexikon mit analytischer Einführung und historischem Überblick*. Tübingen: Max Niemeyer Verlag.

Rees-Miller, J. 1996. Morphological Adaptation of English Loanwords in Algonquian. *International Journal of American Linguistics, 62*(2), 196–202.

Saito, T., Nakamura, J., & Akano, I. 1998. *English Corpus Linguistics*. Tokyo: Kenkyusha.

Serjeantson, M. S. 1961. *A History of Foreign Words in English*. New York: Barnes & Noble.

Smead, R. N. 1998. English Loanwords in Chicano Spanish: Characterization

and Rationale. *The Bilingual Review. La Revista Bilingüe, 23*(2), 113–123.
Smith, R. 1997. English in European Spanish. *English Today 52, 13*(4), 22–25.
Stubbs, M. 1998. German Loanwords and Cultural Stereotypes. *English Today 53, 14*(1), 19–53.
Stubbs, M. 2001. Words in Culture 1: Case Studies of Loan Words in English. In *Words and Phrases —Corpus Studies of Lexical Semantics—*, chap. 8, pp. 170–193. Oxford: Blackwell Publishing.
Tanaka, M. 1992. *Eigo Sinonimu Hikaku Jiten*. Tokyo: Kenkyusha.
The National Institute for Japanese Language (Ed.). 2000. *Kotoba ni Kansuru Mondooshu — Imi no Nita Kotoba —*, Vol. 12 of *Shinkotoba Shiriizu*. Tokyo: Printing Bureau, Ministry of Finance in Japan. (in Japanese).
Todoroki, Y. 1997. Nihongo Kigen no Eigo. *Jinbun, 21*, 29–38. Kagoshima Tanki Daigaku Jinbun Gakkai (in Japanese).
Tokyo Seitoku Eigo Kenkyu-kai. 1995-1998. Seiyou no Nihon Hakken — OED ni Mirareru Nihongo I–VII —. Vol. 1–7 (in Japanese).
Tokyo Seitoku Eigo Kenkyu-kai. 2003. Seiyou no Nihon Hakken — OED Additions Series ni Mirareru Nihongo—. (in Japanese).
Toolan, M. 1997. Recentering English: New English and Global. *English Today 52, 13*(4), 3–10.
Tranter, N. 1997. Hybrid Anglo-Japanese Loans in Korean. *Linguistics, 35*, 133–166.
Ui, H. 1979. A Bilingual Period in England and Scandinavian Loan-words in English. *Bulletin of Daito Bunka University, 17*, 41–54. (in Japanese).
Ui, H. 1980. On Loan-words in English —with Special Reference to the Reason for Their Adoption. *Bulletin of Daito Bunka University, 18*, 1–17. (in Japanese).
Ui, H. 1983. On Non-European Loan-words in English. *Bulletin of Daito Bunka University, 21*, 141–155. (in Japanese).
Ui, H. 1985. *Nichiei Ryougo ni Okeru Gairaigo, Shakuyougo*. Tokyo: Hozuki Shobo. (in Japanese).
Umegaki, M. 1963. *Nihon Gairaigo no Kenkyu*. Tokyo: Kenkyusha. (in Japanese).
Wilkerson, K. T. 1997. Japanese Bilingual Brand Names. *English Today 52, 13*(4), 12–16.
Zamora, J. C. 1998. Quintilian on the Adaptation of Loanwords. *The Bilingual Review. La Revista Bilingüe, 23*(2), 108–112.

Zhang, A. 1997. China English and Chinese English. *English Today 52*, *13*(4), 39–41.

Zipf, G. K. 1935. *Psycho-Biology —An Introduction to Dynamic Philology—*. Boston: Houghton Mifflin Company.

Dictionaries and Corpora

12,000 Words. 1986. *12,000 Words: A Supplement to Webster's Third New International Dictionary.* Springfield: Merriam-Webster.

ARCHER. *A Representative Corpus of Historical English Registers.* Flagstaff: Northern Arizona University. (not publicly distributed).

BNC. 2000. *The British National Corpus* (World edition). Oxford: BNC Consortium. CD-ROM.

BROWN. 1999. The Brown University Corpus of American English. In *the ICAME Collection of English Language Corpora* (2nd edition). Bergen: The HIT Centre, University of Bergen.

FROWN. 1999. The Freiburg-Brown Corpus of American English. In *the ICAME Collection of English Language Corpora* (2nd edition). Bergen: The HIT Centre, University of Bergen.

Koujien. 1998. *Koujien* (5th edition). Tokyo: Iwanami Shoten. EPWING CDROM.

NSOED. 1993. *The New Shorter Oxford English Dictionary*, Vol. 1–2. Oxford: Clarendon Press.

ODFWP. 1997. *The Oxford Dictionary of Foreign Words and Phrases.* Oxford: Oxford University Press.

OED2. 1993. *The Oxford English Dictionary on Compact Disc* (2nd edition). Macintosh Version. Oxford: Clarendon Press. CD-ROM.

OED2v3. 2001. *The Oxford English Dictionary* (2nd edition). Oxford: Oxford University Press. CD-ROM ver. 3.

OEDAD1-2. 1993. *The Oxford English Dictionary Additions Series*, Vol. 1–2. Oxford: Clarendon Press.

OEDAD3. 1997. *The Oxford English Dictionary Additions Series*, Vol. 3. Oxford: Clarendon Press.

PONS. 1999. *PONS Großwörterbuch für Experten und Universität* (4th edition). Stuttgart: Klett.

Readers. 2000. *Readers + Plus.* Tokyo: Kenkyusha. EPWING CD-ROM ver. 2.

RHD. 1987. *The Random House Dictionary of the English Language* (2nd edition). New York: Random House.

RHWD. 1999. *Random House Webster's Unabridged Dictionary: with Illustrations and Recorded Pronunciations.* version 3.0. New York: Random House. CD-ROM.

SOED5. 2002. *The Shorter Oxford English Dictionary* (5th edition). Oxford: Oxford University Press. Book and CD-ROM.

TIME. 1995. *TIME Almanac 1995 for Macintosh.* Cambridge: Softkey. CD-ROM.

TimesCD. 1995. *The Times and the Sunday Times CD-ROM Edition.* London: Times Newspapers Ltd. CD-ROM.

TimesInternet. 1996. *The Times and the Sunday Times Internet Edition.* London: Times Newspapers Ltd. URL: http://www.the-times.co.uk/.

W3. 1986. *Webster's Third International Dictionary of the English Language.* Springfield: Merriam-Webster.

W3CD. 2000. *Webster's Third New International Dictionary, unabridged.* Springfield: Merriam-Webster. CD-ROM.

Wordbanks. 2000. *Wordbanks online.* Birmingham: Collins Cobuild. URL: titania.cobuild.collins.co.uk (renamed from *CobuildDirect*).

Summary in Japanese

借用語の英語化過程と既存語彙に与える影響
—英語における日本語とドイツ語からの借用語を中心に—[1]

1 はじめに

　言語は内的・外的な圧力を受け，常に変化し続ける．その外的な要素の主なものは外国との接触による言語借用である．古英語から現代英語に至るまで，英語は膨大な数の語彙を外国語から借用してきたが，その多くはヨーロッパ系の言語であった．現在でも英語の語彙に占めるヨーロッパ系言語からの借用語の割合は非常に高い．しかし，マルコ・ポーロがヨーロッパに『東方見聞録』をもたらして以来，ヨーロッパと世界の他の国や地域との接触が増加し，その結果，英語話者はヨーロッパ系以外の様々な言語に直接的・間接的に接触し，語彙借用の範囲を広げてきた．

　日本語からも日本の開国前後頃から数多くの単語が英語に借用されてきたが，その数は現在もますます増加する傾向にある．近年，英語に借用されている語のうち日本語はフランス語に次いで 2 番目に多いと言われている（Cannon, 1994b）．借用された語彙は発音・綴り・派生・品詞・意味などの各面で様々な変化を遂げ次第に英語の語彙として広く浸透していく．本研究の特徴の一つは，このような借用語の定着過程に注目していることである．日本語からの借用語がどのようにして英語の語彙に定着していくのかを一般化し，他の言語からの借用語とどのように異なるのか，また共通に見られる現象は何かを明らかにするため，ドイツ語からの借用語を取り上げ比較・対照する．

　本研究のもう一つの特徴は借用語が英語に定着していく過程で既存の語彙体系に与える影響を取り上げたことである．借用された語彙が英語の語彙項目として付け

---

[1] This is a modified version of a summary of this study in Japanese, presented in (Kimura-Kano 2005b).

加えられることにより，語彙の総数が増加するだけでなく，すでに存在する語彙の意味・用法が制限されたり，競合する既存語彙が新しい借用語に置き換えられるなど，様々な共存・競合関係を築き，既存の語彙体系が影響を受ける．このように，本論文は借用によって新しく英語の語彙に加えられる語が，英語に定着するまでの変化の過程を捉えるだけでなく，借用により既存の語彙体系がどのように変化していくのかという側面にも注目することによって，言語接触の結果生じる借用という現象の全体像を，導入される語彙と受け入れる語彙体系の両側面から描き出している（図1）．

```
言語Aの語彙      …日本語, ドイツ語などの語彙
   ⇓           …借用（borrowing）
外国語（Foreign Words）  …定着過程（assimilation）
   ⇓             ● 発音の変化
借用語（Loanwords）      ● 複合語 ● 接尾付加
   ⇓             ● 品詞転換 ● 意味変化など
言語Bの語彙      …英語 ● 語彙の拡大・競合
```

図1：言語借用の流れ

2 日本語からの借用語

2.1 英語辞書の中の日本語からの借用語

現在，英語辞典に登録されている日本語からの借用語は700語以上にのぼり，英字新聞や雑誌では日本語からの借用語がしばしば使用されている．その形態や使用されている意味は多岐にわたるが，それについての体系的な研究は国内外を問わず十分に行われていない．先行研究のほとんどが英語に定着した日本語を列挙しているに過ぎず，借用語の英語化過程に注目した研究のうちでも，その一般化を試みた研究はない．

Oxford English Dictionary 第2版（以下 *OED2*）を始めとする大型英語辞書[2]で借用直後から現在までの用例の変遷をたどり，借用語の時間的な推移を観察すると，日本語からの借用語は以下のような経路をたどり英語の語彙として受け入れられていくことが判明した．つまり，日本語からの借用語は，

---

[2] *ODFWP, RHD, RHWD, SOED5, W3CD*．詳細は巻末の Bibliography を参照のこと．

1. まず，強勢付与，母音の強化・弱化など発音・綴りが英語の規則に従った形に変化し（例：seppuku「切腹」[sɛpúːkuː]；jinrikisha → rickshaw「人力車」），
2. 次に，名詞が限定用法を獲得し，その語を説明する語を伴って繰り返し用いられ（例：bonsai tree「盆栽」；adzuki bean「小豆」），
3. さらには，接辞付加や複合語形成などにより，新たな語を派生する生産性を獲得する（例：kimono「着物」blouse/coat/gown/shirt/sleeve；Shinto「神道」：Shintoistic/Shintoism/Shintoist/Shintonize）．
4. 最終段階では，比喩的用法，意味の拡大・転換により，多義を持つようになり，英語の語彙として浸透し，広く使用されるに至る（例：tycoon「大君（将軍）」→「実業界の巨頭」；kamikaze「神風特攻隊」→「向こう見ずな」）．

しかし，意味転換がみられるほど英語化した日本語からの借用語はまだほんのわずかで，英語に定着した日本語の数の少なさを表している．また，表1のsoy「醬油」のように，意味変化によって新しい語義「大豆」を獲得した語の中には，その新しい意味でStage 2やStage 3に戻り，さらに語形成を行うといった循環的な変化を見せるものもある．日本語からの借用語の英語化の流れを図示すると図2のようになる．

表1：英語化の循環システムの一例

1679年	soy「醬油」の意	←	Stage 1
1795年	soy sauce「醬油」+「ソース」	←	Stage 2
1815年	soy bottle「醬油瓶」, soy frame「醬油立て」	←	Stage 3
1880年	soy「大豆」の意	←	Stage 4
1897年	soy flour「大豆粉」, soy biscuits「大豆ビスケット」,...	←	新義でStage 3

2.2 コーパスの中の日本語からの借用語

上記のように導き出された英語化の過程を検証するために，TIME Almanac (1995)とThe Times and the Sunday Times (1995)を資料として日本語からの借用語が実際にどのように使用されているかを調査した．英語化が進んでいると思われる語を中心に検索した結果，固有名詞や専門用語を除けば，大半が辞書から導き出された結果と合致したが，新たな意味転換の例や辞書には登録されていない派生語も発見され，辞書の記述をアップデートすることができた．日本語からの借用語の数を英語化の段階毎に表2にまとめた．

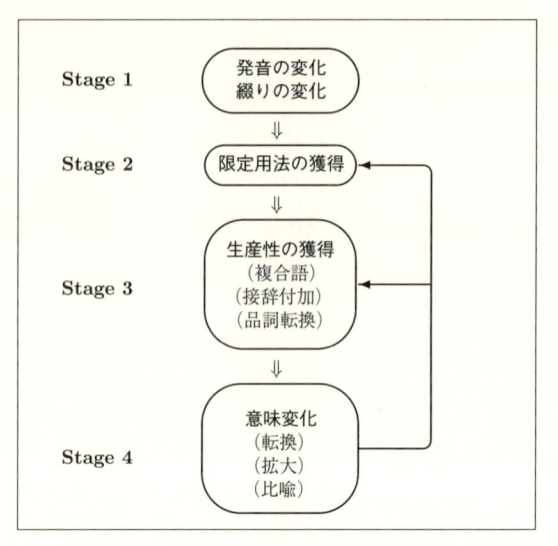

図 2：日本語からの借用語の英語化過程

表 2：日本語からの借用語の英語化度

英語化度	観察される変化	該当語数 (%)
Stage 1	発音，綴り	596 (77.6%)
Stage 2	名詞の限定用法	103 (13.4%)
Stage 3	生産性の獲得	24 (3.1%)
Stage 4	意味変化	15 (2.0%)
その他[a]		30 (3.9%)
Total		768 (100%)

a. 2.3 節で述べる二次的借用語（26 語）と Stage 1 に達しない（=強勢付与がされていない）語（4 語）が含まれる．

(167) に Stage 3, Stage 4 に分類された語を挙げる．

(167) **Stage 3:** *bonsai, ricksha(w)*, *Kabuki*「歌舞伎」, *karaoke*「カラオケ」, *karate*「空手」, *kendo*「剣道」, *kudzu*「葛」, *Meiji*「明治」, *Nippon*「日本」, *Noh*「能」, *Okinawan*「沖縄人」, *origami*「折り紙」, *Ryukyu (an)*「琉球（人）」, *saké*「酒」, *shiatsu*「指圧」, *Shinto*, *sumo*「相撲」, *sushi*「寿司」, *Suzuki*「スズキ（バイオリン）」, *tofu*「豆腐」, *tatami*「畳」, *teriyaki*「照り焼き」, *Tokugawa*「徳川」, *yen*「円」．

Stage 4:
- 意味拡大：*futon*「布団」, *geisha*「芸者」, *honcho*「班長」, *kimono*, *samurai*「侍」, *shogun*「将軍」;
- 意味転換：*kamikaze*, *soy(a)*「醤油・大豆」, *tycoon*;
- 比喩的用法：*hara-kiri*, *jujitsu*, *tsunami*「津波」, *judo*「柔道」, *Zen*「禅」.

2.3 二次的借用語

日本語からの借用語には上記のように日本語の語彙の音をそのまま借用した直接借用語のほかに特殊な借用形態がある．それらは，日本語から導入されたにもかかわらず，英語の語彙で構成された語・句で，本論文では二次的借用語と呼ぶ．二次的借用語は直接借用語とは異なる英語化の過程を持つ可能性があるので，区別して調査を行った．(168) に二次的借用語の例を示す．

(168) a. 翻訳借用：意味だけを借用して英語の単語に直訳・意訳して表す．
　　　　（例：*plum rain*「梅雨」, *black belt*「黒帯」, *bullet train*「新幹線」, *comfort woman*「慰安婦」, *just-in-time*「かんばん方式」など）
　　b. 外来語の借用：日本語に借用された外来語を逆に借用する．
　　　　（例：*beddo*「回転式ベッド」, *shokku*「日本に関する政治・経済事件のショック」など）
　　c. 和製英語の借用：英語を使って日本人が新たに造語した語を借用する．
　　　　（例：*eroduction*「安手の日本向け／日本製のポルノ映画」, *salary man*「サラリーマン」, *Walkman*「ウォークマン」など）

これらの語は英語語源の語彙で構成されているため，発音・綴りを変化させたり，限定用法で語の意味を説明する必要がない場合が多く，直接借用語のように4段階の英語化過程とは異なる過程を経て英語化が進んでいくことを解明した．

2.4 意味と文脈のマトリクス

また本論文では，借用語の意味と使用される文脈に注目して，日本語からの借用語がどのように英語の中で用いられているのかを探った．意味と文脈の組み合わせを行（a：原義，b：新義，c：その他）と列（I：日本，II：日本以外）に取ったマトリクスを用い，それぞれの借用語がどのような意味・文脈で多く使用されているのかを視覚的に捉えられるようにした．その結果，Stage 4 に分類した語の間でも，常

に「日本」という概念から切り離され完全に英語に定着した語（*honcho, tycoon*），「日本」という文脈で使われることもあり，定着途上にあるもの（*futon, kamikaze, kimono, soy*），主に原義で用いられる語（*judo, samurai, zen*）など，定着度に違いがあることが明らかになった．また，英語化がまだあまり進んでいないと思われる Stage 1–3 の語と比較した結果，借用語が英語に導入されてから定着するに至るまでの変化の方向性を見ることができた（表3）．

表3：日本語からの借用語の意味・文脈の変化

	(a) 原義	(b) 新義	(c) 他
(II) 日本以外の文脈 Stage 4 ⇒ Stage 3 ⇧		⇒ Stage 4	
(I) 日本の文脈 ⇧ Stage 3 Stage 1, 2			

3　ドイツ語からの借用語

3.1　英語における各国語からの借用語の推移

Oxford Dictionary of Foreign Words and Phrases (1997) の収録語を調査し，英語に導入された借用語の数の借用元の言語毎の年代別推移を表4にまとめた．それによると，20世紀の借用語の傾向はそれ以前と大きく異なっていることが読み取れる．つまり，ロマンス語系の言語（フランス語・ラテン語・イタリア語・スペイン語）が19世紀までは増加傾向にあるが，20世紀には減少傾向に転じる一方で，ドイツ語・ロシア語・日本語などのロマンス語系以外の言語からの借用語が増加している．

3.2　英語における最近の借用語

近年の借用語の傾向を知り，最近の英語の中の借用語における日本語からの借用語の位置づけを明らかにするために，日本語からの借用語と2つの言語からの最近の借用語を比較した．一つは日本語からの借用語同様20世紀になって増加傾向にあるドイツ語からの借用語，もう一つは20世紀の借用語の数が類似しているスペイン語である．*OED2* の中で1949年以降に初出の語を対象に，付されているラベルや発

Summary in Japanese 217

表 4：上位 11 言語からの借用語数の推移

	Fr	L	It	Sp	G	Gk	Jp	Ar	Sk	R	Y	Total
古英語	1	9	0	0	0	0	0	0	0	0	0	10
中英語	37	24	1	0	1	3	0	0	0	0	0	66
後期中英語	97	136	0	0	0	9	0	0	0	0	0	242
15 世紀	22	14	0	0	0	0	0	0	0	0	0	36
16 世紀	123	289	54	39	1	19	0	11	1	5	0	542
17 世紀	308	366	71	57	6	36	9	19	6	2	1	881
18 世紀	485	175	183	40	13	23	17	20	32	6	0	994
19 世紀	1041	284	229	215	192	63	67	56	46	27	30	2250
20 世紀	615	118	136	126	<u>204</u>	49	<u>99</u>	18	18	<u>57</u>	<u>59</u>	1499
Total	2729	1415	674	477	417	202	192	124	103	97	90	6520

Fr：フランス語，L：ラテン語，It：イタリア語，Sp：スペイン語，G：ドイツ語，Gk：ギリシャ語，
Jp：日本語，Ar：アラビア語，Sk：サンスクリット語，R：ロシア語，Y：イディシュ語

表 5：*OED2* の初例が 1940 年以降の日本語・ドイツ語・スペイン語からの借用語

	日本語	ドイツ語	スペイン語
総数	68	122[a]	48
俗語・口語	4 (5.9%)	18 (14.8%)	5 (10.4%)
学術用語	7 (10.3%)	33 (27.0%)	5 (10.4%)
名詞以外	2 (2.9%)	19 (15.6%)	3 (6.3%)
‖ 付の語	45 (66.2%)	52 (42.6%)	24 (50.0%)
限定用法	13 (19.1%)	8 (6.6%)	0 (0.0%)
不規則変化	2 (2.9%)	11 (9.0%)	3 (6.3%)
外国語的発音[b]	27 (39.7%)	32 (26.2%)	21 (43.8%)
生産性（複合語）	17 (25.0%)	18 (14.8%)	7 (14.6%)
生産性（接辞付加）	4 (5.9%)	28 (23.0%)	1 (2.1%)
生産性（品詞転換）	4 (5.9%)	11 (9.0%)	7 (14.6%)
意味変化	3 (4.4%)	11 (9.0%)	1 (2.1%)

a. イディシュ語を経由した間接借用語 18 語を含む．
b. 強勢のないもの，英語にはない音素が含まれるもの．ドイツ語からの借用語の発音については 3.3 節で述べる．

音や綴りの変化や活用形の規則性，語形成，意味変化などの特徴を調査した結果を表 5 にまとめた．

この 3 言語からの借用語のうち，ドイツ語からの借用語が最も多くなっているが，これはドイツにおける現代科学（鉱物学・化学の分野など）の発展により，学術用語が多く借用されたためである．俗語・口語が多いのはアメリカにおけるユダヤ人系移民が使用するイディシュ語を経由して借用されたものが多いことに因る．また，

名詞以外の借用語の割合が高いことも顕著である．

一方，日本語からの借用語は英語化が進んでいない語に付される ‖ のラベルや，同じく英語化が進んでいない語に多く観察される限定用法の割合が他の2言語からの借用語より高いことから，英語化が進む速度がより遅い，あるいは英語化される語の割合がより少ないことが予測される．また，ドイツ語には英語とは異なる名詞の複数形の体系があるため，ドイツ語からの借用語は原語の複数形を保つ傾向が強く，名詞が不規則変化活用を持つ割合が高いと推測される．発音については，各語とも多かれ少なかれ原語に特徴的な音を残している（[a] [o] [e:] [x] [y] [ø] など）借用語が見られた．

語の生産性についてもそれぞれ異なる特徴が見られる．ドイツ語からの借用語については接辞付加が，日本語からの借用語では複合語が，スペイン語からの借用語では品詞転換が最も多く観察された．本調査は比較的新しい語に限定して行ったため，意味変化は多くは見られないが，それでもドイツ語からの借用語は早くも11語が意味変化をしており，英語化の速度や変化の過程の違いを示唆している．

3.3　英語辞書の中のドイツ語からの借用語

ドイツ語からの借用語については，2節の日本語からの借用語と同様の分析を行い，日本語からの借用語の英語化過程との比較を行った．調査に用いた辞書は日本語からの借用語の分析同様，*OED2* をはじめとする大型辞書[3]である．その結果，ドイツ語からの借用語は日本語からの借用語に見られたような4段階の英語化過程を経るのではなく，様々な側面から順不同に，あるいは同時に英語化が進んでいくことが判明した．

ドイツ語からの借用語の発音の変化には，借用後早い段階で起こる基本的変化（例：'o' [ɔ] → [ɒ]，'b' [p] → [b]）と，それより後に起こる，あるいは変化せずに維持される傾向の強い音素がある（例：'a' [a]，'s' [z]）．変化しにくい音から英語化されやすい音の分布を図3に示した．また，日本語からの借用語にはすべての語に対して強勢付与が必要であるが，ドイツ語からの借用語はドイツ語での強勢を持っているので，それを保持することが多い．

活用語尾の有無，規則性については，日本語では複数語尾が付かない語や集合名詞として扱われる語が多いが，ドイツ語の場合は原語の複数語尾を保持しているもの，英語の規則に則したもの，その両方の複数形をとり得るものの3種類があり，英語の規則に従わない複数形の割合は日本語よりも高い（25.4%）という結果が得ら

---

[3] *ODFWP, RHD, RHWD, SOED5, W3CD*. 詳細は巻末の Bibliography を参照のこと．

			'b' [b]	
'j' [j]	'a' [a]/[æ]	'sp' [ʃp]/[sp]	'd' [d]	
'v' [f]	's' [z]/[s]	'st' [ʃt]/[st]	'er' [ɜː]	
'z' [ts]	'w' [v]/[w]	'u' [ʊ]/[ʌ]	'o' [ɒ]	'r' /ɹ/

← 変化しにくい　　　　　　　　　　　　英語化されやすい →

図3：ドイツ語からの借用語の音素の変化・無変化スペクトラム

れた．

　生産性の獲得に関しては，日本語からの借用語には語を説明するような限定用法が多く見られるが，ドイツ語からの借用語にはそのような用法は21例(5.0%)しか確認されず，日本語からの借用語のように繰り返し用いられる例はほとんどなかった．このことから，ドイツ語からの借用語においては限定用法は英語化過程の一段階とは見なされないことが判明した．ドイツ語からの借用語は日本語からの借用語よりも高い割合(28.9%)で自由な語形成を行う生産性を獲得している（例：*gestalt*「ゲシュタルト，形態」：*psychology/theory/school, -ism/ist* など；*polka*「ポルカ（踊り・音楽）・ポルカ（ジャケット・水玉模様）」：*step/hats, -dot/ist/ic* など；*kindergarten*「幼稚園」：*songs/instruction, -ize/er/ism* など）．

　意味変化をした語は日本語からの借用語より圧倒的に高い割合(21.5%)を占めている（例：*blitz(krieg)*「ロンドン大空襲」→「電撃作戦，大キャンペーン」，*Gestapo*「ゲシュタポ（ナチスの）」→「秘密警察（一般に）」，*Götterdämmerung*「神々のたそがれ（楽劇），崩壊」，*kraut*「ザウワークラウト」→「ドイツ兵」）．しかも，意味変化をした語は必ずしも生産性を獲得しているわけではない．このことから，ドイツ語からの借用語は日本語からの借用語のように，生産性の獲得が意味変化の前段階にあるという体系は成り立たないことが判明した．

　その他の特徴としては，文化的借用が高い割合を占める日本語からの借用語と異なり，ドイツ語からの借用語は科学技術の各分野において学術用語を提供するという役割があること，既存概念の特殊化・専門化が多く行われるため，新概念の借用の割合が低いこと，翻訳借用の多さや翻訳借用された語の直接借用との共存の多さなどが挙げられる．ドイツ語からの借用語の特徴は表6にまとめた．

表6：ドイツ語からの借用語の特徴

総数	418 (100%)	発音の変化[a]	186 (44.5%)
学術用語	95 (22.7%)	不規則変化	106 (25.4%)
‖付の語	284 (67.9%)	限定用法	21 (5.0%)
名詞以外の借用語	33 (7.9%)	生産性の獲得	121[b] (28.9%)
新概念	213 (51.0%)	― 複合語	100 (23.9%)
翻訳借用の併用	43 (10.3%)	― 接辞付加	38 (9.1%)
		― 品詞転換[c]	18 (4.3%)
		意味変化	90 (21.5%)

a. 母音や母音化した [r] の弱化や欠落は除く．
b. 一種類以上の生産性を獲得しているものもある．
c. 名詞から形容詞への品詞転換は叙述的用法のみ含む．

3.4　コーパスの中のドイツ語からの借用語

コーパスに基づく分析では1億語のイギリス英語の話し言葉と書き言葉からなる *British National Corpus*（以下 *BNC*）を用いた．*BNC* での検証では辞書には未登録の新たな語法や語形が見つかり，辞書による調査をアップデートすることができたばかりではなく，辞書での調査とは異なる結果を得た点もあった．辞書での調査では，名詞の複数形の不規則活用形が多く見られたが，実際の英語のテキストにはギリシャ語・ラテン語源でドイツ語経由で借用された語と，ごく限られたドイツ語起源の語しか不規則変化の複数語尾を伴って使用されることはないことを明らかにした（例：*schemata*「概要・略図」，*Lieder*「ドイツ歌曲」，*wunderkinder*「神童」）．また，限定用法については，英語辞書で確認された以外にも数例確認されたものの，日本語からの借用語のように繰り返し用いられることはなく，ドイツ語からの借用語においては限定用法は英語化過程の一段階とは見なされないという辞書での調査結果を支持した．

現在，強い生産性とともに多義を持ち，英語化が進んでいるとみなされるドイツ語からの借用語を (169) に挙げる．

(169) *abseil*「アプザイレン・懸垂下降」，*angst*「不安・苦悩」，*blitz(krieg)*「電撃戦・大キャンペーン」，*delicatessen*「調製食品，総菜屋」，*ersatz*「代替の，代替品」，*Führer*「総統，指導者」，*gestalt*，*hamburger*「ハンバーガー」，*Hanse*「ハンザ同盟，商人組合」，*junker*「貴公子」，*kindergarten*，*kitsch*「キッチュ・低級作品」，*kraut*，*lager*「ラガービール」，*lumpen(proletariat)*「浮浪者的，ルンペンの」，*panzer*「装甲車」，*polka*，*poltergeist*「騒霊，ポルターガイスト」，*shaman*「シャーマン，まじない師」，*sinter*「焼結物・湯の花」

4 英語化過程の比較

ドイツ語からの借用語は，語によって異なる側面から英語化が進み，時には複数の変化が同時進行することもあるので，日本語のように共通した4段階を提示することはできない．しかし，生産性を持ち，複数の意味を持つ，高い英語化の段階に至るまでには，音韻的変化・不規則変化語尾の規則化などはほぼ終了していることが明らかになった．図4，図5は日本語・ドイツ語からの借用語のそれぞれの英語化の時間的流れを図示したものである．

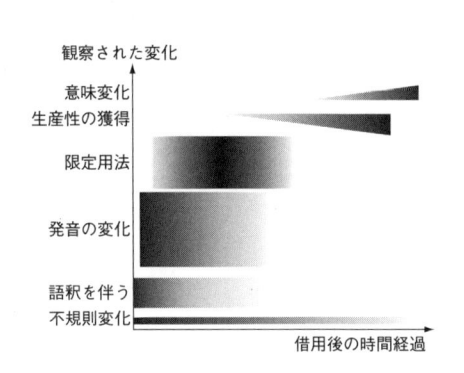

図4：日本語からの借用語の英語化過程

図5：ドイツ語からの借用語の英語化過程

5 借用語と既存語彙の共存・競合パターン

借用語が英語の語彙に加わると，総語彙数が増加するだけではなく，借用元の言語の活用規則を保持し，英語としては不規則な複数形語尾を持つ名詞や，単複同形の名詞など不規則変化の語彙の増加にもつながる．

さらに，借用語の中には英語の既存語彙の中に同じ意味を持つ語彙が存在するものや，英語化の結果，既存語彙と同じ意味を持つようになるものがあり，借用語と既存語彙で同義語のペアまたはグループが生まれる．同義語間で用法に競合が生じると，意味や使用範囲の棲み分けが起こり，共存関係が構築されることや，既存語彙が借用語に置き換えられるなどの現象がみられる．この様な競合関係を分類し，*OED2* をはじめとする英語辞書の記述や *BNC* などの英語コーパスからの用例を基に以下の分析を行った．

- 主に出現する分野・媒体の特徴を探るために，それぞれの分野・媒体での frequency per million（百万語中に出現する頻度）を比較．
- log-likelyhood（ある語の前後に現れる語との結びつきの強さを表す統計値）を用いて，それぞれの語のコロケーションパターンを抽出．

その結果，借用語と既存語彙の競合は以下の 4 パターンに分類できることを解明した．

パターン 1 借用語が限定的な使用範囲を持つ．
（例：*honcho* < *boss, leader*；*kamikaze* < *reckless, self-destructive*；*tsunami* < *tidal wave*；*bergschrund* < *crevasse*；*ersatz* < *substitute*；*gesellschaft*「利益社会」< *association*；*umwelt*「環境」< *environment*；*verstehen*「了解」< *understanding*；*kanban* < *just-in-time, JIT*；*gestalt* < *configuration*）

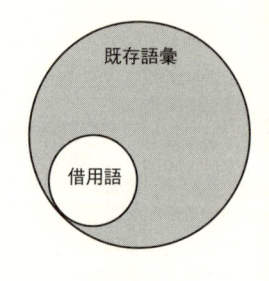

tsunami と *tidal wave* の同義語ペア[4]を例に取ると，*tsunami* は 80 パーセント近くという圧倒的多数が「自然科学」の分野で気象用語として使用されている一方で *tidal wave* は様々な分野で実際の波以外のこと，例えば a tidal wave of supernatural horrors（「超自然的恐怖に襲われること」）のような様々な感情のうねりや，the rising tidal wave of crime（「急速に増加する犯罪」）のような大きな動きを形容し，比喩的に「余暇」や「芸術」の分野でも多用されている．さらに「自然科学」の分野に出現した *tidal wave* は，すべて *tsunami* の前後に現れて *tsunami* の説明をしている．これらのことから *tsunami* は気象学の専門用語として限定的に使用され，しかもまだ *tidal wave* という語で説明を伴わないと認知されないこともある知名度の低い語であるが，今後徐々に *tidal wave* を置き換えると推測される[5]．

---

[4] 元来，英語では「津波」は *tidal wave* と呼ばれ，潮（tide）の満ち引きに関係のある波だと信じられていたが，近年，津波は潮の満ち引きとは関係ないと科学的に証明されたことから，*tidal wave* を改めて *tsunami* と呼ぶようになってきたという経緯がある．

[5] 2004 年 12 月 26 日に発生したスマトラ島沖地震は *tsunami* という単語とその恐怖を世界中に知らしめた．今後の *tsunami* の意味・用法の拡大が予測される．

パターン 2 借用語がより広い使用範囲を持つ.
(例:*harakiri*「切腹」 > *disembowel(ment)*; *glockenspiel*
「鉄琴」 > *carillon*; *shiatsu* > *acupressure*)

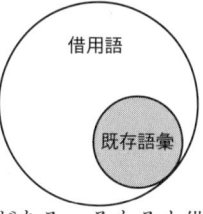

これらの語は同義語の既存語彙のほうが低頻度だという特徴がある.そもそも借用語のほうの頻度も高くないので,これらの概念自体が英語ではそれほど重要度の高いものではないといえる.

パターン 3 既存語彙と借用語が重なる使用範囲を持ち共存する.
(例:*doppelgänger*「生き霊,分身」⇔ *wraith*;
tycoon ⇔ *magnate*; *realpolitik*「現実政策」⇔
practical politics; *wunderkind* ⇔ *prodigy*)

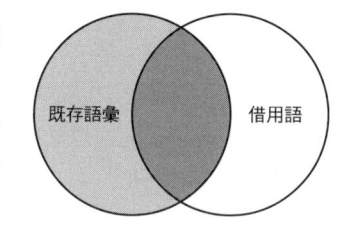

tycoon と *magnate* の同義語ペアは両語とも頻度が高い上に,ほかにも同じ意味を持つ語が多く存在するので,それらの語を併せて 6 節で同義語グループの競合・共存関係として,取り上げる.

パターン 4 それぞれが異なる使用範囲を持つ.
(例:*angst* ⇐ | ⇒ *anxiety*)

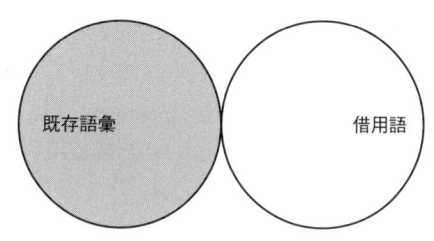

anxiety と *angst* の同義語ペアでは以下のように異なる使用範囲・用法を持っていることが明らかになった.

(170) a. *anxiety*:「応用科学」の分野で主に使用され,社会生活で人が感じる「不安」を指す.ストレス,憂鬱,恐怖,罪悪感などの語句と並列して用いられる.

　　　b. *angst*:「芸術」の分野で主に使用され,哲学的テーマとして／思春期・十代の「苦悩」を指して用いられる.芸術家によって映画や音楽などで表現されることが多いが,国家が抱える「不安」を指すこともある.

この4つのパターンのうち，借用語と既存語彙の同義語のペアはパターン1の関係にあるものが多く，借用語がごく限られた分野でのみ用いられる専門用語としての地位しか持たないことが多いことが分かる．一方で，パターン2, 3, 4の同義語ペアも複数存在し，中には様々な言語からの借用語と複数の既存語彙で同じ意味を表す同義語群を成し，それぞれ異なる使用範囲を持ちつつ共存するものや，借用語の頻度が既存語彙の頻度を大きく上回り，語彙の置き換えが起こりつつあるのではないかと思われるものもあり，借用語が確実に英語の既存語彙体系を変化させていることを示した．

6 ケーススタディ：*magnate* と *tycoon*

借用語と既存語彙の同義語ペアのケーススタディとして「実業界の巨頭」を表す *tycoon* と *magnate* を取り上げ，*OED2*, *BNC* を用いて様々な側面から分析・比較を行った．その結果，この同義語ペアは使用される時代の範囲が違い，*magnate* には新旧2種類の用法があること，*tycoon* と *magnate* の現代の用法は類似しているものの，それぞれ異なる傾向を持っていることが判明した．例えば，この2語と共起する語を頻度順に並べると，その人物が富を築いている業界を示す単語や人物名が上位に並ぶ．2語に共通する部分はあるものの，*tycoon* は商業・事業名（property, media, business）と，*magnate* は工業・製造業名（industorial, oil, shipping）と共起して用いられるという傾向が見られる．また，使用されるテキストの分野別に出現頻度を比較すると *tycoon* は「レジャー」の分野で，*magnate* は「美術」の分野で多く用いられるという特徴が明らかになった．さらに，それぞれのテキストの内容を分析すると，「レジャー」の分野での *tycoon* の使用は汚職スキャンダルやプライベートでの豪遊，離婚劇などを主にタブロイド紙に書き立てられたものである一方，「芸術」の分野での *magnate* は骨董品や美術品に財を投じたりコレクションを美術館に寄贈するなどの内容の芸術関係の新聞・雑誌の記事の中で使用されていることが多く，これら2語で表される人物像に相違があることを述べた．その他，指示する人物，同格の名詞の位置，主に使用される数（単数・複数）などにそれぞれ異なる傾向を持っていることなどを明らかにした．

さらに，*tycoon* と *magnate* のその他の同義語（例：*mogul*, *tsar*, *mandarin* ; *baron*, *king*, *lord*, *prince* ; *bigwig*, *big-gun*, *big-shot*, *big man*）を取り上げ，同義語グループとしてそれらとの相互関係に焦点をあて，それらが使用される分野や共起する語の分布を示し，共存・競合関係を詳説した．使用される分野としては，*prince* 以外の同義語は *tycoon* と *mangate* で重なり合う4つの分野（「芸術」,「商

業・通商」,「レジャー」,「世界情勢」)のいずれか,あるいは複数の分野と重なり合っている. prince はそのいずれとも重ならない「小説」の分野で主に用いられる. それぞれの使用分野の重なりを図 6 に示した.

この同義語グループの語が用いられている文中で,その前後に現れる語を頻度の高いものから並べると,それぞれの巨頭が力を持っている業界に違いがあることを示唆する語が並ぶ. 図 7 では,実業界の巨頭の意味で用いられる例が多かった 3 つの語 (*tycoon, magnate, baron*) を中心にそれぞれの語で表される巨頭が力を持っている業界を表した. media, newspaper はこの 3 語すべてに共通する共起語であるが, *tycoon* に固有なのは business, film, publishing などビジネス・マスコミ関係の語, *magnate* に固有なのは industrial, oil, shipping, cotton, steel, press など工業・産業の名前, *baron* と共起するのは drug が圧倒的多数を占める. これらのことから, *tycoon* は商業界, *magnate* は工業界, *baron* は麻薬取引組織などが権力の及ぶ範囲として典型的であることが読みとれる.

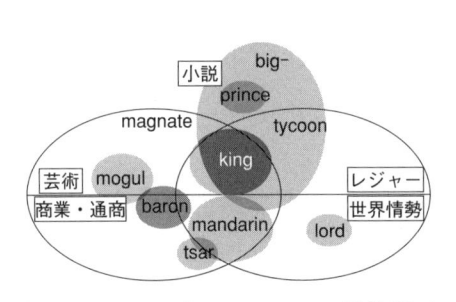

図 6: *Tycoon* と *Magnate* の類義語グループの使用分野

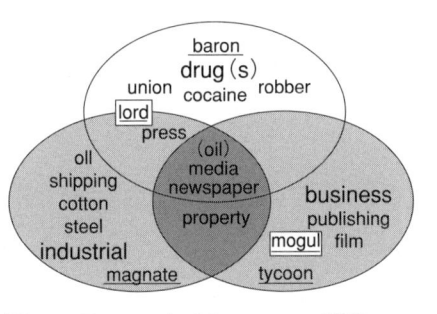

図 7: *Tycoon* と *Magnate* の類義語グループのコロケーション

7 まとめと今後の展望

本研究では英語における日本語からの借用語とドイツ語からの借用語に焦点を当て,借用語に見られる形態的・意味的変化を捉え,それぞれの言語からの借用語の英語化の過程を解明した. また借用語が既存の語彙に与える影響の一つとして借用語と既存語彙の共存・競合関係を観察し,4 つの競合パターンに分類した. 現代英語において借用は新語彙導入の主要な方法ではないが,英語話者が他言語話者と接触する限り英語に新しい語彙を提供し続けるであろう. 特に,増加傾向にあると言われている日本語からの借用語には,今後どのような語が加えられ,英語の語彙として定着していくのか,またそれらが既存の語彙体系にどのように影響を与えていくのか注目していきたい.

Appendix A Productive Forms of Japanese Loanwords in *TIME Almanac*

Classification	Items
Compounds	geisha girls
	harakiri tactic
	hiragana script
	judo style, judo doll, judo competitor
	jujitsu coup, jujitsu skill
	Kabuki theater, Kabuki star, Kabuki whiteness, Kabuki drama
	kamikaze mission, kamikaze reputation, kamikaze competition,
	kamikaze attack, kamikaze airmen, kamikaze team, Kamikaze plane,
	kamikaze bandanna, kamikaze flight, kamikaze right-winger
	kamikaze corps, kamikaze kids, kamikaze band,
	kamikaze Yankee owner
	karaoke parlor, karaoke bars
	karate ring, karate black belt, karate chop, karate classes,
	karate instructor, karate expert
	Meiji Restoration, Meiji Constitution, Meiji era
	Nippon hysteria
	Nisei outcasts, Nisei students, nisei son
	Okinawa bunkers and foxholes
	ricksha pullers
	eel-and-sake dinner
	samurai sword, samurai class, samurai warrior, samurai epic,
	samurai work ethic, pseudo-samurai businessman, samurai comic,
	samurai work ethic, Samurai Night Live gang, samurai biker,
	Samurai Spuds-san
	soy sauce, soy bean(s), soy ink, soy diesel fuel, soy milk
	soybean rust fungus, soybean crop(s), soybean king,

Classification	Items
	soybean formulas, soybean processor, soybean farmers, soybean pit, soybean traders, soybean brokers, soybean oil, soybean contract, soybean crackers and milk, soybean bran, soybean future price
	tsunami alerts, tsunami wave
	shiatsu massage, shiatsu person, shiatsu masseuse
	Shinto shrine, Shinto ceremony, Shinto priests, Shinto ritual, Shinto beliefs, Shinto sun goddess Amaterasu, Shinto high priest
	sushi bar, sushi chefs, sushi lovers, sushi eater, sushi deliveries, sushi waitress
	tatami mat
	teriyaki salsa, beef, burger
	Tokugawa seclusion
	Zen politics, Zen expressionism, Zen retreat, Zen meditation, Zen genius, Zen experience, Zen teacher, Zen name, Zen practice, Zen approach, Zen instructor, Zen garden, Zen mode, Zen rock gardening, Zen machismo, Zen student, Zen candidate, Zen bunkers, Zen Buddhism, Zen roshi, Zen characters, Zen state, Zen archery, Zen Buddhist, Zen manner, pseudo-Zen profundities, Zen state of suspended agitation
Hyphenation	kamikaze-style(d)
	samurai-like
	soy-based, soy-sunflower soy-bean, soybean-futures
	tsunami-sized
	karate-skilled,
	Meiji-era
	Zen-heavy, Zen-like, Zen-minded, Zenned-out
Suffixation	kimonoed
	shogunate, shogunism, shogunist
	tycoonery
	karatecize
	Okinawan
	Nipponese
	zenlike, Zenned
Functional Shifts	kamikaze (*adj.*), karate-kick (*v.*), karate-chop (*v.*)

Appendix B Productive Forms of Japanese Loanwords in *The Times*

Classification	Items
Compounds	geisha artwork, geisha doll, geisha girls, geisha houses, geisha persona
	judo centre, judo champion, judo championship, judo club, judo coach, judo competition, judo contestants, judo countries, judo dictum, judo event, judo fighter, judo gold medallist, judo mat, judo medal, judo nations, judo perfection, judo players, judo squad, judo star, judo success, judo talent, judo team, judo title, judo tournament, Judo Union
	kamikaze actor, kamikaze attacker, kamikaze campaign, kamikaze challenge, kamikaze flight, Kamikaze Ken, kamikaze man, kamikaze manoeuvres, kamikaze mission, kamikaze mood, kamikaze overtaking manoeuvre, kamikaze performance, kamikaze plane, Kamikaze Redoubler, kamikaze resignations, kamikaze satellite, kamikaze stakes, kamikaze terrorism, kamikaze troops
	kimono designer, kimono design
	Kabuki actor, Kabuki actor and dancer, kabuki Hamlet, kabuki musical, kabuki theatre
	karaoke backing, karaoke bars, karaoke channel, karaoke classic, karaoke club, karaoke Conservatism, karaoke craze, karaoke evenings, karaoke facility, karaoke king, karaoke machine, karaoke microphone, karaoke night, karaoke novelty record, karaoke outing, karaoke parlours, karaoke party, karaoke renditions, karaoke restaurant, karaoke rig, karaoke session, Karaoke sex, Karaoke Shakespeare, karaoke song, karaoke tape, karaoke videos
	karate attack, karate belt, karate black belt, karate bout, karate buddies, karate brown belt, karate business,

Classification	Items
	karate champion, karate club, karate championships,
	karate chop, karate display, karate expert, karate highkick,
	karate instructor, karate kick, karate moves, karate pyjamas,
	karate school, karate showman, karate techniques,
	karate tournament, Karate Union
	Noh drama, Noh movements, Noh Music Concert, Noh play,
	Noh theatre
	origami night, origamist
	Rickshaw Company, rickshaw drivers, rickshaw riders,
	rickshaw service, Rickshaw snag, rickshaw wallahs
	Ryukyu islands
	Samurai Cowboy, samurai epics, samurai family, samurai palace,
	Samurai sword-wielding, samurai swords, samurai warrior,
	samurai version
	sayonara pet
	shiatsu massage
	Shinto doctrine, Shinto element, Shinto gods, Shinto priests,
	Shinto religion, Shinto rituals, Shinto shrines,
	Shinto value-systems
	soy products, Soy protein, soy sauce
	Soya beans, soya flour, soya flour or oil, soya milk, soya oil,
	soya products, soya sauce
	soy(a)bean
	Sushi restaurant, sushi knives, sushi box, Sushi chic, sushi bars,
	sushi chef, sushi rolls
	Suzuki weekend music course
	tatami mat-weaver, tatami mats
	teriyaki sauce
	Ukiyo-e school, Ukiyo-e artists
	Zen master, Zen Buddhism, Zen practices, Zen Buddhist method,
	Zen meditation, Zen Central, Zen Video Theatre, Zen novel,
	Zen harmony
Hyphenation	karaoke-entertainment, karaoke-fashion, karaoke-singing,
	karaoke-style,
	karate-kick, karate-kicking, karate-like, karate-style, karate-type

Classification	Items
	noh-theatre
	shiatsu-practising
	soya-based
	sushi-making
Suffixation	Nipponese
	Shintoism
Functional Shifts	kamikaze (*adj.*), karate-kick (*v.*), Zen (*adj.*)

Appendix C Japanese Loanwords in English Dictionaries

	Item	O	W	R	S5	FW	Dic.	→	Corp.
1	abukumalite			○			1		
2	aburachan seed			○			1		
3	aburagiri			○			1		
4	acupressure	M	○	M		M	×		
5	adzuki (bean)	L	○	○	○	○	2		
6	aikido	L	○	○	○	○	1		
7	akamatsu			○			1		
8	akamushi mite			○			1		
9	Akashi		D				1		
10	Akebi(a)	L	○	○			1		
11	akeki			○			1		
12	akenobeite			○			1		
13	Akihito		D				1		
14	Akita	E	D	○		○	1		
15	ama	L	○	○	○	○	1		
16	amado	L				○	1		
17	Amagasaki		D	○			1		
18	amanori			○			1		
19	Amidism (-st)			○			1		
20	anime		○			○	×		
21	ansu			○			1		
22	Aomori		○				1		
23	Aoyama's fluid			○			1		
24	arakawaite			○			1		
25	arame					○	1		
26	arigato			○			1		
27	arisaka			○			2		
28	Arita (ware)	D		○		○	3	→	1
29	Asahik(/g)awa		D	○			1		
30	Ashikaga		D				1		
31	ashura			○			1		
32	Asosan		D				1		
33	aucuba	L	○	○		○	1		
34	awabi	L		○	○	○	1		
35	Awaji		D				1		

O: *OED2*, **W:** *W3*, **R:** *RDH*, **FW:** *ODFWP*, **S5:** *SOED5* ○: Registered, **E:** Etymology Search, **D:** Definition Search, **T:** Text Search, **M:** Manual Search **Dic.:** The Result of Dictionary Study, **Corp.:** The Result of Corpus Study **0:** No Assimilation ×: Not Applicable (Secondary Loanwords) **1:** Pronunciation and Orthography Assimilation **2:** Attributive Use **3:** Productivity Acquisition **4:** Semantic Shift

Appendix C 233

	Item	O	W	R	S5	FW	Dic.	→	Corp.
36	ayu/ai			○			1		
37	Azuchi-Momoyama		○				1		
38	bai-u	L		○			1		
39	baka bomb			○			1		
40	bancha			○		○	1		
41	bandaite			○			1		
42	banzai	L	○	○	○	○	4	→	2
43	banzuke				○	○	1		
44	baren	L		○			1		
45	Basho [poet]		○				1		
46	basho [sumo]	L			○	○	1		
47	bekko	L					1		
48	bento, obento		D			○	1		
49	Beta(max)	L					×		
50	Biwa [lake]		○				1		
51	biwa [music]		D	○			1		
52	Bizen ware				○		2		
53	black belt	T	○	M		M	×		
54	bokken					○	1		
55	bon-seki			○			1		
56	Bon, Obon	L	○	○			2		
57	bonsai	L	○	○	○	○	2	→	3
58	bonze	L	D	○		○	1		
59	brown belt	M	○			M	×		
60	bu (1) [coin]			○			1		
61	bu (2) [length]			○			1		
62	budo			○			1		
63	bugaku		○	○	○	○	1		
64	bullet train	D	D	M		D	×		
65	bunraku	L	○	○	○	○	2		
66	Burakumin		D				1		
67	bushido	L	D	○	○	○	1		
68	butoh			○			1		
69	butsu		○				1		
70	butsudan			○			1		
71	cat(t)an			○			1		
72	chanoyu		○	○			1		
73	chiba		D	○			1		
74	cho			○			1		
75	chorogi		○	○			1		
76	chosenese			○			1		
77	daibutsu		○				1		
78	daikon		○	○			1		
79	daimio (-myo)	L	○	○	○	○	3	→	1
80	dairi	L				○	1		
81	daisho	L					1		

O: *OED2*, **W**: *W3*, **R**: *RDH*, **FW**: *ODFWP*, **S5**: *SOED5* ○: Registered, **E**: Etymology Search, **D**: Definition Search, **T**: Text Search, **M**: Manual Search **Dic.**: The Result of Dictionary Study, **Corp.**: The Result of Corpus Study **0**: No Assimilation ×: Not Applicable (Secondary Loanwords) **1**: Pronunciation and Orthography Assimilation **2**: Attributive Use **3**: Productivity Acquisition **4**: Semantic Shift

	Item	O	W	R	S5	FW	Dic.	→	Corp.
82	dan	L	○	○	○	○	2		
83	daruma		○				1		
84	dashi	L		○			1		
85	do			○			1		
86	dojo [judo]	L	○	○	○	○	4		
87	dojo (2) [fish]			○			1		
88	dotaku	L			○	○	1		
89	elder statesman	D	○	M		D	×		
90	emakimono	(L)M				○	1		
91	enalite				○		1		
92	engawa		○				1		
93	enoki(dake)		D	○		○	2		
94	Eta, eta	L		○		○	2		
95	fugu		D	○	○	○	1		
96	fuji(yama/san)		D				1		
97	fuji (2) [apple]					○	1		
98	fuji (3) [flower]			○			1		
99	Fujisawa		D				1		
100	Fujiwara		D				1		
101	fukuoka		D	○			1		
102	Fukushima		D				1		
103	Fukuyama						1		
104	fun			○			1		
105	funori(n)			○			1		
106	furo, ofuro		D			○	1		
107	fusuma	L	○	○			1		
108	futon	L	○	○	○	○	4		
109	gagaku	L	○	○	○	○	1		
110	gaijin	L	○		○	○	2		
111	geisha	L	○	○		○	4		
112	Genro		D	○		○	1		
113	Genroku		○				1		
114	geta	L	○	○		○	1		
115	(judo)gi, gie	(L)	○	○			1		
116	gifu		D	○			1		
117	ginkgo	L	○	○		○	2		
118	Ginza		D				1		
119	go	L	○	○	○	○	1		
120	goban(g)	L	○		○	○	1		
121	gobo			○			1		
122	god-shelf	T					×		
123	gomoku		○				1		
124	graphic novel	M	○			M	×		
125	gumi (goumi)		○	○			1		
126	gyokuro			○			1		
127	habu	L		M			1		

O: *OED2*, **W:** *W3*, **R:** *RDH*, **FW:** *ODFWP*, **S5:** *SOED5* ○: Registered, **E:** Etymology Search, **D:** Definition Search, **T:** Text Search, **M:** Manual Search **Dic.:** The Result of Dictionary Study, **Corp.:** The Result of Corpus Study **0:** No Assimilation ×: Not Applicable (Secondary Loanwords) **1:** Pronunciation and Orthography Assimilation **2:** Attributive Use **3:** Productivity Acquisition **4:** Semantic Shift

Appendix C   235

	Item	O	W	R	S5	FW	Dic.	→	Corp.
128	habutai(/e)	L	○	○	○	○	2		
129	Hachioji		D				1		
130	hagi			○			1		
131	haikai	(L)	○	○			1		
132	haiku	L	○	○	○	○	1		
133	hakama	L			○	○	1		
134	hakodate		D	○			1		
135	hamamatsu		D	○			1		
136	hanami	L					0		
137	hanashika	L					0		
138	haniwa	L	○	○	○	○	2		
139	haori	L	D	○		○	1		
140	happi-coat	L	○			○	2		
141	happy dispatch	M				M	×		
142	hara(-)kiri	L	D	○	○	○	4		
143	harai goshi	L			○	○	1		
144	Hashimoto('s disease)	D		○		○	3	→	1
145	hatamoto	L					0		
146	hechima	L		○			1		
147	Heian	L	D	○		○	3	→	1
148	heimin	L		○		○	1		
149	hiba arborvitae			○			1		
150	hibachi	L	○	○	○	○	4	→	1
151	himeji		D	○			1		
152	hibakusha		D		○	○	1		
153	Hideyoshi		D				1		
154	higashiosaka		D				1		
155	Higashiyama		D				1		
156	high profile			○		M	×		
157	hinin	L				○	1		
158	hinoki (cypress)	L	D	○		○	2		
159	Hirado (ware)	D		○		○	2		
160	hiragana	L	○	○	○	○	3	→	2
161	Hirakata		D				1		
162	Hiranuma		○				1		
163	Hirohito		D				1		
164	hiroshima		D	○			1		
165	Hizen (ware)	D		○		○	2		
166	chediak-higashi syndrome			○			×		
167	Hojo		D				1		
168	Hokkaido		D				1		
169	hokku	(L)M	○	○	○	○	1		
170	hondo			○			1		
171	honcho	L	○	○	○	○	4		
172	Honshu		D				1		
173	hoo(t)ch(ie)	L	○	○		○	1		

O: *OED2*, **W**: *W3*, **R**: *RDH*, **FW**: *ODFWP*, **S5**: *SOED5* ○: Registered, **E**: Etymology Search, **D**: Definition Search, **T**: Text Search, **M**: Manual Search **Dic.**: The Result of Dictionary Study, **Corp.**: The Result of Corpus Study **0**: No Assimilation ×: Not Applicable (Secondary Loanwords) **1**: Pronunciation and Orthography Assimilation **2**: Attributive Use **3**: Productivity Acquisition **4**: Semantic Shift

	Item	O	W	R	S5	FW	Dic.	→	Corp.
174	ibota (/ibolium) privet		○	○			1		
175	ibotenic	L				○	1		
176	Ichikawa		D				1		
177	Ichinomiya		D				1		
178	icho			○			1		
179	ikebana	E	○	○	○	○	2		
180	ikunoite	L					1		
181	Imari (ware)	D	○	○		○	3	→	1
182	inkyo	L					3	→	1
183	inro	L	○		○	○	1		
184	ippon	L			○	○	1		
185	iroha	L		○		○	1		
186	Ishiguro		D				1		
187	Ishihara (test)	D	○	○		○	3	→	1
188	ishikawaite	L		○			1		
189	Issei		○	○		○	1		
190	itai-itai	L					1		
191	itzebu, -boo	E				○	1		
192	Iwaki		D				1		
193	Iwo Jima		D				1		
194	Izanagi		D				1		
195	janken	L			○	○	1		
196	jigotai	L			○	○	1		
197	(jin)ricksha(w)	L	D	○	○	○	3		
198	jito	L					1		
199	Jodo	L	○	○		○	1		
200	johachidolite	L					1		
201	Jomon	L	○	○		○	3	→	1
202	joro	L				○	1		
203	joruri	L			○	○	2		
204	judo	L	○	○	○	○	3	→	4
205	judoka	(L)	○	○		○	1		
206	ju(-)jitsu	L	D	○	○	○	4		
207	juku		D		○	○	1		
208	junshi	L					1		
209	kabane	L				○	1		
210	kabuki	L	D	○	○	○	3		
211	Kagawa		○				1		
212	kago	L	D	○		○	1		
213	Kagoshima		D	○			1		
214	kagura	L		○	○	○	1		
215	kainic (acid)	L	○	○		○	1		
216	kaizen	L			○	○	1		
217	kakebuton		○				1		
218	kakemono	L	○	○	○	○	1		
219	kaki	L	○	○		○	2		

O: *OED2*, **W:** *W3*, **R:** *RDH*, **FW:** *ODFWP*, **S5:** *SOED5* ○: Registered, **E:** Etymology Search, **D:** Definition Search, **T:** Text Search, **M:** Manual Search **Dic.:** The Result of Dictionary Study, **Corp.:** The Result of Corpus Study **0:** No Assimilation ✕: Not Applicable (Secondary Loanwords) **1:** Pronunciation and Orthography Assimilation **2:** Attributive Use **3:** Productivity Acquisition **4:** Semantic Shift

Appendix C 237

	Item	O	W	R	S5	FW	Dic.	→	Corp.
220	Kakiemon	L		○		D	2		
221	kakke	L				○	1		
222	Kamakura	D	D			D	3	→	1
223	Kambara earth			○			1		
224	kami	(L)		○	○	○	2		
225	kami-dana	L					1		
226	kamikaze	L	○	○	○	○	4		
227	kana	L	○	○	○	○	2		
228	kana-majiri		○	○			1		
229	Kanazawa		D	○			1		
230	kanban	L	○		○	○	2		
231	kanji	L	○	○	○	○	2		
232	kanten				○		1		
233	karaoke	L	○	○	○	○	3		
234	karate	L	D	○	○	○	3		
235	karateka			○		○	1		
236	Karatsu ware				○		1		
237	karoshi				○	○	1		
238	kata	L	○	○	○	○	1		
239	katakana	L	○	○	○	○	2		
240	katana	L		○		○	1		
241	Katayama			○			1		
242	katsu			○			1		
243	katsuo (katsuwonidae)	L		○	○	○	1		
244	katsura	L		○		○	1		
245	katsura (tree)			○			1		
246	katsura(mono)	L		○		○	1		
247	Kawaguchi		D	○			1		
248	Kawasaki		D				1		
249	Kawasaki disease			○		○	1		
250	kaya	L		○		○	1		
251	Kegon			○			1		
252	keiretsu		D	○	○		1		
253	Kempeitai	L		○	○		1		
254	ken (1) [lenght]	L				○	1		
255	ken (2) [prefecture]	L				○	1		
256	ken (3) [fist]	L		○	○	○	1		
257	kendo	L	○	○	○	○	1	→	3
258	kesa-gatame	L					1		
259	keyaki (kia-)			○		○	1		
260	ki-mon	L				○	1		
261	Kibei		D	○			1		
262	kiku			○			1		
263	Kikuchi	L				○	2		
264	kikumon			○			1		
265	kikyo	L					1		

O: *OED2*, **W**: *W3*, **R**: *RDH*, **FW**: *ODFWP*, **S5**: *SOED5* ○: Registered, **E**: Etymology Search, **D**: Definition Search, **T**: Text Search, **M**: Manual Search **Dic.**: The Result of Dictionary Study, **Corp.**: The Result of Corpus Study **0**: No Assimilation ✕: Not Applicable (Secondary Loanwords) **1**: Pronunciation and Orthography Assimilation **2**: Attributive Use **3**: Productivity Acquisition **4**: Semantic Shift

	Item	O	W	R	S5	FW	Dic.	→	Corp.
266	kimono	L	○	○	○	○	4		
267	kin			○			1		
268	kiri	L		○		○	2		
269	kirimon			○			1		
270	kirin	L			○	○	1		
271	Kitakyushu		D				1		
272	Kitsato		○				1		
273	koan	L	○	○	○	○	1		
274	koban(g)	L		○		○	1		
275	Kobe (beef)		D	○			1		
276	kobeite	L					1		
277	Kochi		D	○			1		
278	Kofu		D	○			1		
279	kogai	L					1		
280	koi	L	D	○	○	○	1		
281	koi-cha	L				○	1		
282	koji	L	○	○		○	1		
283	kokeshi	L				○	2		
284	Kokka		D				1		
285	koku	L	○	○		○	1		
286	Kokura		○	○			1		
287	kombu	L		○	○	○	1		
288	koni(/j)ak(u)	L		○		○	1		
289	Kōrin	D				D	2		
290	Koriyama		D				1		
291	koro	L		○	○	○	1		
292	kotatsu	L				○	1		
293	koto	L	○	○	○	○	2		
294	kotoite				○		1		
295	kozo				○		1		
296	kudzu (vine)	L	○	○	○	○	2	→	3
297	Kuge	L				○	1		
298	Kumamoto		D	○			1		
299	kumaso			M			1		
300	kumite					○	1		
301	Kuniyoshi		D				1		
302	kura	L				○	1		
303	Kurashiki		D				1		
304	kure		D	○			1		
305	Kurosawa		○				1		
306	Kuroshi(w)o	L	D			○	1		
307	kuruma	L		○		○	2		
308	Kurume (azalea)		D		○	○	2		
309	Kurusu			○			1		
310	Kutani (ware)	E	○	○		○	2		
311	kuzushi	L			○	○	1		

O: *OED2*, **W**: *W3*, **R**: *RDH*, **FW**: *ODFWP*, **S5**: *SOED5* ○: Registered, **E**: Etymology Search, **D**: Definition Search, **T**: Text Search, **M**: Manual Search **Dic.**: The Result of Dictionary Study, **Corp.**: The Result of Corpus Study **0**: No Assimilation ✕: Not Applicable (Secondary Loanwords) **1**: Pronunciation and Orthography Assimilation **2**: Attributive Use **3**: Productivity Acquisition **4**: Semantic Shift

Appendix C 239

	Item	O	W	R	S5	FW	Dic.	→	Corp.
312	kwaiken		○				1		
313	kwazoku			○			1		
314	kyogen	L	○		○	○	1		
315	kyoto	D	○				1		
316	kyu	L			○	○	2		
317	Ky(/i)ushu	D					1		
318	low profile	M	○			M		×	
319	Macanese	L	○	○		○	1		
320	machi			○			1		
321	Maebashi	D					1		
322	magatama	L				○	1		
323	mai			○			1		
324	maiko	L				○	1		
325	makimono	L	○	○	○	○	1		
326	makiwara	L					1		
327	maki(/-)zushi		○			○	1		
328	mama-san	L			○	○	1		
329	mamushi			○			1		
330	mana			○			1		
331	manga		○		○	○	1		
332	manyogana	L				○	1		
333	martial art	D	○	M		D		×	
334	maru			○			1		
335	marumi kumquat		○	○			1		
336	matsu	L	○	○		○	1		
337	matsucoccus			○			1		
338	Matsudo	D					1		
339	Matsuoka		○				1		
340	matsuri	L				○	1		
341	matsu(-)take	D					1		
342	Matsuyama	D	○				1		
343	mebos	L		○		○	1		
344	mechatronics					D		×	
345	medaka		○	○		○	1		
346	Meiji	L	○	○		○	3		
347	metake	L				○	1		
348	miai	L				○	1		
349	Mikado	L	D	○		○	2		
350	mikan	L				○	1		
351	Mikimoto (pearl)	D				D	2		
352	Minamata disease	E	○	○		○	1		
353	Minamoto		D				1		
354	mingei	L			○	○	1		
355	mirin					○	1		
356	Mishima		○	○			1		
357	miso	L	○	○	○	○	2		

O: *OED2*, **W**: *W3*, **R**: *RDH*, **FW**: *ODFWP*, **S5**: *SOED5* ○: Registered, **E**: Etymology Search, **D**: Definition Search, **T**: Text Search, **M**: Manual Search **Dic.**: The Result of Dictionary Study, **Corp.**: The Result of Corpus Study **0**: No Assimilation ×: Not Applicable (Secondary Loanwords) **1**: Pronunciation and Orthography Assimilation **2**: Attributive Use **3**: Productivity Acquisition **4**: Semantic Shift

	Item	O	W	R	S5	FW	Dic.	→	Corp.
358	mitsukurina			○			1		
359	mitsumata	L		○		○	2		
360	Miyagawanella			○			1		
361	Miyazaki		D				1		
362	mizuna					○	1		
363	mochi	L			○	○	1		
364	Moji		○	○			1		
365	mokum	L		○			1		
366	momme	D	○	○		○	1		
367	Momoyama			○			1		
368	mompe(i)	L			○	○	1		
369	mon	L		○		○	1		
370	mondo	L	○	○	○	○	1		
371	mondo (2)					○	2		
372	moose (musume)	L				○	1		
373	Morioka			○			1		
374	moxa	L	○	○		○	4	→	1
375	mume			○			1		
376	mura	L	D	○		○	1		
377	muraji	L					1		
378	Murasaki Shikibu		○				1		
379	Mutsuhito		D				1		
380	Nabeshima (ware)	D		○		○	2		
381	nagami kumquat		○	M			1		
382	Nagano		D				1		
383	Nagasaki		D	○			1		
384	nagatelite			○			1		
385	Nagoya		D	○			1		
386	Naha		D				1		
387	nakodo	L				○	1		
388	nandin(a)	L	○	○			1		
389	Nanga	L				○	2		
390	napa		○			○	1		
391	Nara	E	D	○		D	3	→	1
392	narikin	L			○	○	1		
393	nashi					○	1		
394	Nashiji	L				○	2		
395	nembutsu		○	○	○	○	1		
396	netsuke	L	○	○	○	○	1		
397	Nichiren (Buddhism)		○	○		D	2		
398	nightingale floor	D				D	×		
399	nigiri(/-)zushi		○			○	1		
400	Niigata		D	○			1		
401	Nikkei	L	○			○	2		
402	Nikko		D	○			1		
403	Nikko fir		D	○			1		

O: *OED2*, **W**: *W3*, **R**: *RDH*, **FW**: *ODFWP*, **S5**: *SOED5* ○: Registered, **E**: Etymology Search, **D**: Definition Search, **T**: Text Search, **M**: Manual Search **Dic.**: The Result of Dictionary Study, **Corp.**: The Result of Corpus Study **0**: No Assimilation **×**: Not Applicable (Secondary Loanwords) **1**: Pronunciation and Orthography Assimilation **2**: Attributive Use **3**: Productivity Acquisition **4**: Semantic Shift

Appendix C 241

	Item	O	W	R	S5	FW	Dic.	→	Corp.
404	ningyoite	E					1		
405	Ninigi	D					1		
406	ninja	L	○	○	○	○	2		
407	ninjutsu	L	○		○	○	1		
408	Nip(pon(ese/ian)), Nihon	L	D	○		○	3		
409	Nisei	L	○	○	○	○	3		
410	Nishinomia		D	○			1		
411	No(h)	L	D	○	○	○	3		
412	nogaku	L	○	○	○	○	2		
413	nokyo			○			1		
414	nori	L		○	○	○	1		
415	norimon	L		○		○	1		
416	norito			○			1		
417	noshi	L				○	1		
418	notan			○			1		
419	nunchaku	L	○	○	○	○	2		
420	Obaku	L				○	1		
421	oban(g)	L		○		○	1		
422	obi	L	○	○	○	○	1		
423	odori			○			1		
424	o-goshi	L				○	1		
425	Oh		D				1		
426	oiran	L				○	1		
427	Oita		D				1		
428	ojime	L			○	○	1		
429	okayama		D	○			1		
430	Okazaki [place]		D				1		
431	Okazaki [person]	D				○	2		
432	okimono	L				○	1		
433	Okinawan	L	D	M		D	3		
434	omi [title]	L					1		
435	Omi [place]		○				1		
436	Omiya		D				1		
437	Omuta		D	○			1		
438	on	L					1		
439	onnagata	L	○		○	○	1		
440	onsen	L				○	1		
441	origami	L	○	○	○	○	3		
442	orihon	L	○	○	○	○	1		
443	osaekomi( )waza	L				○	1		
444	Osaka		D	○			1		
445	oshibori	L				○	2		
446	O-soto-gari	L				○	1		
447	otaku					○	1		
448	Otaru		D	○			1		
449	oyama [=onnagata]	L			○	○	1		

O: *OED2,* **W:** *W3,* **R:** *RDH,* **FW:** *ODFWP,* **S5:** *SOED5* ○: Registered, **E:** Etymology Search, **D:** Definition Search, **T:** Text Search, **M:** Manual Search **Dic.**: The Result of Dictionary Study, **Corp.**: The Result of Corpus Study **0:** No Assimilation ✕: Not Applicable (Secondary Loanwords) **1:** Pronunciation and Orthography Assimilation **2:** Attributive Use **3:** Productivity Acquisition **4:** Semantic Shift

	Item	O	W	R	S5	FW	Dic.	→	Corp.
450	Oyama [person]		○				1		
451	Oyashio Current		D				1		
452	Pac-Man (defense)					M	×		
453	pachinko	L	○	○	○	○	2		
454	plum rain	L					×		
455	rain-door	D				D	1		
456	raku (ware)	L	○	○	○	○	2		
457	ramanas (rose)	L		○		○	2		
458	ramen	L	○		○	○	1		
459	randori	L		○	○	○	1		
460	red belt					M	1		
461	red tai		○	M			1		
462	reiki					○	1		
463	renga	L	○		○	○	1		
464	ri	L		○		○	1		
465	rikishi					○	1		
466	rikka	L			○	○	2		
467	rin	L	D	○		○	1		
468	Rinzai	L				○	1		
469	rishitin	L				○	1		
470	Ritsu	L		○			1		
471	Roju	L					1		
472	romaji	L	○	○		○	2		
473	ronin	L			○	○	1		
474	Roshi	L	○			○	1		
475	rotenone	L	○	○		○	1		
476	rumaki	L	○	○		○	1		
477	ryo	L				○	1		
478	Ryobu (Shinto)			○			1		
479	ryokan	L	○			○	1		
480	ryu	L			○	○	1		
481	Ryukyu(an) (luchuan)	L	D	○		○	3		
482	sabi	L			○	○	1		
483	Sagamihara		D				1		
484	sai	L				○	1		
485	Sakai		D	○			1		
486	sakaki			○			1		
487	saké	L	○	○	○	○	3	→	2
488	sakura	L		○		○	1		
489	salaryman		D			D	×		
490	samisen	L	○	○	○	○	1		
491	samurai	L	D	○	○	○	4		
492	(-)san	L	○		○	○	1		
493	Sanda ware			○			1		
494	sanpaku	L			○	○	2		
495	sanron			○			1		

O: *OED2,* **W:** *W3,* **R:** *RDH,* **FW:** *ODFWP,* **S5:** *SOED5* ○: Registered, **E:** Etymology Search, **D:** Definition Search, **T:** Text Search, **M:** Manual Search **Dic.:** The Result of Dictionary Study, **Corp.:** The Result of Corpus Study **0:** No Assimilation ×: Not Applicable (Secondary Loanwords) **1:** Pronunciation and Orthography Assimilation **2:** Attributive Use **3:** Productivity Acquisition **4:** Semantic Shift

Appendix C   243

	Item	O	W	R	S5	FW	Dic.	→	Corp.
496	sansei	L	○	○	○	○	1		
497	Sapporo		D	○			1		
498	sasanqua	L		○		○	1		
499	Sasebo		D	○			1		
500	sashimi	L	○	○	○	○	1		
501	satori	L	○	○	○	○	3	→	1
502	Satsuma (ware)	E	D	○	○	○	2		
503	Satsuma [orange]	E	○	○	○	○	2		
504	sawara cypress				○		1		
505	sayonara	L	○	○	○	○	3	→	1
506	seiza	L			○	○	1		
507	sen	L	D	○		○	1		
508	Sendai	D	D	○		○	2		
509	sennin	L			○	○	2		
510	senryu	D			○	○	1		
511	sensei	L	○		○	○	1		
512	sentoku	L				○	1		
513	seoi nage	L					0		
514	seppuku	L	○	○	○	○	1		
515	Seto (ware)	D		○		○	2		
516	sewamono	L					1		
517	shabu-shabu	L			○	○	1		
518	shaku	L			○	○	1		
519	shakudo	L			○	○	2		
520	shakuhachi	L			○	○	1		
521	shiats(/z)u	L	○	○	○	○	3		
522	Shibayama	D				○	2		
523	shibui	L			○	○	2		
524	shibuichi	L		○		○	2		
525	Shiga (bacillus)	D		M		○	2		
526	shigella	M	○	○		M	2		
527	Shihan	L				○	1		
528	shiitake	L	○	○	○	○	3	→	2
529	Shijō	E					2		
530	shikibuton		○				1		
531	shikii			○			1		
532	shikimi(c) acid	L		○		○	2		
533	shikken			○			1		
534	Shikoku		D				1		
535	shimada	D				○	2		
536	shime-waza	L				○	1		
537	Shimazaki		○				1		
538	Shimonoseki		D	○			1		
539	Shimose	L		○			1		
540	Shin(-shu)	L	○	○		○	3	→	1
541	Shingon	L	○	○		○	3	→	1

O: *OED2*, W: *W3*, R: *RDH*, FW: *ODFWP*, S5: *SOED5* ○: Registered, E: Etymology Search, D: Definition Search, T: Text Search, M: Manual Search Dic.: The Result of Dictionary Study, Corp.: The Result of Corpus Study 0: No Assimilation ✕: Not Applicable (Secondary Loanwords) 1: Pronunciation and Orthography Assimilation 2: Attributive Use 3: Productivity Acquisition 4: Semantic Shift

	Item	O	W	R	S5	FW	Dic.	→	Corp.
542	Shinkansen	L				○	4	→	1
543	shintai			○			1		
544	Shinto	L	D	○		○	3		
545	Shippo	L			○	○	1		
546	shirakashi			○			1		
547	shishi	L				○	1		
548	shizoku			○			1		
549	shizuoka		D	○			1		
550	sho	L					1		
551	sho (2)	L				○	1		
552	shochu	L				○	1		
553	shodan	L					1		
554	shogaol			○			1		
555	shogi	L	○	○	○	○	1		
556	shogoin turnip			M			1		
557	shogun	L	D	○	○	○	3	→	4
558	shoji	L	○	○		○	3	→	1
559	shokku	L					×		
560	Shorin ryu	L					1		
561	shosagoto	L			○	○	1		
562	shosha	L			○	○	1		
563	Shotokan	L				○	2		
564	Showa	L	○			○	1		
565	shoyu	L		○	○	○	2		
566	shubunkin	L		○		○	1		
567	shugo	L				○	1		
568	Shuha		○				1		
569	shunga	L		○	○		1		
570	shunto	L	○				1		
571	shuriken	L			○	○	1		
572	shuto	L				○	1		
573	sika	L	○	○		○	2		
574	skibby			○			1		
575	skimmia	L	○	M		○	1		
576	skosh	L	○	○		○	1		
577	soba	L			○	○	1		
578	sodoku	L		○		○	1		
579	sogo shosha	L			○	○	1		
580	Sohyo	L					1		
581	Soka Gakkai	L		○		○	1		
582	sokaiya	L			○	○	1		
583	soogee			○		M	1		
584	soroban	L	○	○		○	1		
585	sosaku hanga	L					1		
586	Soseki, Natsume		○				1		
587	soshi	L			○	○	1		

O: *OED2,* **W:** *W3,* **R:** *RDH,* **FW:** *ODFWP,* **S5:** *SOED5* ○: Registered, **E:** Etymology Search, **D:** Definition Search, **T:** Text Search, **M:** Manual Search **Dic.:** The Result of Dictionary Study, **Corp.:** The Result of Corpus Study **0:** No Assimilation ×: Not Applicable (Secondary Loanwords) **1:** Pronunciation and Orthography Assimilation **2:** Attributive Use **3:** Productivity Acquisition **4:** Semantic Shift

Appendix C

	Item	O	W	R	S5	FW	Dic.	→	Corp.
588	Soto	L				○	2		
589	soy (bean)	(L)	○	○		○	4		
590	soya(/ja) (bean)	L	○	○	○	D	4		
591	stone	D				D	×		
592	sudoite	L					1		
593	sugamo			○			1		
594	sugi	L	D	○		○	1		
595	suiboku	L			○	○	1		
596	suimono	L					1		
597	suiseki	L					1		
598	Suita	D					1		
599	sukiya				○	○	2		
600	sukiyaki	L	○	○	○	○	3	→	1
601	sumi	L	○	○	○	○	2		
602	sumi-e	L	○	○		○	2		
603	sumi-gaeshi	L				○	1		
604	sumo	L	D	○	○	○	2	→	3
605	sumotori	L			○	○	1		
606	sun	L				○	1		
607	Suntory	D					1		
608	Suribachi		○				1		
609	surimi		○	○			1		
610	surimono	L			○	○	1		
611	sushi	L	○	○	○	○	3		
612	sutemi-waza	L					1		
613	Suzuki	L				D	3		
614	suzuribako	L			○	○	1		
615	Tobata		○				1		
616	tabi	L	D		○	○	1		
617	tachi	L				○	1		
618	tai	L	D	○		○	1		
619	tai-otoshi	L				○	1		
620	Taira	D					1		
621	tai-sabaki					○	1		
622	taiko				○	○	1		
623	Taisho		○			○	1		
624	Taka-diastase	L		M		○	1		
625	takamakie				○	○	1		
626	Takamatsu		D	○			1		
627	Takaoka			○			1		
628	Takatsuki		D				1		
629	Takayasu	L					2		
630	tamagotchi		○		○	○	1		
631	tamari	L		○	○	○	2		
632	tamo		○	○			1		
633	tan (1) [field]	L		○		○	1		

O: OED2, **W**: W3, **R**: RDH, **FW**: ODFWP, **S5**: SOED5 ○: Registered, **E**: Etymology Search, **D**: Definition Search, **T**: Text Search, **M**: Manual Search **Dic.**: The Result of Dictionary Study, **Corp.**: The Result of Corpus Study **0**: No Assimilation ×: Not Applicable (Secondary Loanwords) **1**: Pronunciation and Orthography Assimilation **2**: Attributive Use **3**: Productivity Acquisition **4**: Semantic Shift

	Item	O	W	R	S5	FW	Dic.	→	Corp.
634	tan (2) [cloth]	L				○	1		
635	Tanabata	L					1		
636	tanka	L	○	○	○	○	1		
637	tansu	L				○	1		
638	tanto	L				○	1		
639	tanyosho pine			○			1		
640	tara vine		D	○			1		
641	tatami	L	○	○	○	○	3		
642	tea ceremony	T		M		D	×		
643	tea master	M				D	×		
644	teinite			○			1		
645	temmoku	L			○	○	2		
646	tempo	L			○	○	1		
647	tempura	L	○	○	○	○	3	→	2
648	Tempyo			○			1		
649	Tendai	L			○	○	2		
650	tenko	L				○	1		
651	tenno				○		1		
652	teppan-yaki	L			○	○	2		
653	terakoya	L					1		
654	teriyaki	L	○	○	○	○	3		
655	to	L				○	1		
656	tobira		D	○			1		
657	todorokite	E					1		
658	tofu	L	○	○	○	○	1	→	3
659	togidashi	L			○	○	2		
660	Tojo	L	○			○	1		
661	tokkin	L				○	2		
662	tokonoma	L	○	○		○	2		
663	Tokugawa	L	D			○	3		
664	Tokushima		D	○			1		
665	Tokyo(ite) (Bay)	E	D	○		○	1		
666	tomoe-nage	L					1		
667	tonari gumi	L				○	1		
668	tori	L				○	1		
669	torii	L	D	○	○	○	2		
670	toringin			○			1		
671	Tosa [dog]	E				○	1		
672	Tosa [painting]	D				○	2		
673	Toyama			○			1		
674	toyo			○			1		
675	Toyohara		○				1		
676	Toyohashi		D	○			1		
677	Toyonaka		D				1		
678	Toyota		D				1		
679	tsuba	L			○	○	1		

O: *OED2*, W: *W3*, R: *RDH*, FW: *ODFWP*, S5: *SOED5* ○: Registered, E: Etymology Search, D: Definition Search, T: Text Search, M: Manual Search Dic.: The Result of Dictionary Study, Corp.: The Result of Corpus Study 0: No Assimilation ×: Not Applicable (Secondary Loanwords) 1: Pronunciation and Orthography Assimilation 2: Attributive Use 3: Productivity Acquisition 4: Semantic Shift

Appendix C 247

	Item	O	W	R	S5	FW	Dic.	→	Corp.
680	tsubo	L		○		○	1		
681	tsuga(resinol)			○			1		
682	tsugi ashi	L				○	1		
683	Tsukahara	L				○	2		
684	tsukemono	L			○	○	1		
685	tsukuri	L				○	1		
686	tsunami	L	○	○	○	○	4		
687	tsurikomi	L				○	1		
688	Tsushima Current(/Strait)		D				1		
689	tsutsugamushi disease(/mite)	L	○	○		○	2		
690	tsutsumu	L			○	○	1		
691	tycoon	L	D	○	○	○	4		
692	Ube		D	○			1		
693	uchimata	L				○	1		
694	uchiwa	L			○	○	1		
695	ude	L					1		
696	ude-garami					○	1		
697	ude-gatame					○	1		
698	udo		D	○			1		
699	udon	L			○	○	1		
700	uguisu	L				○	1		
701	uji			○			1		
702	uji (2)	L				○	1		
703	ujigami	L				○	1		
704	uke	L				○	1		
705	ukemi	L			○	○	1		
706	uki	L			○	○	1		
707	ukiyo-e	L	D	○	○	○	3	→	2
708	umami					○	1		
709	ume				○		1		
710	Urawa		D	○			1		
711	ura-nage	L				○	1		
712	urushi(ol/-ic acid)	L	○	○		○	3	→	1
713	urushiye			○			1		
714	uta	L				○	1		
715	Utsunomiya		D				1		
716	wabi	L			○	○	1		
717	wacadash (wakizashi)	L				○	1		
718	waka	L	○		○	○	1		
719	wakame	L			○	○	1		
720	Wakamatsu		○				1		
721	Wakayama		D	○			1		
722	Walkman	T	○			M	×		
723	warabi			○			1		
724	wasabi	L	○	○	○	○	2		
725	washi	L			○	○	1		

O: *OED2*, **W**: *W3*, **R**: *RDH*, **FW**: *ODFWP*, **S5**: *SOED5* ○: Registered, **E**: Etymology Search, **D**: Definition Search, **T**: Text Search, **M**: Manual Search **Dic.**: The Result of Dictionary Study, **Corp.**: The Result of Corpus Study **0**: No Assimilation ×: Not Applicable (Secondary Loanwords) **1**: Pronunciation and Orthography Assimilation **2**: Attributive Use **3**: Productivity Acquisition **4**: Semantic Shift

	Item	O	W	R	S5	FW	Dic.	→	Corp.
726	waza-ari	L					1		
727	white belt		○			M	×		
728	Yagi (antena)	D	○	○		○	2		
729	yakitori	L	○	○	○	○	1		
730	yakuza	L	○		○	○	1		
731	Yamaguchigumi	L					1		
732	yamamai			○			1		
733	Yamamoto		○				1		
734	Yamasaki		○				1		
735	Yamashita		○				1		
736	Yamato(-damashii)	L		○			1		
737	yamato(-e/-ryu)	L	○	○		○	3	→	1
738	yashiki	L				○	1		
739	Yaw(/h)ata		○	○			1		
740	Yayoi	D	D	○		D	3	→	1
741	Yed(d)o (sprunce/hawthorn)	D	○	○		D	3	→	1
742	yellow belt	M				M	×		
743	yen	L	D	○		○	1	→	3
744	Yezo		○				1		
745	Yokkaichi		D	○			1		
746	yoko-shiho-gatame	L				○	1		
747	Yokohama	D	D	○		○	1		
748	Yokosuka		D	○			1		
749	yokozuna	L			○	○	1		
750	yondan	L					1		
751	Yoshihito		D				1		
752	Yoshino paper			○			2		
753	Yoshiwara	D				○	2		
754	yugawaralite	E					1		
755	yugen	L			○	○	1		
756	yukata	L	○		○	○	1		
757	Yukawa	D	○			○	3	→	1
758	yusho	L				○	1		
759	yūzen	D				○	2		
760	zabuton	L	D		○	○	1		
761	zaibatsu	L	D	○	○	○	1		
762	zaikai	L			○	○	2		
763	zaitech	L			○		1		
764	za(-)zen	L	○	○	○	○	2		
765	Zen	L	D	○	○	○	3	→	4
766	zendo	L	○	○	○	○	1		
767	Zengakuren	L				○	2		
768	zori	L	○	○	○	○	1		

O: *OED2*, **W:** *W3*, **R:** *RDH*, **FW:** *ODFWP*, **S5:** *SOED5* ○: Registered, **E:** Etymology Search, **D:** Definition Search, **T:** Text Search, **M:** Manual Search **Dic.:** The Result of Dictionary Study, **Corp.:** The Result of Corpus Study **0:** No Assimilation ×: Not Applicable (Secondary Loanwords) **1:** Pronunciation and Orthography Assimilation **2:** Attributive Use **3:** Productivity Acquisition **4:** Semantic Shift

Appendix D Unchanged and Anglicized Phonemes of German Loanwords

Word	Unchanged	Dual Usage	Anglicized
ablaut	'a' [a]		'b' [p] → [b]
abseil		's' [z]/[s]	'b' [p] → [b]
		'ei' [aɪ]/[eɪ]	
Anschluss		'a' [a]/[æ]	
Blitzkrieg		'g' [k]/[g]	
doppelgänger		'ä' [ɛ]/[æ]	'o' [ɔ] → [ɒ]
Dummkopf	'pf' [pf]		'o' [ɔ] → [ɒ]
ersatz	's' [z]	'a' [a]/[æ]	
		'er' [ɛr]/[ɜː]	
Gedankenexperiment	'a' [a]		'e' [e] → [ɛ]
Gesamtkustwerk	'a' [a]		'er' [ɛr] → [ɜː]
	'w' [v]		
	's' [z]		
Gesellschaft	's' [z]		'a' [a] → [ɑː]/[æ]
Gestapo		'e' [ɛ]/[ə]	('st' [ʃt] → [st])
			'o' [o] → [əʊ]
glockenspiel		'sp' [ʃp]/[sp]	'o' [ɔ] → [ɒ]
gneiss		'gn' [gn]/[n]	
goldwasser	'o' [ɔ]		'd' [t] → [d]
	'w' [v]		
Hakenkreuz	('a' [a(ː)])		'eu' [ɔʏ] → [ɔɪ]
Hanse		'a' [a]/[æ]	
		's' [z]/[s]	
Herrenvolk		'ol' [ɔl]/[əʊ]	

Word	Unchanged	Dual Usage	Anglicized
inselberg		's' [z]/[s]	'er' [ɛr] → [ɜː] 'g' [k] → [g]
jäger	'j' [j]		('ä' [ɛː] → [eː])
klaberjass	'j' [j]		'a' [a] → [ɑ] 'er' [ər] → [ɪ]
konditorei	'i' [i]		'o' [o] → [ɔ]
krummholz	'z' [ts]		'u' [ʊ] → [ʌ] 'o' [ɔ] → [ɒ]
krummhorn		'u' [ʊ]/[ʌ]	'or' [ɔr] → [ɔː]
landwehr	'a' [a] 'w' [v]		'd' [t] → [d] ('e' [eː] → [ɛː])
lebensraum	'e' [eː]		's' [s] → [z]
leitmotiv	'v' [f]		'o' [o] → [əʊ]
loess		'oe' [œ]/[əʊ]	
panzer		'a' [a]/[æ] 'z' [ts]/[z]	
putz	'z' [ts]	'u' [ʊ]/[ʌ]	
quark	'qu' [kv]		'ar' [ar] → [ɑː]
sauerbraten		's' [z]/[s] 'a' [aː]/[ɑː]	
schappe		'a' [a]/[æ]	'e' [ə] → φ
spätzle	'sp' [ʃp]	'tzle' [tslə] → [ts(ə)l]	
spritzer		'sp' [ʃp]/[sp]	
Stollen	'st' [ʃt]		'o' [ɔ] → [ɒ]
stoss	'o' [oː]	'st' [ʃt]/[st]	
streusel	's' [z]	'st' [ʃt]/[st] 'eu' [ɔY]/[ɔɪ]/[uː]	
strudel		'st' [ʃt]/[st]	
thalweg	'w' [v] 'th' [t]	'a' [aː]/[ɑː]	
vorlage	'v' [f]	'o' [oːr]/[ɔ] 'a' [aː]/[ɑ]	
wanderlust		'w' [v]/[w] 'a' [a]/[ɑ]	

Word	Unchanged	Dual Usage	Anglicized
		'u' [ʊ]/[ʌ]	
wurst		'w' [v]/[w]	'ur' [ur] → [ɜː]
zollverein	'z' [ts]		'o' [ɔ] → [ɒ]

Appendix E Productive Forms of German Loanwords in English Dictionaries

Items	Productive Forms
\multicolumn{2}{c}{(a) and (d): Strong Productivity}	
blitz(krieg)	Blitzkrieg method, Blitz bombing, blitz babies, blitz (v.) blitzed, blitzing, blitzer
ersatz	ersatz reserve, ersatz name, Ersatz Parliament, Ersatz-religion, Ersatz materials, Ersatz butter, ersatz uniform, ersatz coffee, ersatz facts, ersatz culture, ersatz morality
Gestalt	Gestalt psychology, Gestalt-psychologist, Gestalt theory, Gestalt school, Gestaltism, Gestalist
Hanse	hanse-house, hanse-penny, hanse-gild, Hanse merchant, Hanse city, Hanse town, Hanse association, Hanse league, hansing, hansing-silver
junker	Junker papistes, junker feeling, Junker stupidity, junkerdom, junkerish, junkerism
kindergarten	Kinder Garten songs, Kindergarten Amusements, kindergarten toy, kindergarten soldiers, kindergarten work, kindergarten instruction kindergarten (v.), kindergartenize, kindergartener, kindergartenism
kitsch	kitsch masterpiece, kitsch-culture, kitschfests, kitsch (v.), kitschy (a.), kitschily (adv.), kitschiness (n.)
kraut	Kraut Forks, Kraut Stamper, Kraut Cutters, krautfurter, Krautheads, kraut machine guns, Kraut bullet, krautland, Kraut sub, Kraut-bashing
lager	lager beer, lager description, lager lout, lager (v.), lagered, lagering, lagering time
loden	loden cloak, loden cloth, loden coat, loden jacket, loden mantle, loden skirt, loden green
lumpenproletariat	lumpenproletarian (a.), lumpen (a.) lumpenproletarian element

Appendix E 253

Items	Productive Forms
panzer	lumpen-proletarian fringe, lumpen(-)bourgeoisie, lumpen Right, lumpen-avant-garde, lumpen aesthetics, lumpen linguist panzer wire attacks, Panzer inrush, panzer division, Panzer troops, Panzer-man, Panzer Corps, Panzer battalion, panzer-spearheads, panzer major
polka	Polka step, polka time, Polka-mazurka, Polka song book, polka hats, polka curtain-band, polka-gauze, polka-dot ($n., v.$), polka-dotted, polka ($v.$), polkaic, polkamania, polkist(e)
poltergeist	poltergeist medium, poltergeist activity, poltergeistic, poltergeistism
putsch	putsching, putschism, putschist, putschist group/attempt/character
shaman	Shaman religion, Shaman Buritas, Shaman-office, shamanism, shamanian, shamanic, shamanka, shameness, shamanin
sinter	Sinter coal, sinter plant, sinter ($v.$), sintering
wedeln	wedel track, wedel turn, wedeln series, wedeln style, wedeln ($v.$), wede(l)ing
Kaiser	Kaiser (Wilhelm/Bill) moustache, Kaiserate, Kaiserdom, Kaiserish Kaiserism, Kaisership
umlaut	Umlaut form, umlaut plural, Umlaut vowels, Umlaut ($v.$) umlauted, umlauting
(b) and (e): Some Productivity	
bund	Bundist, Bund members
delicatessen	delicatessen store, delicatessen shop, delicatessen dinner, Delicatessen Department, Delicatessen Goods, deli
Führer	fuehrer complex, führer-commissar, führer order, Führer-principle
Herrenvolk	herrenvolk creed, Herrenvolk ideas, herrenvolk attitude, herrenvolk arrogance
jäger	jäger-companies, jäger costume
katzenjammer	Katzenjammer spirit, Katzenjammer Kids
pretzel	pretzel man, pretzel stick, pretzel bender
sauerkraut	sauerkraut barrel, sauerkraut cutter, sauerkraut-eater
schiller	Schiller asbestos, Schiller rock, Schiller-stone, Schiller-plane
schuss	schuss position, schuss ($v.$) schussing
zollverein	Zollverein-Departments, Zollverein-Governments
ablaut	ablaut-form, ablaut-grade, ablaut-relation, ablaut-pattern, ablaut variations

Items	Productive Forms
abseil	abseil (v.), abseiling
angst	angst-forming, angst-ridden, angst-wrought
anschluss	Anschluss idea, anschluss (v.)
barouche	Barooch seat, barouche-driver, barouche-landau, barouche (great-)coat
fest	shooting fest, talk fest, rat fest, liquor-fest, hen fest, filmfest
firn	firn-field, firn stoss, firn line, firnification
Jungendstil	Jungendstil painters, jungendstil period, Jungendstil décor, Jungendstil Parsifal
ländler	Ländler rhythms, Ländler-like
langlauf	Langlaufers, langlauf race
schappe	Schapping, schappe yarns, schappe (v.)
schottische	Highland Schottische, Balmoral Schottische, Military Schottische
wanderlust	wander(-)luster, wanlerlusting, wanderlust-club

Appendix F Selected German Loanwords in English Dictionaries

	Item	O	W	R	S5	FW	Dic.	→	Corp.
1	Abitur	O	×	×	O	O			
2	abiturient	O	×	×	O	O			
3	ablaut	O	O	O	O	O	(e)		
4	abseil	O	O	O	O	O	(e)	→	(a)
5	alpenhorn	O	O	O	O	O			
6	alpenstock	O	O	×	O	O			
7	althorn	O	O	O	O	O			
8	an sich	O	×	×	O	O			
9	angst	O	O	O	O	O	(e)	→	(a)
10	anlaut	O	O	O	O	O			
11	Anschauung	O	O	O	O	O	(c)		
12	Anschluss	O	O	O	O	O	(e)	→	(c)
13	apfelstrudel	O	×	×	O	O			
14	Aufklärung	O	O	O	O	O			
15	Auslese	O	×	O	O	O			
16	autobahn	O	O	O	O	O		→	(b)
17	automat	O	O	O	O	O	(c)		
18	backfisch	O	O	×	O	O			
19	barouche	O	O	O	O	O	(e)		
20	Bauhaus	O	O	O	O	O		→	(d)
21	bebung	O	O	×	O	O			
22	beerenauslese	O	×	×	O	O			
23	bergschrund	O	O	O	O	O			
24	bierhaus	O	×	×	O	O			
25	Bierstube	O	O	O	O	O			
26	Bildungsroman	O	O	O	O	O			
27	blitz(krieg)	O	O	O	O	O	(a)	→	(a)
28	blutwurst	O	O	×	O	O			
29	bratwurst	O	O	O	O	O			
30	brei	O	O	O	O	O			
31	breitschwanz	O	O	×	O	O			
32	buckling	O	O	×	O	O			
33	buhl	O	O	O	O	O			

O: *OED2*, **W**: *W3*, **R**: *RDH*, **FW**: *ODFWP*, **S5**: *SOED5*, O: Registered, ×: Not Registered, **Dic.**: The Result of Dictionary Study, **Corp.**: The Result of Corpus Study, **(a)** New Senses and Strong Productivity, **(b)** New Senses and Some Productivity, **(c)** New Senses and Little or No Productivity, **(d)** Strong Productivity but No Semantic Variation, **(e)** Some Productivity but No Semantic Variation

	Item	O	W	R	S5	FW	Dic.	→	Corp.
34	bund	○	○	○	○	○	(b)	→	(b)
35	conservatorium	×	×	×	○	○			
36	Dasein	○	○	×	○	○			
37	delicatessen	○	○	○	○	○	(b)	→	(a)
38	diktat	○	○	○	○	○	(c)	→	(c)
39	Ding an sich	○	○	○	○	○			
40	dirndl	○	○	○	○	○			
41	Dobos Torte	○	○	×	○	○			
42	docent	○	○	○	○	○			
43	doctorand	○	○	×	○	○			
44	dom	○	×	×	○	○			
45	doppelgänger	○	○	○	○	○		→	(c)
46	Drang	○	×	×	○	○			
47	Drang nach Osten	○	×	×	○	○			
48	dummkopf	○	○	○	○	○			
49	durchkomponiert	○	○	×	○	○			
50	echt	○	○	○	○	○			
51	Einfühlung	○	×	×	○	○			
52	Eiswein	○	×	×	○	○			
53	Entscheidungsproblem	○	×	×	○	○			
54	erbswurst	○	×	×	○	○			
55	Erlebnis	○	×	×	○	○			
56	ersatz	○	○	○	○	○	(a)	→	(a)
57	euchre	○	○	○	○	○			
58	Ewigkeit	○	×	×	○	○			
59	Fach	○	×	×	○	○			
60	fasching	○	×	○	○	○			
61	feldgrau	○	×	×	○	○			
62	felsenmeer	○	○	×	○	○			
63	fest	○	○	○	○	○	(e)		
64	Festschrift	○	○	×	○	○			
65	firn	○	○	○	○	○	(e)		
66	flügelhorn	○	○	○	○	○	(c)		
67	föhn	○	○	○	○	○	(c)		
68	Formgeschichte	○	×	×	○	○			
69	Fraktur	○	○	○	○	○			
70	frankfurter	○	○	○	○	○			
71	Frau	○	○	○	○	○			
72	Frauendienst	○	×	×	×	○			
73	Fräulein	○	○	○	○	○	(c)	→	(c)
74	Führer	○	○	○	○	○	(b)	→	(a)
75	Führerprinzip	○	×	×	×	○			
76	galant	○	○	×	○	○			
77	Galgenhumor	○	×	×	○	○			
78	Gastarbeiter	○	×	○	○	○			
79	gasthaus	○	○	○	○	○			

O: *OED2*, **W:** *W3*, **R:** *RDH*, **FW:** *ODFWP*, **S5:** *SOED5*, ○: Registered, ×: Not Registered, **Dic.**: The Result of Dictionary Study, **Corp.**: The Result of Corpus Study, **(a)** New Senses and Strong Productivity, **(b)** New Senses and Some Productivity, **(c)** New Senses and Little or No Productivity, **(d)** Strong Productivity but No Semantic Variation, **(e)** Some Productivity but No Semantic Variation

Appendix F 257

	Item	O	W	R	S5	FW	Dic.	→	Corp.
80	gasthof	O	×	×	O	O			
81	Gebrauchsmusik	O	O	×	O	O			
82	Gedankenexperiment	O	O	O	O	O			
83	Gelehrte	×	×	×	O	O			
84	Gemeinschaft	O	O	O	O	O			
85	gemshorn	O	O	×	O	O			
86	gemütlich	O	O	O	O	O			
87	Gemütlichkeit	O	O	O	O	O			
88	Gesamtkunstwerk	O	O	O	O	O			
89	Gesellschaft	O	O	O	O	O			
90	gestalt	O	O	O	O	O	(a)	→	(a)
91	Gestapo	O	O	O	O	O	(c)	→	(c)
92	giro	O	O	×	O	O		→	(d)
93	Gleichschaltung	O	O	×	O	O			
94	glockenspiel	O	O	O	O	O			
95	glühwein	O	O	×	O	O			
96	gneiss	O	O	O	O	O		→	(d)
97	goldwasser	O	O	O	O	O			
98	Götterdämmerung	O	O	O	O	O	(c)	→	(c)
99	Graf	O	×	O	O	O			
100	graupel	O	O	O	O	O			
101	Grenzbegriff	O	×	×	O	O			
102	Grübelsucht	O	×	×	O	O			
103	gugelhupf	O	O	×	O	O			
104	haff	O	O	×	O	O			
105	Hakenkreuz	O	O	O	O	O			
106	Hanse	O	O	O	O	O	(a)	→	(a)
107	hausfrau	O	O	O	O	O			
108	hausmaler	O	×	×	O	O			
109	Heft	O	×	×	O	O			
110	Heilsgeschichte	O	O	×	O	O			
111	Heimweh	O	×	×	O	O			
112	Heldentenor	O	O	O	O	O			
113	Herrenvolk	O	O	O	O	O	(b)		
114	heurige	O	×	O	O	O			
115	hochgeboren	O	×	×	O	O			
116	horst	O	O	O	O	O			
117	Identitätsphilosophie	O	×	×	O	O			
118	idioticon	O	×	×	O	O			
119	inselberg	O	O	O	O	O			
120	Interimsethik	O	×	×	O	O			
121	jäger	O	O	O	O	O	(b)		
122	judenrain	O	×	×	×	O			
123	Judenrat	O	×	×	O	O			
124	Jugendstill	O	O	O	×	O	(e)		
125	junker	O	O	O	O	O	(a)	→	(a)

O: *OED2*, **W**: *W3*, **R**: *RDH*, **FW**: *ODFWP*, **S5**: *SOED5*, O: Registered, ×: Not Registered, **Dic.**: The Result of Dictionary Study, **Corp.**: The Result of Corpus Study, **(a)** New Senses and Strong Productivity, **(b)** New Senses and Some Productivity, **(c)** New Senses and Little or No Productivity, **(d)** Strong Productivity but No Semantic Variation, **(e)** Some Productivity but No Semantic Variation

	Item	O	W	R	S5	FW	Dic.	→	Corp.
126	Kaffeeklat(s)ch	○	○	✕	○	○			
127	Kaiser	○	○	○	○	○	(d)		
128	kamerad	○	○	✕	○	○			
129	kapellmeister	○	○	○	○	○			
130	kaput	○	○	○	○	○	(c)		
131	karabiner	○	○	○	○	○			
132	Karren	○	○	✕	○	○			
133	Karrenfeld	○	✕	✕	○	○			
134	karst	○	○	✕	○	○			
135	katzenjammer	○	○	○	○	○	(b)		
136	keller	○	✕	✕	○	○			
137	kinder, kirche, küche	○	✕	✕	○	○			
138	kindergarten	○	○	○	○	○	(a)	→	(a)
139	kinderspiel	○	✕	✕	○	○			
140	kirsch(wasser)	○	○	○	○				
141	kitsch	○	○	○	○	○	(a)	→	(a)
142	klaberjass	○	○	○	○				
143	klat(s)ch	○	○	○	○				
144	kletterschuh	○	✕	✕	○	○			
145	klippe	○	○	○	○	○			
146	klops	○	✕	✕	○	○			
147	knödel	○	○	✕	○	○			
148	knallgas	○	✕	✕	○	○			
149	Kneipe	○	✕	✕	○	○			
150	kobold	○	○	○	○	○			
151	kohlrabi	○	○	○	○	○			
152	Kommers	○	○	✕	○	○			
153	konditorei	○	○	○	○	○			
154	kraut	○	○	○	○	○	(a)	→	(a)
155	kriegspiel	○	○	○	○				
156	krimmer	○	○	○	○				
157	krug	○	✕	✕	○	○			
158	krum(m)horn	○	○	○	○				
159	krummholz	○	○	○	○				
160	kuchen	○	○	○	○				
161	kultur	○	○	○	○	○	(d)		
162	kulturgeschichte	○	✕	✕	○	○			
163	kulturkampf	○	○	○	○	○			
164	kümmel	○	○	○	○	○			
165	Kunstforscher	○	✕	✕	○	○			
166	Künstlerroman	○	✕	✕	○	○			
167	Kunstgeschichte	○	✕	✕	○	○			
168	Kunsthistoriker	○	✕	✕	○	○			
169	Kunstprosa	○	✕	✕	○	○			
170	Kur	○	✕	✕	○	○			
171	Kurhaus	○	✕	✕	○	○			

O: *OED2*, **W**: *W3*, **R**: *RDH*, **FW**: *ODFWP*, **S5**: *SOED5*, ○: Registered, ✕: Not Registered, **Dic.**: The Result of Dictionary Study, **Corp.**: The Result of Corpus Study, **(a)** New Senses and Strong Productivity, **(b)** New Senses and Some Productivity, **(c)** New Senses and Little or No Productivity, **(d)** Strong Productivity but No Semantic Variation, **(e)** Some Productivity but No Semantic Variation

Appendix F

	Item	O	W	R	S5	FW	Dic.	→	Corp.
172	Kurort	O	×	×	O	O			
173	kursaal	O	×	×	O	O			
174	lachsschinken	O	O	×	O	O			
175	lager	O	O	O	O	O	(a)	→	(a)
176	lammergeyer	O	O	O	O	O			
177	Land	O	O	×	O	O			
178	landau	O	O	O	O	O			
179	ländler	O	O	O	O	O	(e)		
180	Landsturm	O	O	O	O	O			
181	Landwehr	O	O	O	O	O	(c)		
182	langlauf	O	O	O	O	O	(e)	→	(e)
183	Lebensform	O	×	×	O	O			
184	Lebenslust	O	×	×	O	O			
185	lebensraum	O	O	O	O	O	(c)	→	(c)
186	lebensspur	O	×	×	O	O			
187	Lebenswelt	O	×	×	O	O			
188	leberwurst	O	O	×	O	O			
189	lederhosen	O	O	O	O	O			
190	Lehrjahre	O	×	×	O	O			
191	leitmotiv(/f)	O	O	O	O	O	(c)	→	(c)
192	liebchen	O	×	×	O	O			
193	Liebestod	O	×	×	O	O			
194	liebling	O	×	×	O	O			
195	lied	O	O	O	O	O		→	(e)
196	Linzer( )torte	O	O	O	O	O			
197	litzendraht	O	×	×	O	O			
198	loden	O	O	O	O	O	(a)		
199	loess	O	O	O	O	O		→	(d)
200	lumpen(proletariat)	O	O	O	O	O	(a)	→	(a)
201	maar	O	O	O	O	O	(c)		
202	Macht(-)politik	O	O	×	O	O			
203	malerisch	O	×	×	O	O			
204	Märchen	O	O	×	O	O			
205	meerschaum	O	O	O	O	O	(c)		
206	mensur	O	O	×	O	O			
207	Methodenstreit	O	×	×	O	O			
208	Mettwurst	O	O	×	O	O			
209	Minnelied	O	O	×	O	O			
210	Minnesinger	O	O	O	O	O			
211	Mischsprache	O	O	×	O	O			
212	mit	O	×	×	O	O			
213	Mitbestimmung	×	×	×	O	O			
214	Mitsein	O	×	×	O	O			
215	Mittelschmerz	O	O	O	O	O			
216	Mittelstand	×	×	×	O	O			
217	Modernismus	O	×	×	O	O			

O: *OED2*, W: *W3*, R: *RDH*, FW: *ODFWP*, S5: *SOED5*, O: Registered, ×: Not Registered, Dic.: The Result of Dictionary Study, Corp.: The Result of Corpus Study, (a) New Senses and Strong Productivity, (b) New Senses and Some Productivity, (c) New Senses and Little or No Productivity, (d) Strong Productivity but No Semantic Variation, (e) Some Productivity but No Semantic Variation

	Item	O	W	R	S5	FW	Dic.	→	Corp.
218	mordent	○	○	○	○	○			
219	motiviert	○	×	×	○	○			
220	muesli	○	×	○	○	○			
221	Nachlass	○	×	×	○	○			
222	Nachschlag	○	○	×	○	○			
223	Nacht und Nebel	○	×	×	○	○			
224	Naturphilosophie	○	×	×	○	○			
225	nebelwerfer	○	×	×	○	○			
226	Neue Sachlichkeit	○	×	×	○	○			
227	nicht wahr	○	×	○	○	○			
228	nockerl	○	○	×	○	○			
229	noumenon	○	○	○	○	○		→	(d)
230	orterde	○	○	×	○	○			
231	ortstein	○	○	×	○	○			
232	Ostpolitik	○	×	○	○	○			
233	palatschinken	○	○	×	○	○			
234	panzer	○	○	○	○	○	(a)	→	(a)
235	pickelhaube	○	○	×	○	○			
236	polka	○	○	○	○	○	(a)	→	(a)
237	poltergeist	○	○	○	○	○	(a)	→	(a)
238	posaune	○	○	×	○	○			
239	Prägnanz	○	×	×	○	○			
240	pralltriller	○	○	○	○	○			
241	pretzel	○	○	○	○	○	(b)		
242	prosit	○	○	○	○	○			
243	pumpernickel	○	○	○	○	○			
244	putsch	○	○	○	○	○	(a)	→	(c)
245	putz	○	○	○	○	○	(c)		
246	quark	○	○	○	○	○			
247	quatsch	○	×	×	○	○			
248	Quellenforschung	○	×	×	○	○			
249	rac(/n)kett	○	○	○	○	○	(c)		
250	randkluft	○	○	×	○	○			
251	rauschpfeife	○	○	×	○	○			
252	realpolitik	○	○	○	○	○		→	(c)
253	realpolitiker	○	○	○	○	○			
254	Rechtsstaat	○	×	×	○	○			
255	Reeperbahn	○	×	×	○	○			
256	Reich	○	×	○	○	○			
257	ressentiment	○	○	×	○	○			
258	riegel	○	○	×	○	○			
259	rinderpest	○	○	○	○	○	(c)		
260	ritter	○	○	○	○	○			
261	roesti	○	×	×	○	○			
262	Romanze	○	×	×	○	○			
263	Sachertorte	○	○	○	○	○			

O: *OED2*, **W:** *W3*, **R:** *RDH*, **FW:** *ODFWP*, **S5:** *SOED5*, ○: Registered, ×: Not Registered, **Dic.:** The Result of Dictionary Study, **Corp.:** The Result of Corpus Study, **(a)** New Senses and Strong Productivity, **(b)** New Senses and Some Productivity, **(c)** New Senses and Little or No Productivity, **(d)** Strong Productivity but No Semantic Variation, **(e)** Some Productivity but No Semantic Variation

Appendix F

	Item	O	W	R	S5	FW	Dic.	→	Corp.
264	Sachlichkeit	O	×	×	O	O			
265	Sängerfest	O	O	×	O	O			
266	sastruga	O	O	O	O	O			
267	sauerbraten	O	O	O	O	O			
268	sauerkraut	O	O	O	O	O	(b)		
269	Schadenfreude	O	O	O	O	O			
270	schappe	O	O	O	O	O	(e)		
271	schema	O	O	O	O	O	(c)	→	(b)
272	schiller	O	O	O	O	O	(b)		
273	Schimpfwort	O	×	×	O	O			
274	schinken	O	×	×	O	O			
275	Schlag(obers)	O	×	O	O	O			
276	schlag(sahne)	O	×	×	O	O			
277	Schlamperei	O	×	×	O	O			
278	schlemiel	O	O	O	O	O			
279	schloss	O	O	O	O	O			
280	schmelz	O	O	×	O	O			
281	Schmelzglas	O	×	×	O	O			
282	Schmerz	O	×	×	O	O			
283	schmierkäse	O	O	O	O	O	(c)		
284	schnapps	O	O	O	O	O		→	(e)
285	schnitzel	O	O	O	O	O			
286	schnook	O	O	O	O	O			
287	schottische	O	O	O	O	O	(e)		
288	Schrecklichkeit	O	×	O	O	O			
289	schreierpfeife	O	×	×	O	O			
290	schrund	O	O	×	O	O			
291	Schuhplattler	O	O	×	O	O			
292	schuss	O	O	O	O	O	(b)		
293	schwa	O	O	O	O	O			
294	schwarm	O	×	×	O	O			
295	schwärmerei	O	O	O	O	O			
296	Schweinerei	O	×	×	O	O			
297	schwerpunkt	O	×	×	O	O			
298	Schwung	O	×	×	O	O			
299	Sehnsucht	O	×	×	O	O			
300	Seilbahn	O	×	×	O	O			
301	Sekt	O	×	O	O	O			
302	Sezession	O	×	×	O	O			
303	Sezessionsstil	O	×	×	O	O			
304	shaman	O	O	O	O	O	(a)	→	(a)
305	Sicherheitsdienst	O	×	×	O	O			
306	Sieg Heil	O	×	O	O	O			
307	singspiel	O	O	O	O	O			
308	sinter	O	O	O	O	O	(a)	→	(a)
309	Sitzfleisch	O	×	×	O	O			

O: *OED2*, W: *W3*, R: *RDH*, FW: *ODFWP*, S5: *SOED5*, O: Registered, ×: Not Registered, Dic.: The Result of Dictionary Study, Corp.: The Result of Corpus Study, (a) New Senses and Strong Productivity, (b) New Senses and Some Productivity, (c) New Senses and Little or No Productivity, (d) Strong Productivity but No Semantic Variation, (e) Some Productivity but No Semantic Variation

	Item	O	W	R	S5	FW	Dic.	→	Corp.
310	Sitz im Leben	○	×	×	○	○			
311	sitzkrieg	○	○	○	○	○	(c)		
312	skat	○	○	○	○	○			
313	Spätlese	○	×	×	○	○			
314	Spätzle	○	○	○	○	○			
315	Spielraum	○	×	×	○	○			
316	Sprechgesang	○	×	○	○	○			
317	Sprechstimme	○	○	○	○	○	(c)		
318	spritzer	○	○	○	○	○		→	(c)
319	spritzig	○	×	×	○	○			
320	spurlos	×	×	×	○	○			
321	stadthaus	○	×	×	○	○			
322	staffage	○	○	×	○	○			
323	Stimmung	○	×	×	○	○			
324	stollen	○	○	○	○	○			
325	stoss	○	○	○	○	○	(c)		
326	streusel	○	○	○	○	○			
327	strudel	○	○	○	○	○		→	(b)
328	Stube	○	○	×	○	○			
329	Sturm und Drang	○	○	○	○	○	(c)		
330	sympathisch	○	×	×	○	○			
331	Tafelmusik	○	×	×	○	○			
332	Tafelwein	○	×	×	○	○			
333	tendenz	○	○	×	○	○			
334	tendenzroman	○	×	×	○	○			
335	textura	○	×	×	○	○			
336	thalweg	○	○	○	○	○			
337	thuringer	○	○	○	○	○			
338	Torschlusspanik	○	×	×	○	○			
339	torte	○	○	○	○	○			
340	Totentanz	○	×	×	○	○			
341	treff	○	×	×	○	○			
342	tremolant	○	○	○	○	○			
343	Trinkhalle	○	×	×	○	○			
344	Trockenbeerenauslese	○	×	×	○	○			
345	turnverein	○	○	○	○	○			
346	tusche	○	○	○	○	○			
347	U-bahn	○	×	×	○	○			
348	über alles	○	×	×	○	○			
349	Überfremdung	○	×	×	○	○			
350	überhaupt	○	×	×	○	○			
351	Übermensch	○	×	○	○	○			
352	umlaut	○	○	○	○	○	(d)		
353	Umwelt	○	×	×	○	○			
354	unberufen	○	×	×	○	○			
355	Unding	○	×	×	○	○			

O: *OED2*, **W**: *W3*, **R**: *RDH*, **FW**: *ODFWP*, **S5**: *SOED5*, ○: Registered, ×: Not Registered, **Dic.**: The Result of Dictionary Study, **Corp.**: The Result of Corpus Study, **(a)** New Senses and Strong Productivity, **(b)** New Senses and Some Productivity, **(c)** New Senses and Little or No Productivity, **(d)** Strong Productivity but No Semantic Variation, **(e)** Some Productivity but No Semantic Variation

Appendix F

	Item	O	W	R	S5	FW	Dic.	→	Corp.
356	und so weiter	○	×	○	○	○			
357	unheimlich	○	×	×	○	○			
358	Untergang	○	×	×	○	○			
359	Untermensch	○	×	×	○	○			
360	ur-	○	×	○	○	○			
361	Urfirnis	○	○	×	○	○			
362	Urheimat	○	×	○	○	○			
363	Ursprache	○	○	○	○	○			
364	Urtext	○	×	○	○	○			
365	Vaterland	○	×	×	○	○			
366	verboten	○	○	○	○	○			
367	Verfremdung	○	×	×	○	○			
368	Versöhnung	○	×	×	○	○			
369	Verstandesmensch	○	×	×	○	○			
370	Verstehen	○	○	×	○	○			
371	Völkerwanderung	○	○	×	○	○			
372	völkisch	○	×	×	○	○			
373	volksgeist	○	×	×	×	○			
374	volkslied	○	○	○	○	○	(c)		
375	vorlage	○	○	○	○	○			
376	vorlaufer	○	×	×	○	○			
377	Vorspiel	○	○	○	○	○			
378	Vorstellung	○	×	×	○	○			
379	waldhorn	○	○	×	○	○			
380	Waldsterben	○	×	×	○	○			
381	Walpurgisnacht	○	○	×	○	○			
382	Wanderjahr	○	×	○	○	○			
383	wanderlust	○	○	○	○	○	(e)		
384	Wandervogel	○	×	×	○	○			
385	wedeln	○	○	○	○	○	(a)		
386	Wehmut	○	×	×	○	○			
387	Wehrmacht	○	○	○	○	○		→	(d)
388	Wehrwirtschaft	○	×	×	○	○			
389	weinkraut	○	×	×	○	○			
390	Weinstube	○	×	×	○	○			
391	Wein, Weib, und Gesang	○	×	×	○	○			
392	Weisswurst	○	×	×	○	○			
393	Weltanschauung	○	○	○	○	○			
394	Weltbild	○	×	×	○	○			
395	Weltliteratur	○	×	×	○	○			
396	Weltpolitik	○	○	×	○	○			
397	Weltschmerz	○	○	○	○	○			
398	Weltstadt	○	×	×	○	○			
399	wertfrei	○	×	×	○	○			
400	wertfreiheit	○	×	×	○	○			
401	Westpolitik	○	×	○	○	○			

O: *OED2*, **W**: *W3*, **R**: *RDH*, **FW**: *ODFWP*, **S5**: *SOED5*, ○: Registered, ×: Not Registered, **Dic.**: The Result of Dictionary Study, **Corp.**: The Result of Corpus Study, **(a)** New Senses and Strong Productivity, **(b)** New Senses and Some Productivity, **(c)** New Senses and Little or No Productivity, **(d)** Strong Productivity but No Semantic Variation, **(e)** Some Productivity but No Semantic Variation

	Item	O	W	R	S5	FW	Dic.	→	Corp.
402	wiener	○	×	×	○	○	(c)		
403	wiener(wurst)	○	○	○	○	○			
404	wili	○	×	×	○	○			
405	Wirtschaft	○	×	×	○	○			
406	Wirtschaftswunder	○	×	×	○	○			
407	Wissenschaft	○	○	×	○	○			
408	Wunderkammer	○	×	×	○	○			
409	wunderkind	○	○	○	○	○	(c)	→	(c)
410	wurst	○	○	○	○	○	(c)		
411	zeitgeber	○	○	○	○	○			
412	Zeitgeist	○	○	○	○	○			
413	Zigeuner	○	×	×	○	○			
414	zollverein	○	○	○	○	○	(b)		
415	Zugunruhe	○	×	×	○	○			
416	zugzwang	○	○	○	○	○	(c)		
417	zwieback	○	○	○	○	○			
418	zwischenzug	○	×	×	○	○			

O: *OED2*, **W:** *W3*, **R:** *RDH*, **FW:** *ODFWP*, **S5:** *SOED5*, ○: Registered, ×: Not Registered, **Dic.:** The Result of Dictionary Study, **Corp.:** The Result of Corpus Study, **(a)** New Senses and Strong Productivity, **(b)** New Senses and Some Productivity, **(c)** New Senses and Little or No Productivity, **(d)** Strong Productivity but No Semantic Variation, **(e)** Some Productivity but No Semantic Variation

【著者紹介】

加野（木村）まきみ（かの（きむら）まきみ）

文化女子大学室蘭短期大学コミュニティ総合学科講師．
博士（言語文化学）．
京都生まれ．
- 1990 年 関西外国語大学外国語学部英米語学科入学．
- 1992 年 ファーマン大学（米国サウスカロライナ州）編入．言語学を学ぶ．在学中に *The Oxford English Dictionary on Compact Disc(2nd edition)* に出会う．以来、電子化資料（辞書・コーパス）に興味を持つ．
- 1994 年 同校卒業．
- 1995 年 関西外国語大学外国語学部英米語学科卒業．
- 2004 年 大阪大学大学院言語文化研究科博士課程修了．
- 2002 年より現職．

Hituzi Linguistics in English No. 1

Lexical Borrowing and its Impact on English
with Special Reference to Assimilation Process of Newer Loanwords from Japanese and German and Impact on the Existing Lexical System in English

発行	2006 年 2 月 20 日　初版 1 刷
定価	8000 円＋税
著者	Ⓒ加野（木村）まきみ
発行者	松本　功
装丁	向井裕一（glyph）
印刷所	三美印刷株式会社
製本所	田中製本印刷株式会社
発行所	株式会社 ひつじ書房
	〒112-0002 東京都文京区小石川 5-21-5
	Tel.03-5684-6871　Fax.03-5684-6872
	郵便振替 00120-8-142852
	toiawase@hituzi.co.jp　http://www.hituzi.co.jp/

ISBN4-89476-268-4　C3082

造本には充分注意しておりますが、落丁・乱丁などがございましたら、小社かお買上げ書店にておとりかえいたします。ご意見、ご感想など、小社までお寄せ下されば幸いです。

Hituzi Linguistics in English

No. 1 Lexical Borrowing and its Impact on English
Makimi Kimura-Kano 8400YEN

No. 2 From a Subordinate Clause to an Independent Clause
Yuko Higashiizumi 13440YEN

No. 3 ModalP and Subjunctive Present
Tadao Nomura 15750YEN